ABOVE: 27in (68.6cm) *Little Lady Gibson Girl* by Effanbee, circa 1950. *Photograph by John Axe.*

TITLE PAGE: 33in (83.8cm) Kestner 171. Open mouth, sleep blue eyes, original human hair wig, fully jointed composition body. *Photograph by Robert and Karin MacDowell.* ©1980 Hobby House Press, Inc.

FRONT COVER: Left to right - Mimerle by Käthe Kruse, 1975, *Agnes Smith Collection;* composition Kewpie; *Running Bear* by North American Bear Company, Inc.; Toby of the *Calico Kids. Photographs by John Axe.*

BACK COVER: *Lucie with Baby* by Heidi Ott. *Photograph by John Axe.*

The Doll Catalog

3rd Edition

A Photographic Guide to the Doll World

edited by
Donna H. Felger

ANTIQUE & COLLECTIBLE DOLLS

Published By

HOBBY HOUSE PRESS, INC.
Cumberland, Maryland 21502

Additional Copies of this book may be purchased at $8.95

from
HOBBY HOUSE PRESS, INC.
900 Frederick Street
Cumberland, Maryland 21502
or from your favorite bookstore or dealer.
Please add $1.25 per copy postage.

LISTING COORDINATOR
Luanne Arnold

TYPOGRAPHY
Tonyia Kendall

LAYOUT & DESIGN
Matthew Barb
Ellen Cutter
John Rafter
Brenda Yates

ISBN: 0-87588-188-2

Table of Contents

How To Use THE DOLL CATALOG

A book is only as useful as one's ability to use and reference this knowledge. The third edition of THE DOLL CATALOG is a comprehensive compendium of firms and individuals associated with doll collecting/making organized with you, the reader, in mind. The entries are placed within the themes as chosen by the companies who participated. By listing under these headings the companies or individuals are indicating the emphasis of their products or services they can offer.

This book is a "Photographic Guide to the Doll World." There are over 600 photographs, 13 different categories showing products and services on dolls running the gamut of antique to modern. Not only are individual artist dolls shown but spectacular examples of antique and collectible dolls as well. Words alone cannot accurately convey the beauty of dolls. One can always differ with a written interpretation but, aided by a photograph, the beauty of a doll is not as elusive.

DOLL ARTISTS AND MAKERS. Many are making dolls. Usually artists are worried about their artistry and do not have enough time to devote to properly market or sell their creations. As in art, there is quite a range of mediums and quality in which dolls are available. Now you can see representative samples of artist dolls from all over the world so that you can follow through on artists whose works appeal to you. Reproduction dolls are also included in this section.

DOLL DEALERS. Included are doll dealers, doll stores and mail order doll firms. Because antique and collectible dolls are one-of-a-kind items, their catalogs are constantly changing. Therefore, one should see how dealers specialize (in the readers' particular area of interest) and send for a larger catalog. Searching for that elusive doll is easier when you have more places to look! Make sure that you are not limiting your choice of dolls and consider a wider range of dealers.

DOLL MANUFACTURERS. This section includes collector quality dolls and related items made by large scale doll producers. Although made in large quantities, from tens of thousands to the millions, such dolls at some time will become first collectible and then later antique. Doesn't it make good sense to buy the doll at an introductory price rather than at a "scarce" or "antique" price? In order to give ideas of which dolls will appeal to you, numerous "collectible" dolls are shown and discussed. If you are a dealer you can inquire from these companies about buying and selling their products. This section is a "wish list" for the individual collector as manufacturers CANNOT sell their products to individuals.

DOLL AND CLOTHING PATTERNS. Whether you want to buy ready-made doll clothes or make your own, this grouping of firms and individuals will aid your collecting/making. "Rescue" torn dolls clothes or do your own handiwork. Remember when making a new garment, do not dispose of the old garment. One should put in a plastic bag (carefully marked). The "old" clothes should be transferred with the doll. The new owner should have the use of both garments.

DOLL MUSEUMS. Learning is one of the most important facets of doll collecting. The more one knows, the better buyer one can become. One of the best places to learn is at a doll museum where specific examples are available for study. As one travels, it would be good to check out this doll museum selection to make sure a collector does not miss these opportunities. Because seasons change and interest levels are different it is recommended that you write ahead before traveling great distances. You will note there is a geographical listing of museums for your convenience.

AUCTION HOUSES. There has been an increase in the number of auctions being held for doll collectors. In addition to established auctioneers, some new firms have come to light. Whether you are interested in selling your collection or buying antique and collectible dolls, one must carefully consider their options. Write these firms with particular questions or to obtain a listing of their upcoming auctions.

DOLL KITS. Collectors have an option of creating a finished doll from parts. This section illustrates and highlights doll kits offered by different companies. Start your check list of kits to obtain.

DOLL MAKING SUPPLIES. If you are one of the many who are now trying out your own artistic expression in making or repairing dolls, you will need sources of supply. Nothing is more frustrating than to get a project started only to fall short or not have all supplies necessary. Once you have decided which companies can best help you, order complete company catalogs which list many more items than could fit in this section.

DOLL RELATED ITEMS. The doll world would not be complete without its products that embellish collecting. Included in this miscellaneous section are notecards, calendars, stationery, giftwrap, doll stands, and many other items.

TEDDY BEARS. Collectors love the Teddy Bear! Originally called a "fad" when introduced, the Teddy Bear has become one of the most pervasive playthings of the 20th Century. This section is offered as a guide to collector-oriented Teddy Bears. One is sure to enjoy *On Collecting Teddy Bears* by Patricia Schoonmaker, the author of the definitive collectors identification guide *A Collector's History of the Teddy Bear,* plus *Bears at Toy Fair 1982* by the editors of the **Doll Reader**.

PUBLICATIONS. The printed word is one of the best ways to store knowledge. Should we have to refer or to acquire knowledge, a photograph, piece of information, or a process is available when we need it. Photographs allow one to observe many different types of dolls without actually owning them. Enclosed in this section are books, magazines, and periodicals related in any way to dolls. There are collector and how-to oriented materials.

DOLL REPAIR AND RESTORATION. As doll collecting becomes more popular and with the limited number of older dolls existing, more "hurt" dolls will appear on the marketplace. As prices for the older dolls esculate, it becomes practical to have dolls repaired. This section provides a selection of firms or individuals to consider to retain the originality of the doll as well as preserving the doll for the future.

INDEX. If you are looking for a specific dealer or dealers in a particular area, this is the book for you. There are FOUR separate indexes. The first index is an *alphabetical company index* of all companies or individuals included in the book. The pages that these firms or individuals appear on are listed. A separate *geographical index* enables one to see all dealers in a particular local area or section. The museums are listed geographically in the *museum section*. It is suggested that one always check the complete book listing before traveling as some firms do not have an open place of business or set hours. (Some firms are mail-order oriented and do not have retail display.) Lastly, a *cross index* enables a person to look for specific areas of interest within and across themed sections.

The editor, publisher, typesetter, listing coordinator, and layout artists have through their presentation communicated through photographs and text the information you, the doll collector/maker, need to widen your knowledge of doll firms and doll individuals. With this knowledge comes more appreciation for your hobby.

15in (38.1cm) *Toni* by Ideal, 1950. *Photograph by John Axe.*

Introduction

As interest in the field of doll collecting and making continues to increase dramatically, so does the need for a comprehensive source of dolls and all related items. Hobby House Press, Inc. is happy to present the third edition of *The Doll Catalog.*

Doll enthusiasts will find this photographic reference an integral part of their library, furnishing sources for both manufactured and artist's dolls, doll clothing and patterns, doll making supplies, kits and related items, doll repair and restoration as well as listings of museums and auction houses. A special feature in the museum section of the second edition is a geographical list of many of the museums on this continent and abroad either devoted entirely to dolls and related subjects or which have a display of dolls as one of their exhibits.

You are, of course, aware that the scope of dolls and related items has broadened extensively and *The Doll Catalog* will enable you, the doll collector/maker to be selective. You will find the more than 700 photographs herein very useful in making intelligent choices.

Innumerable catalogs, lists and other informative materials are listed as available at no or minimal cost . . . another aid in your decision making as well as helping you become educated on what is available on the current market.

The geographical index will be invaluable in your travels. The alphabetical index and product index will also serve to assist you in your doll collecting/making.

Have a nice trip through the "doll world."

Donna H. Felger

Donna H. Felger
Editor

DOLL ARTISTS and MAKERS

Marie Antoinette - $450.

Sheila Wallace

Individually directly modeled one-of-a-kind historic costume dolls, each with carefully researched, authentic costuming and accessories. Wax heads and hands, cloth bodies. Price range $400. - $1,000. Photographs $1.00 each; color brochure. (Wholesale and retail.)

407 Garden Avenue
Grove City, PA 16127
(412) 458-6940

18in (45.7cm) Pam, K★R 121.

Dolls by B. Frank

Porcelain reproductions of Jumeau, Kestner, etc., original limited editions, 19th century rag dolls; kits, cradles, doll beds, clothing. Sold in USA, South America, Australia, England in better shops. Catalog $3.00. Retail price range $22. - $380. + postage and insurance. (Wholesale and retail.)

1042 Minnetonka Road, Dept. RC
Severn, MD 21144
(301) 969-0283

11in (27.9cm) Martha Washington in cream satin-$130.

"Gay '90's Couple" with baby - $66. per set

Sheila Wallace

Cast wax doll house dolls, scale 1" = 1', adults, babies, children, maids in "Victorian" or "Gay '90's" styles, all from my own original molds. Also larger cast wax costume dolls. Price range $30. - $250. Photographs $1.00 each; color brochure. (Wholesale and retail.)

407 Garden Avenue
Grove City, PA 16127
(412) 458-6940

Ann Parker

English characters and costumes, 11in (27.9cm). Carved portrait likenesses reproduced in tough resin and painted by the artist. Price range $100. - $150. Catalog $2.00. (Mail order only.)

67 Victoria Drive
Bognor Regis, Sussex, PO212TD
England

Alice's Wonderland

Original dolls signed and dated. Jointed arms and legs. Baby $30.; 2in (5.1cm) boy or girl dressed $35.; 3½in (8.9cm) child, boy or girl dressed $40. New 3in (7.6cm) clowns, Hobo or polka dot outfit $40. Catalog $1.00. (Retail only.)

P. O. Box 45
Niantic, CT 06357

29in (73.7cm) H — Heuret.

Rita Gordon, Doll Artist

Exquisite dolls you will love and treasure. Larger dolls my specialty. Send $1.00 for list or call (914) 735-3997. Price range $65. - $500. Printed list $1.00; photographs $1.00 each. (Wholesale and retail. Shop and mail order.)

19 Valley Court
Pearl River, NY 10965
(914) 735-3997

A. T. Heather.

Claridge Dolls

A. T. Heather, incised A-14-T, (C-11½) 20in (50.8cm) doll dressed as a French child in various colors and trims by Clarice Aldridge - $350. Approximately 50 dolls available. Doll brochure $1.00+LSASE. Blank head list $.50+SASE. (Shop and mail order. Retail only.)

RD #2, Route 12B, Box 190
Hamilton, NY 13346

Layne's Little Ladies.

Layne's Little Ladies

Porcelain reproduction dolls, classes, supplies, fabric, trims, composition bodies. Available for seminars. Everything needed to make and complete your doll. Shop open Monday through Friday 12 noon -5pm. Doll price range $35. - $700. SASE for printed list. (Wholesale and retail. Shop and mail order.)

174 East 8th Avenue
Chico, CA 95926
(916) 891-1432

Kestner Gibson Girl 172.

H Belle Dolls

Antique doll replicas by Hazel Murphy. Available 40 different porcelain bisque dolls. Dressed in authentic period costumes or undressed. Price range: $45. - $350. Postage and insurance additional. Catalog: $2.00 (Refunded with order). (Retail only.)

Rt. 4, Box 4144, Mt. Carmel Woods
LaPlata, MD 20646
(301) 934-2730

18in (45.7cm) A.T., human hair wig on composition body.

Sarah Beardshear

Sixty porcelain reproduction dolls ranging in price from $25. - $175. Doll pictured dressed in 1905 antique wedding dress. Available dressed or ready-to-dress. Printed list $.50 + SASE. (Retail only. Shop and mail order.)

P. O. Box 234
Homer, NE 68030
(402) 698-2120

8in (20.3cm) Peter or Polly all-bisque Caucasian or black porcelain with bear -$110.

Lois Beck Originals

Ten original porcelain dolls ranging from $110. to $275. each postpaid. SASE for information. (Retail only. Shop and mail order.)

10300 Southeast Champagne Lane
Portland, OR 97266
(503) 777-2131

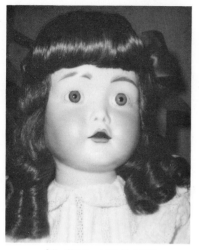

34in (86.4cm) K★R 117N.

Rita Gordon, Doll Artist

Exquisite dolls you will love and treasure. Larger dolls my specialty. Send $1.00 for list or call (914) 735-3997. Price range $65. - $500. Printed list $1.00; photographs $1.00 each. (Wholesale and retail. Shop and mail order.)

19 Valley Court
Pearl River, NY 10965
(914) 735-3997

Reproduction peg wooden sitting on Shaker bed.

Dr. Fred Laughon, Jr.
Miniatures from Cheswick

Nine authentic replicas of peg wooden and Queen Ann dolls of the 18th and 19th centuries. Jointed, pegged and carved with delicate hand painting on faces. Salesman sample furniture available (reproductions). Price range $30. -$800. SASE for printed list. (Wholesale and retail. Shop and mail order.)

8106 Three Chopt Road
Richmond, VA 23229
(804) 288-7795

Tiny bisque dolls.

Kay's Doll House

1¾in (4.5cm) porcelain dolls beautifully painted and dressed. Mohair wigs. No moving parts. SASE for price. (Retail only. Shop and mail order.)

P. O. Box 367, 222 East Vine
Ellettsville, IN 47429
(812) 876-2237

Doll house Family.

Kay's Doll House

1in (2.5cm) to 1ft (30.5cm) doll house people. All handmade. Beautifully featured, completely hand dressed. Available either bisque or wire armature body. $25. - $60. each. Postage & insurance additional. Printed list $1.00. (Retail only. Shop and mail order.)

P.O. Box 367 - 222 East Vine
Ellettsville, IN 47429
(812) 876-2237

Seeley mold - Annie-Anne and Heubach's Henry.

Claridge Dolls

Quality reproductions. The "Dolls with a Personal Touch" by Clarice $95.-$500., postage and insurance additional Doll brochure $1.00 + LSASE. Blank head list $.50 + SASE. (Shop and mail order. Retail only.)

RD #2, Route 12B, Box 190
Hamilton, NY 13346

K★R 117 Mein Liebling.

Jo Conn Dolls

Award-winning porcelain replica doll, hand decorated, glass eyes, human hair, composition body, 17in (43.2cm), clothing copied from K★R catalog 1927. Money back guarantee. Send SASE for picture and information. Price $155. + postage and insurance. Sixty dolls available, porcelain and composition, retail price range $45. - $575. (Wholesale and retail. Shop and mail order.)

2548 Cranston Street
Cranston, RI 02920
(401) 942-2256

28in (71.1cm) Bru Jne - $350.

Antique Doll Replicas
by Yolanda

Tomorrow's heirlooms are here today with each doll being made of the finest quality materials available; reproduced with the craftsmanship of days gone by. All porcelain dolls are signed and dated. Price: $85. - $350. Postage and insurance additional. Free printed list. $1.00 each for photographs. 150 different types. (Wholesale and retail. Shop and mail order.)

**6021 North Encinita Avenue
Temple City, CA 91780
(213) 286-8146**

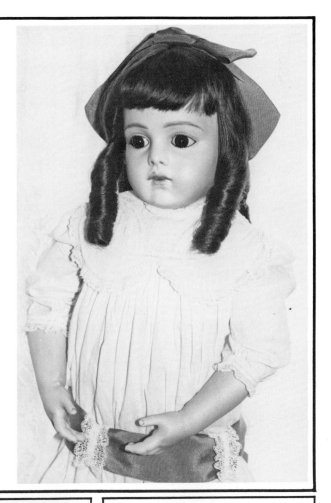

Dream Maker's Dolls

Authentic reproductions guaranteed to please you. Send SASE for wholesale price list.

**Box 219
Winona, MO 65588**

Steiner A-9 Bride - $125.

Barbara Anne's Babies

Expertly painted porcelain reproductions. Greatest care given to detail. Available in kit form or finished. Patterns, wigs, composition bodies, porcelain slip, china paints, other supplies available. Doll list $1.00 + SASE. Sixty dolls ranging from $15. to $350. (Retail only. Shop and mail order.)

**13820 Spriggs Road
Manassas, VA 22111**

14in (35.6cm) jointed Laughing Jumeau, $200.

MAm Porcelain Dolls

Porcelain reproductions, original angels and clowns. All exquisitely dressed using only the finest fabrics and laces. Can be personalized. Retail price range $25. - $300. + postage and insurance. Printed lists and photographs $1.50. (Wholesale and retail. Mail order, home and shows.)

**2117 - 68th Terrace South
St. Petersburg, FL 33712
(813) 867-2723**

Edna Henderson Dolls

Artist editions modeled from portraits especially for collectors. Appropriate colors of porcelain. Young, older, men, women, Indians. Special requests considered. SASE quarantees reply. Pictures, prices shown in catalog for $3.00. Single photographs $1.00. (Retail only. Mail order only.)

**200 Swarthmore Avenue
Charleston, WV 25302
(304) 343-7304**

Original sculptured portrait doll by Edna Henderson.

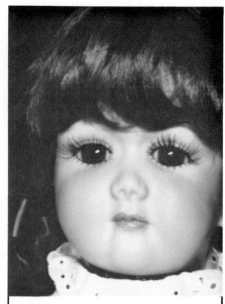

Patricia Proctor Originals

Porcelain dolls - Copyrighted limited editions of 100. Send a LSASE for descriptive list and prices. For photographs include $1.00. (Shop and mail order.)

**4618 Stillwater Court
Concord, CA 94521
(415) 685-6431**

Patricia Proctor Originals

Porcelain dolls - Copyrighted limited editions of 100. Send a LSASE for descriptive list and prices. For photographs include $1.00. (Shop and mail order.)

**4618 Stillwater Court
Concord, CA 94521
(415) 685-6431**

Patricia Proctor Originals

Porcelain dolls - Copyrighted limited editions of 30. Send a LSASE for descriptive list and prices. For photographs include $1.00. (Shop and mail order.)

**4618 Stillwater Court
Concord, CA 94521
(415) 685-6431**

Patricia Proctor Originals

Porcelain dolls - Copyrighted limited editions of 100. Send a LSASE for descriptive list and prices. For photographs include $1.00. (Shop and mail order.)

**4618 Stillwater Court
Concord, CA 94521
(415) 685-6431**

TIF N' TODDS

731 W. Knox
SPOKANE, WASHINGTON 99205
1-509-327-3452
Wholesale Available

No. 1

"Grannie" 29½in (75.0cm) Tall
She has soft bosoms, pearl ear-rings, long panties, when she is held, her arms "hug" Poem on bib of apron reads: "If Your Grandma lives very far away, Here's one to love and talk to, Every Day!" Stock No. 82 ..Reg. Price. $75., This Ad..$65. (No two alike, unless requested.)

No. 3

"Sweetie"

28in (71.1cm) Tall
She has slip fancy panties (appears to have a broken elastic in one leg), freckles..Choice of hair color, eyes. Stock No. S-82 Reg. Price, $60., Spec. $45.

No. 2

"Girl with Sucker"

28in (71.1cm) Tall
Lovely pleated dress with fancy panties. Blonde hair (pictured) or your choice, hair, eyes. Reg Price: $60. Spec. Price: $45. Stock No. 12

No.5

"Snyder"

29½" (75.0cm) Tall. Freckles. Also designed for restaurant, same choice of what he is holding as No. 4 and color choice. Back pocket with hankie, can have bow tie, or cook's kerchief. Can be Oriental, Spanish, black, or as shown. Reg. Price $80. Spec. Price: $60. Stock No. P-W-82 with sturdy stand $68. (No two alike, unless requested.)

No.4

"Pioneer Polly"

29½in (75.0cm) Tall
Designed for restaurants. Can be holding any menu, or sign, "Please Wait to be Seated," or "Welcome to (Your Restaurant.") She is very fancy, knee panties, ruffles, slip, calf-length dress, pinafore, high-button shoes. Can be dressed to $80. Spec Price: $60. with Sturdy Stand $68.00. Stock No. P-P-82 (No two alike, unless requested.)

No. 6 Baby Boy with spoon, Baby Girl

14in (35.6cm) Tall, Jointed Arms, Legs
Boy in rompers, gingham shirt, white hair. Girl fancy panties, gingham dress, white hair. Hair and eyes color choice available. Dolls are saying, "Yum, Yum, here comes Mom with our food." Single orders, or matched pair. Stock No. Boy, B-62..Girl No. 62. Reg Price: $65. Special, this ad, $50. ea.

Full Amt, Prepaid with order, or C.O.D.-U.P.S. (extra charge)

Limited Editions, 500 each.
Nos. 1-2-3-6.

Allow 2-3 weeks Del.

13

Larkin F.F. Jumeau by Jean Nordquist.

Collectible Doll Company

Presenting the fabulous Jean Nordquist dolls. Museum quality originals and antique reproductions. Porcelain doll kits. Dealer inquiries invited. Retail price range $20. - $1,000. 150+ porcelain bisque items available. Lists, photographs $.50 each - LSASE appreciated.

**6233 2nd Avenue Northwest
Seattle, WA 98107
(206) 782-5576**

Lovely E.J. Jumeau reproduction by Jeri Ann.

Dainty Darling Dolls
by Jeri Ann Ray

Exquisite antique reproductions of yesterday's cherished dolls for the discriminating collector. All-bisque baby dolls, German and French character children, doll house dolls and many beautiful French Jumeaus, Brus and others. Award-winning workmanship - 100% guaranteed. Retail price range $35. - $500. + postage and insurance. $1.00 for list. Photographs available. (Wholesale and retail. Shop and mail order.)

**645 Roxanne Drive
Antioch, TN 37013
(615) 834-1675**

Sweet Dolls by Laurie.

Sweet Dolls
by Laurie

100 porcelain reproduction antique dolls. Composition bodies, glass eyes, beautifully dressed. Marque, Brus, Jumeaus, A.T., Poulbot, Just Me, French wrestler, Poutys, Wee Ones, Googlies and Orientals. Retail price range $30. - $265. + postage and insurance. $1.00 + LSASE. (Wholesale and retail. Shop and mail order.)

**1217 Hanover
Owosso, MI 48867
(517) 725-7747**

Mikuen's Dolls

Ten antique porcelain reproduction dolls $69. to $200. Send $1.50 for brochure with pictures. French fashion lady doll 8in (45.7cm), kid body, glass eyes, 1890 style dress as shown in photograph above. $1.00 photograph LSASE (refundable). (Retail only. Mail order only.)

**1394 Coates Avenue
Holbrook, NY 11741**

Melissa and her Kestner, limited edition.

Reja Dolls

Porcelain bisque reproductions and one-of-a-kind limited editions. Reasonably priced and professionally painted and costumed. Over five years of quality workmanship. 150 dolls available, price range $50. - $500. Catalog $.50. (Retail only. Shop and mail order.)

**510 Ellington Road
South Windsor, CT 06074
(203) 289-8782**

Original portrait dolls of John Michael III and Nita.

Bonnie-Lee Portrait Doll Makers

We'll make an original doll to look like your child. Facial features are hand-sculptured in earthenware china w/earthenware limbs attached to a sturdy muslin body. Clothing in picture copied. Details send $.50. Depending on size - price: $175. - $250. (Mail order only.)

**2005 George Washington Road
Vienna, VA 22180
(703) 893-7780**

A Touch of the Blarney, original porcelain sculpture.

Lucille Sabad Tovcimak IDMA

Enchanting new series of original limited edition character dolls. Sculptured porcelain head, arms, legs with cloth, wire armature body. Each 10in (25.4cm) doll signed, numbered, dated and copyrighted. Price range $145. - $365. + postage and insurance. Color photographs and information $2.00. (Retail only. Shop by appointment, mail order and shows.)

401 North Main Street
Moscow, PA 18444
(717) 348-0947

Marandy Dolls, Etc.

signed . . . *Elfoe* 19 © ...

shown:
1. Marandy
2. Marandy as Laura
3. Lady J.
4. E 1 Googly
5. Gibby

ARTIST
Eleanor G. Bridgers
Studio - 2811 Jeffers Drive
Richmond, VA 23235
804-272-4029
By appointment

Doll's-N-Things

Porcelain reproductions. Over 200 dolls to choose from. Picture on request. SASE for list and prices. (Wholesale and retail. Shop and mail order.)

1416 Rees Street
Breaux Bridge, LA 70517
(318) 332-2622

Jeff Blue, doll by Sarah Burton.

Sarah Burton's Doll Depot

Tall, dark and handsome. A masculine doll to escort your finest lady dolls. Original porcelain portrait doll of country singer, Jeff Blue. 19in (48.3cm) tall, wired cloth body. Limited edition. Price $175. Also 100 reproductions. Retail price range $5. - $250. Send business number for wholesale information. List $.50. Jeff Blue doll photograph $1.00 + SASE. (Shop and mail order.)

560 Locust Street
Middletown, IN 47356
(317) 354-4885

Ellen McAdams by Terri people

Baby Kevin and Sallie, 2¼in (5.8cm), porcelain. Original copyright design. Silk curls, safety pin in diaper. Limited orders. Shoes extra. $75. + $10. for shoes. Cute fingers and toes. Printed list free features dolls $75. and up. (Retail only.)

3711 Page Street
Redwood City, CA 94063

Baby Kevin and Baby Sallie by Terri.

Elegant needle sculptured dolls with adorable modeled babies.

Nerissa

Adult dolls: 20in (50.8cm) seated. Mixed media babies: 6in (15.2cm) toddler and 3in (7.6cm) infant. Needle sculpture and polyform. Individually signed, named or numbered and copyrighted. Six designs, retail price range $40. - $290. SASE for catalog. (Wholesale and retail. Shop and mail order.)

P. O. Box 200
Edinborg, PA 16412
(814) 734-3174

Jamie doll originals.

Jamie Doll Originals

Expressive faces and detailed modeling are characteristic of the beautiful porcelain doll artist originals created by Jamie. Several designs currently available. Sizes from 9in (22.9cm) - 30in (76.2cm). Price range $75. - $350. Send SASE for list. Catalog $2.00. (Retail and wholesale. Mail order.)

5476 Burtch Road
Jeddo, MI 48032

Bru Jne 11 and Laughing Jumeau.

Tomorrow's Treasures

Collector quality antique reproduction porcelain dolls. Dressed authentically or ready-to-dress. Retail price $100. up. $1.00 + LSASE for list. (Shop and mail order.)

RD #1, Box 2815
Norway, ME 04268

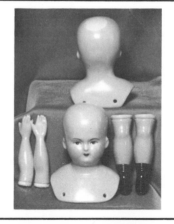

Milano's Creative Clay Cottage

Will work with you to create a doll kit or dressed doll, customized for your own wants and dreams, from your photo and description. (Bride, christening or prom?) Kits: $3.50 -$45. Dressed to order only $35. -$450. Postage and insurance additional. Catalog $2.50. (Wholesale and retail. Shop and mail order.)

625 Rowe Avenue
Yuba City, CA 95991

Reproduction A. Marque in pure silk taffeta dress.

The Dollsmith Studio
Mary Evans Smith, Doll Artist

Fifty porcelain reproductions of original antique dolls. Specialize in French bébés and German and SFBJ character children. Bodies of composition, porcelain or cloth. Human hair wigs, glass eyes. Lay-a-ways. Price range $20. - $300. Printed list $1.00 + LSASE. Photographs. (Retail only. Shop and mail order.)

8339 Carrbridge Circle
Towson, MD 21204
(301) 825-8744

Kestner's Hilda.

Priscilla's Ceramics & Porcelain

Beautiful porcelain reproductions include Kestner's Hilda (2 sizes), Pouty (3 sizes), Paris Twirp, Bye-Lo (2 sizes), Gibson Girl, Robbie, doll house dolls and more. Retail price range $75. - $250. + postage and insurance. Send $.75 for list today. (Wholesale and retail. Shop and mail order.)

**5705 Fisher Road
Temple Hills, MD 20748
(301) 567-9630**

Betty Reeder
Bru-Bet's Dolls

My dolls are faithfully reproduced from the antiques. They are beautifully china painted and well costumed; composition bodies are used. My originals are ready now. Catalog $1.00 and LSASE please. Price range $115. - $450. Postage and insurance additional. (Retail only. Shop and mail order.)

**2737 Southwest 63rd Street
Oklahoma City, OK 73159
(405) 685-6878**

Betty Reeder's Promise, an original.

Three-year-old in silk dress.

Tanya Heyrend

10in (25.4cm) loving representation of two to five year old child in porcelain. Finest quality material used. Dressed to suit. 8in (20.3cm) celebrity dolls, also porcelain originals available. Price range $50. - $100. Printed list available; photograph of other work $2.00 (refundable). (Retail only. Mail order only.)

**Box 753, 54630 South Circle Drive
Idyllwild, CA 92349**

Doll Corner

Approximately 250 kits available, also dressed dolls complete or will dress dolls to order. Catalog $3.50, refundable first $15. order. Kit prices range from $3. to $45. (Wholesale and retail. Shop and mail order.)

**940 Richie
Lima, OH 45805**

Tiffany, our "Birthday Girl."

Dolls by Dolores

Cloth doll originals of the highest quality, dressed in the finest fabrics. Because each doll is hand painted, it is unique. Retail price range of 12 dolls $16. - $75. each. $1.00 + SASE for brochure. (Wholesale and retail.)

**112 Dunham Hill Road, RD4
Binghamton, NY 13905
(607) 729-3291**

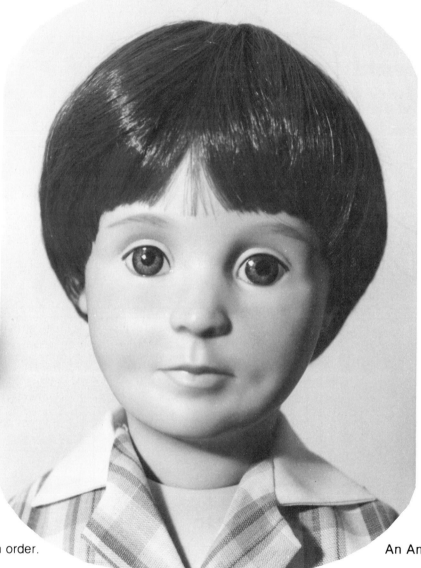

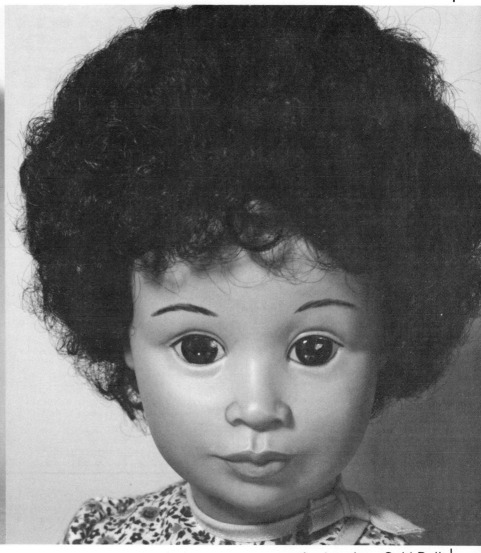
Doll Artists & Makers

Original Doll Artists Council of America

Original Rose Petal Dolls

Rabbit Jester©1981, $495.

Wendy Brent (ODACA)

Hand sculptured using a unique rose petal composition. (See article *DOLL READER,* April/May 1981) also, Cat Jester, Flower Fairy, Wood Elf, Cat Angel, Fairy Godmother. Ms. Brent's work has been purchased for exhibition by the Smithsonian Museum. For brochure send LSASE & $1.00. (Retail only.)

**42751 Road 409
Mendocino, CA 95460**

Bobi's Doll Creations

For something unusual, award-winning wax creations not effected by heat or cold. Also, one-of-a-kind sculpted from polyform. Limited editions. Priced from $12. to $175., ranging in size 6in (15.2cm) to 18in (45.7cm). Printed list free. Send SASE for brochure with photographs. UFDC, ODACA, IDMA.

**306 Riverview Court
Portage, WI 53901
(608) 742-6803**

Ball-jointed colonial lady and child; lady $130., child $65.

Sharon Lee Dolls now at Treasure Chest of Dolls

Hand sculpted one-of-a-kind children and adult dolls of low fire fimo clay. Made with cloth or ball-jointed bodies. All made by artist. Glass or painted eyes. Price range $65. - $130. + postage and insurance. (Retail only. Shop and mail order.)

**15930 Main Street
Hesperia, CA 92345
(714) 948-3121**

20in (50.8cm) wax lady of 1895 - $200.

Sharon Lee Dolls now at Treasure Chest of Dolls

Original hand sculpted one-of-a-kind wax over papier-mâché. Glass eyes. Artist makes clothes. Doll sizes 6in (15.2cm) to 22in (55.9cm). Mohair wigs. Original cloth dolls also available. Price range $100. -$200. + postage and insurance. (Retail only. Shop and mail order.)

**15930 Main Street
Hesperia, CA 92345
(714) 948-3121**

Original Doll Artists Council of America

Original doll, The Spirit of '76 from the painting by Archibald M. Willard. Price $250. plus postage and insurance.

Virginia Little

Carved bass wood head, hands and feet. Wire armature body, also Super Sculpy. Authentic costume. Photograph and description of historical American dolls available. (Shop and mail order.)

**Locust Lane Dolls
R. D. 1, Box 207
Beech Creek, PA 16822
(717) 726-4507**

Boy of the 1860s with two small friends.

Pipsqueekers
Cathy J. Ellis

One-of-a-kind miniature (under 6in, 15.2cm) dolls. Made of Sculpy with wired cloth body and lovingly dressed. Mini marionettes, carousel animals and multi-faced dolls also available. Retail price range $30. - $150. SASE for information. Photographs. (Shop and mail order.)

**6335 North Moore
Portland, OR 97217
(503) 285-2910**

Donna G. Guinn,
Original Doll Creations

Original doll artists dolls in limited editions. Photo/information packet $2.00 (USA). Fifteen or more porcelain/ceramic dolls ranging in price from $25. - $225. ODACA member artist. (Retail only. Shop, mail order and personal appearances.)

**RD #4 - Box 154-B2
Guinn Ridge Road
Norwich, NY 13815**

24in (61.0cm) Danny, circa, 1880 - $450.

Original Dolls by Fae Morris

Danny is available in a limited edition of 30 in all sizes, 24in (61.0cm), 15in (38.1cm) and 13in (33.0cm). Other dolls available are Chloe, Petite Chloe, Patty and Wendy. Porcelain bisque. Price range $175. - $450. Portrait dolls start at $500. Postage and insurance additional. (Retail only.)

**16128 Escobar Avenue
Los Gatos, CA 95030
(408) 356-2398**

17in (43.2cm) St. Nicholas ©1981 Beverly Port.

Beverly Port Originals

Forty porcelain, wax and cloth people, fantasy and animal figures. Price range $45. - $600. + postage and insurance. UFDC national ribbons. Member of ODACA. Waiting list. Photographic article and prices. $.50. (Retail only.)

**P. O. Box 711
Retsil, WA 98378
(206) 871-1633**

Original porcelain sculpture dolls.

Benner-Disbro Studio (ODACA)

We create only original porcelain 19th and 20th century character dolls, baby dolls, gnomes and fantasy dolls, and portrait dolls. Retail price range $60. - $400. Photographs available. (Wholesale and retail.)

**373-B West Oak Hill Road - RD 2
Jamestown, NY 14701
(716) 488-9473**

Original Doll Artists Council of America

Timothy lamb, Billy (mask face) and Blossom.

Mary Ann Oldenburg (ODACA)

A unique collection of original patterns and instructions for teddy bears, baby animals, toddlers and baby dolls. Instructions for needle sculpture and mask face dolls. SASE + $.50 for brochure. Also porcelain and fabric children and toddler dolls. (Retail only. Mail order.)

**5515 South 12th Street
Sheboygan, WI 53081**

Karmie.

Arden 1 Originals

Original porcelain and polyform children and adults (small people). Six dolls available, price range $125. - $300. + postage and insurance. Photographs available. (Retail only.)

**1969 Potomac Drive
Toledo, OH 43607
(419) 535-1881**

Anne Luree Dolls

ODACA porcelain artist dolls. Custom designs. Characters, adults, children, historical, Kewpie, fantasy, portraits. Many styles immediately available, originals and replicas. Quantity designs, UFDC national Denver, region 4 souvenir, club dolls. Price range $10. - $350. plus postage. Printed list: SASE. (Wholesale and retail. Mail order and shop.)

**P.O. Box 7164
Sacramento, CA 95826
(916) 363-5733**

Rebecca Biedermann (ODACA)

Original Asian - Quan and Mai.

Original creations, detailed and sensitively depicting babies and children (a specialty). Pictured are Quan and Mai - $260. each. Coming soon - doll portraits of the artist's small children, Nicole, Mariah and Gabriel. Approximately ten porcelain and cloth limited edition dolls with price range $190.-$275. SASE + $.50 for photographs and prices. (Retail only. Mail order only.)

**6510 Maple Drive
Rockford, MN 55373
(612) 477-5161**

Felt Theresa and furry Timmy, $135.

Originals
by Bettina (ODACA)

A limited edition of felt dolls, entirely handcrafted. Uniquely flexible heads molded over original sculpture with hand-painted faces. Swivel heads, jointed arms and legs. Retail price range $135. - $395. Printed list with color photograph $1.25. (Primarily mail order.)

**6120 North Orange Tree Lane
Tucson, AZ 85704**

"The Plain Folk"
by Jan Painter

One-of-a-kind originals including Appalachian mountain people, peddlers, southwestern Indians, immigrants, Santas, others. Polyform head, hands and feet. Padded wire bodies. Approximately 9in (22.9cm) tall. $110. and up + postage and insurance. SASE for information and photographs. (Retail only. Mail order and shows.)

**900 Cheyenne Drive
Fort Collins, CO 80525
(303) 484-4518**

Appalachian Mountain Musicians.

Barb Corning's
"REFLECTIONS"*

PROUDLY PRESENTS, FOR THE PREFERRED COLLECTOR, RARE RECREATIONS OF OLD WORLD QUALITY BISQUE DOLLS.

ALL PHASES OF DOLLS ARE DONE ENTIRELY BY THE ARTIST. DOLLS ARE SIGNED, DATED, AND ARE LIMITED EDITIONS, IN QUANTITIES OF 200 WITH EXCEPTION OF A MARQUE. ALL COSTUMING HAS BEEN RESEARCHED AND RECREATED FROM OLD TYPE FABRICS, AND FOR THE SECURITY OF THE BUYER, HAVE BEEN COPYRIGHTED

BOTH FRENCH, GERMAN, AND CHARACTER DOLLS ARE AVAILABLE.

ORIGINAL DOLLS ARE IN THE WORKS.

**BARB CORNING
7727 BOLTON AVE.
RIVERSIDE, CAL. 92503
(714) 785-0260**

lg. dl. stamped S.A.S.E.
VIEWING BY APPOINTMENT
ONLY

*BARB CORNING'S "REFLECTIONS" NOT ASSOCIATED OR AFFILIATED WITH ANY PERSON, PERSONS OR COMPANIES USING THE WORD "REFLECTIONS".

Precious Babes
by Beth

Limited edition 18in (45.7cm) Beth. Copyrighted, original head on composition body, signed and dated. Price $300 + postage and insurance. Information and two color photographs, please send $2.00 (refundable with order) and SASE. New dolls forthcoming. (Retail only. Shop and mail order.)

980 Robin Hood Avenue
Eugene, OR 97401
(503) 686-8175

Beth, © 1982.

Fashions of 1870.

Dolls of Yesteryear by Robert Archer

Ceramic ladies of fashion authentically costumed to period. Wigs of cotton floss. Approximately 11½in (29.2cm) tall. Classes in costume design and pattern making for the doll maker. Dolls priced from $75. up + postage and insurance. (Retail only. Shop and mail order.)

420 North Broad Street
Suffolk, VA 23434
(804) 539-2924

30in (76.2cm) Jumeau reproduction.

Chére Amie Dolls

Over 30 antique reproduction dolls, porcelain and composition. Doll price list $1.00 and SASE. (Retail only. Mail order only.)
P. O. Box 4491
Scottsdale, AZ 85258

Elizabeth Vigee Lebrum, French 1755-1842.

L Bro

Elizabeth Vigee Lebrum, court portraitist to Queen Marie Antoinette. First in a series of six original sculptures portraying famous women artists. Each doll handcrafted of finest French porcelain and authentically dressed. Edition limited to 120. Retail price $250 + postage and insurance. Printed list and photographs available. (Wholesale and retail.)
33620 Hillcrest
Farmington, MI 48024

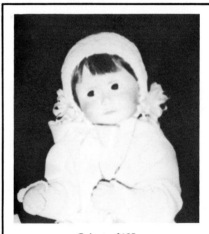

Celeste, $135.

Elva Weems

ODACA artist porcelain dolls. Layaway available. $25. deposit on dolls. Satisfaction or money refunded. Two stamps for brochure. (Retail only. Shop and mail order.)

10510 East Polk Street
Tacoma, WA 98445
(206) 531-4127

Charlotte in wax, 26in (66.0cm) or bisque 20in (50.8cm).

Gillie Dolls

I make 40 different original wax and bisque dolls, also a few reproductions all with good quality glass eyes and human hair; the smaller dolls have mohair. Mainly dressed in antique fabrics. Retail price range £60 - £200 ($105.- $350.) + postage and insurance. Catalog $4.00. (Wholesale and retail. Shop and mail order.)

69 Babylon Lane, Anderton, Nr. Chorley Lancs., England
0257   482074

Lady and Gentleman of 1870.

Teresa Thompson

English historical costume dolls, handmade from cotton stockinette with wired arms, molded and painted faces. Approximately 9in (22.9cm) high. Member of British Doll Artists Association. Price range of 52 different dolls, $25.- $30. Catalog $1.00. (Mail order only.)

35 Lonsdale Way
Oakham, Leicestershire
LE15 6LP England
Oakham 3907

Claudine - £195 ($341.) sterling.

Margaret Glover

Wide range of dolls including babies, orientals, black, boys and fashion, all with wax head and limbs, soft bodies. Rooted hair, lashes and brows. Beautiful handmade costumes. Wax restoration and repair also undertaken. Fifty dolls ranging from £85 - £350 ($149. - $613.) + postage and insurance. Descriptions and photographs available. (Retail. Mail order.)

42 Hartham Road, Isleworth
Middlesex, England

Portrait Series, Brooks, $325.

House of Wright
Phyllis Wright

Porcelain bisque toddler, 13in (33.0cm) tall. Soft-sculptured polyester body, bisque swivel-head/ shoulder plate, arms and legs. Human hair wig. Original sculpture; edition limited to 25. Other children and sizes available. $135.- $375. Up-dated catalog to be printed soon. $1.50.

P. O. Box 456
St. James, NY 11780

Collector's Series, Empire Couple, 1810, $500. pair.

House of Wright
"The Wright People"

Undressed dolls, bisque head, hands and legs. Handsewn kid bodies, wire armiture for articulation. Handmade period mohair wigs. Select from 1750 - 1900 time periods. Dressed Collectors Series - special order. Catalog $1.00. (Retail only. Mail order and shows.)

P. O. Box 456
St. James, NY 11780

U.S. Naval Lt., Summer Whites 1852-62, $275.

House of Wright
Gary Wright

12in (30.5cm) articulated figures of men and women representing fashions from American history. Porcelain bisque head, hands and legs. Wigs handmade period styled mohair. Available dressed and undressed. Limited edition collectors series. Price range: $175. - $375. Postage and insurance additional. Catalog $2.00. (Retail only. Mail order and shows.)

P.O. Box 456
St. James, NY 11780

A real pine cone body 10in (25.4cm) high.

Sharing Joy with Sharon & Jeanne

and their original pine cone dolls with plush fabric faces and sweet hand-painted expressions; quilted hands, wooden feet. A dozen different dolls - write for free color brochure. $6. wholesale, $12. retail (Kits available on 3 Christmas dolls @ $3. wholesale and $6. retail.)

607 17th Street Northwest
Rochester, MN 55901
(507) 285-1271

8in (20.3cm) Hilda: sizes range 6½-18in (16.5 - 45.7cm).

Main Street Emporium

Blue ribbon winning dolls from 1978 through 1982. Internationally acclaimed and currently producing over 200 different reproduction dolls. Retail price range: $15. - $385. + postage and insurance. Catalog $1.00. (Wholesale and retail. Shop and mail order.)

41 Main Street
Brockport, NY 14420
(716) 637-5400

Heirloom Dolls

French and German reproductions, originals and Bye-los. Finest workmanship and materials. Beautifully dressed, careful attention given to finishing details. Porcelain heads with composition, leather or porcelain bodies. Eight dolls; retail price range $80. - $300. + postage and insurance. Send SASE for photographs. (Wholesale and retail. Shop and mail order.)

5604 5th Court South
Birmingham, AL 35212
(205) 595-7861

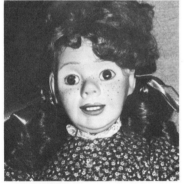

Red haired Bridget, Irish child, limited edition 10 - $150.

Brenda L. Stewart

The Peddler's Workshop

Unique character children, all original. Porcelain heads and limbs, cloth body with complete armature. Dolls available in signed and dated limited editions. Certificate of authenticity with each doll. Price range $150. - $200. Visa/Mastercard. (Retail only. Shop and mail order.)

1562 Rooker Road
Mooresville, IN 46158

Meet the Gypsies, $149.50 each or $275. pair postpaid.

Treasures

by Trulove

First in series of four by Judy Trulove, French bisque from rare old S & H character. Composition body, glass eyes, colorful costuming, leather shoes, beads, bangles. Limited edition of 150. Price range $149. - $195. postpaid. Money back guarantee. (Retail only. Shop and mail order.)

101 East Avenue C
Lampasas, TX 76550
(512) 556-2355

16in (40.6cm) Abagail and 21in (53.3cm) Matthew.

Carole Bowling Dolls

Small limited edition fine fabric dolls based on portraits of real children. Price range $350. - $1,000. NIADA registered dolls shown: Abagail $390.; Matthew $600. + postage and insurance. SASE for printed list. (Retail only. Mail order only.)

P. O. Box 272
West Roxbury, MA 02132
(617) 327-5094

Doll Artists & Makers

Dolls
by Corazon Ugalde-Yellen
Superior quality porcelain doll replicas; costumes designed and hand-sewn by herself. Photographs.

1615 Benedict Canyon Drive
Beverly Hills, CA 90210

Poker Alice - $150.

Original Porcelain Character Dolls
by Filis Coit
Animal, portrait, folk, fantasy and western character dolls by Filis Coit. Porcelain heads. Retail price range $35. - $300. Printed list $.50. Photographs. (Wholesale and retail.)

1846 Fuller Road
Colorado Springs, CO 80918
(301) 598-3925

Lovely Anna.

The Doll Emporium
First in a series of four porcelain and cloth lady dolls by Ginger. Exquisite in basque, pantalettes, laced corset, hoops, billowing petticoat and a dress of pale pink satin and candy pink velvet. Limited edition of 200. $185. postpaid. Series $175. - $225. Send SASE for printed list. (Retail only. Shop and mail order.)

Route 2, Box 187, South Hiway 183
Lampasas, TX 76550

Littlest Angel.

Judith W. Little
Original dolls with flexible, cloth covered wire armature bodies. Each uniquely costumed in period styles. Size range 4in (10.2cm) to 18in (45.7cm). Price range $10. - $50. SASE for list. Photographs available. (Retail only. Mail order only.)

1912 Adams Court
Mt. View, CA 94040

Doll house family.

Granny & Me
René E. Wells
Each porcelain doll is a work of art, meticulously crafted with quality materials, insuring you the finest authentic reproductions available. By award-winning artist, René E. Wells. Thirty dolls miniature size to 16in (40.6cm). Price range $35. and up + postage and insurance. (Shop and mail order.)

136 "F" Street
Port Townsend, WA 98368
(206) 385-6269

Boots Tyner Originals

5027 Whispering Falls
Houston, Texas 77084

"SARA"
PLAYMATE SERIES
Limited Edition of 600

"CASEY"
TODDLER SERIES
Limited Edition of 600

The **Boots Tyner** collection of limited edition character dolls made from original sculptures, meticulously crafted with only the finest quality materials. Each porcelain doll is completely hand painted and comes with its own plexiglas stand, engraved nameplate and Certificate of Authenticity. Price range $275 - $450. For more information and color photos send SASA and $2.00.

DOLL ARTISAN GUILD

15in (38.1cm) Sally Jane Goes to Market, porcelain shoulder head, $75.

Stuffins Dolls by Sheila Meadows

Award-winning porcelain originals in limited editions. Character dolls and portrait dolls. (Send detailed description for estimate on portrait or custom work.) Price range $60. - $500. Send $1.00 + SASE for printed list. (Retail only. Mail order and shows.)

P. O. Box 227
Collinsville, AL 35961
(205) 524-2218

16in (40.6cm) Twirp SFBJ 247.

The Enchanted Doll

Fifty beautiful and authentic porcelain reproductions of antique dolls. Blanks to dressed dolls from $25. - $400. Each doll custom made with care and attention to detail. Illustrated catalog $1.50. Photographs. (Retail only. Shop and mail order.)

1038 Heritage Hill Drive, Apt B
Naperville, IL 60540
(312) 420-0178

A treasure of love in shades of velvet.

Geraldine Ives

Beautiful porcelain reproduction SFBJ 252 Pouty in velvets or delicate fabrics, ginghams or dotted swiss. State color and fabric choices. Blonde or brunette $105. - $125. Send $1.50 for photograph. (Wholesale and retail. Shop and mail order.)

18 Asbury Court
Binghamton, NY 13905
(607) 722-9544

Dolls by Karen Petersen Wirth (D.A.G.).

Les Petits Amis

Authentic French and German reproductions accurately and beautifully costumed, signed and dated by artist. Dolls made to order, can be musical, composition or cloth bodies. Modern paperweight eyes, distinctive colors. Wide price range. Write for information. (Wholesale and retail.)

1526 Benton Street
Alameda, CA 94501
(415) 865-7803

Scotty, "Children of the Past" series.

Lois Moore's House of Dolls

Original artist's edition in porcelain, representing my "Children of the Past" series (5 different dolls). Expertly china painted. Cloth bodies are wired for mobility. Toys included with doll. Very limited edition. Price range $150. -$200 + postage and insurance. Picture brochure available January 1983 $1.00 + LSASE. (Retail only.)

19 Crestview Drive
York, PA 17402
(717) 741-2601

A Marqué doll.

Susan Hawkins Dolls

Highest quality award-winning porcelain reproductions made by skilled artist. Beautifully costumed or dress them yourself. Forty dolls, retail price range $60. - $500. Printed list $1.00. Photographs available. (Shop and mail order.)

Route 4, Box 256-B
Harrisonburg, VA 22801
(703) 867-5188

19in (48.3cm) Steiner.

Betty's Dolls

The finer porcelain reproductions by Betty Schreiner. Each doll signed, numbered and dated. Satisfaction guaranteed. Distributor for Shirmar, Seeley and IMSCO. We carry a full line of doll making supplies. Printed list $1.00. (Shop, mail order and shows.)

1244 Agency Street
Burlington, IA 52601
(319) 752-2289

Bru Jne 24"   *A.14T. 25"*

Yesterday's Charmers

For information and photo, please send $1.00 and a self-addressed, stamped envelope to:

Yesterday's Charmers
1525 N.W. Woodland Dr.
Corvallis, OR 97330
503/757-7362 (by appointment)

Yesterday's Charmers
Fine Antique Doll Reproductions
by
Charleen Thanos

Armand Marseille doll.

Glady's Ceramic Chalet

Antique reproduction dolls of finest porcelain, delicately china painted and assembled. Price range $25.-$300. + postage and insurance. Illustrated catalog $1.50. List only send SASE. (Retail only. Shop and mail order.)

691 Keystone Road
Traverse City, MI 49684
(616) 947-4149

Claudia Gooch-Zamzow

Needlemaid ™ Designs. Fully-jointed 1/12th scale costume dolls for the discriminating collector. Each one-of-a-kind original is finely hand-stitched in delicate detail. SASE for more information. Printed list or photograph $1.00. (Retail only.)

P. O. Box 4610
Santa Clara, CA 95054
(408) 294-2327

1¾in (4.5cm) bride dressed in antique lace - $50.

Verity's Dolls

Original limited edition miniature dolls, ¾in (2.0cm) to 2in (5.1cm) tall. Fimo, latex, composition. Authentic antique types including French Bébés, Parisiennes, Queen Annes, etc. Also fantasy figures. Will reproduce your favorite doll in miniature. Retail price range $20. - $100. Wholesale (Latex dolls only) price $10. Printed list $1.00. (Mail order only.)

Route 1, Box 429
Eureka, CA 95501

Past and present.

13in (33.0cm) girl by Lenci, circa
1920s. Made in Italy. The little
dog was made in England by
Farnell Alpha Toys, circa 1920s.
Photograph by John Axe.

Be sure to tell that
You found it in
THE DOLL CATALOG

DOLL DEALERS

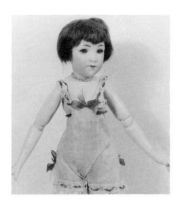

R.H. Stevens

Antique and modern doll list $.50; paper doll list $.50. Will lend photographs. (Wholesale and retail.)
Rt. 1, Box 476D
Umatilla, FL 32784
(904) 821-3276

Cher and Farrah.

Coppola's

Cher and Farrah 12in (30.5cm) dolls by Mego. Discontinued, mint in package. Jointed arms, legs, turning head, rooted hair (Cher's hair 9in long). Special sale - great opportunity. Sample pair $7.50; any six for $18.; your choice $29. per dozen. Postage + handling $2.50. Offer good through 1982 or until stock depleted. Visa/Mastercard/COD.
Berry Road
Derry, NH 03038
(603) 432-2446

Roslyn Linda Herman

Catalog of over 3,000 items. *Ginny* to Jumeau. Many M.I.B. box lots. Hard to find old accessories. Toys. Send 5 stamps with large envelope. You will be overwhelmed and delighted! Free catalog. Photographs $1.00 each. (Mail order only.)

124-16 84th Road
Kew Gardens, NY 11415

Rare French A.T.

The Doll Gallery

Florence Kotanjian

Dolls new and old. Doll houses and miniatures. Teddy bears. Doll supplies. (Retail only. Shop and mail order.)

1276 East Main Street
Ventura, CA 93001
(805) 648-5566

Westwood Ceramic Supply Co.

Doll supply source for collectors and dealers. Fast service. We manufacture Sun Dynasty™porcelain. Wigs, eyes, cord; all your doll needs. Dealers please write on letterhead. Catalog and printed list available. (Wholesale and retail.)

14400 Lomitas Avenue
Industry, CA 91746
(213) 330-0631

Shirley's Dollhouse

We carry the largest inventory of collector dolls, old and new, in the Midwest. Fliers and lists available upon request. Send long double-stamped envelope for same. (Retail only. Shop and mail order.)
20509 N. Hwy 21, P.O. Box 99A
Wheeling, IL 60090
(312) 537-1632

Bru Jne. 11, 24in (61.0cm)

Lynne's Doll House

Limited edition character and portrait dolls in porcelain. Authentic porcelain reproductions of highest quality, dressed in appropriate costumes. Price range $60. - $400. plus postage and insurance. Printed list $.25, photograph $.50. (Retail only. Shop and mail order.)

**P.O. Box 1637
Silsbee, TX 77656
(713) 385-3660**

Alice in Wonderland dolls

Something Special

Antique and collectible dolls, toys and bears for sale. Shop open Monday, Thursday, Friday and Saturday from May to October. Always interested in buying or trading. Doll repair, dressing and appraisals. Photographs $1.00. (Shop and mail order.)

**Route 9
Garrison, NY 10524
(914) 424-3779**

Wanda's Dolls

We buy and sell antique to modern collectible dolls. If traveling through, stop and shop (by appointment only). Also mail order and shows. Postage and insurance additional. Pictured list $1.00 or large double-stamped SASE and $.50. (Retail only.)

**274 Benita
Youngstown, OH 44504
(216) 743-9715**

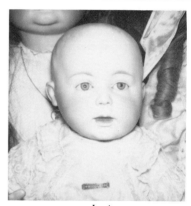

Lori.

Cookie's Dolls

Discontinued personality dolls, TV stars, sport figures, character dolls, paper dolls, Barbies, much more. Everything mint-in-box. Postage paid. Satisfaction guaranteed. Price range $5. - $25. Send SASE for free list. (Mail order only.)

**15315 S.W. Village Lane
Beaverton, OR 97007
(503) 644-6157**

Lovely Dolly Parton in colonial dress.

8in (20.3cm) Just Me.

Victorian Vintage

Collector favorites in porcelain and sculpted. Elegant ladies and children, period dolls and character dolls. $75. - $200. When writing send LSASE and state what you are interested in. (Mail orders and shows.)

**P.O. Box 761
Clark, NJ 07066**

Second Childhood

Antique reproduction dolls in porcelain. 8in (20.3cm) Just Me $50.; undressed $40. plus $2.00 postage. Other dolls start at $20. SASE plus $1.00 for list. Mastercharge and Visa. Satisfaction guaranteed. (Wholesale and retail. Shop and mail order.)

**473 North Palm Canyon Drive
Palm Springs, CA 92262
(714) 320-6151 or 320-7171**

Doll Repair Parts, Inc

Wigs, crowns, glass eyes, plastic eyes, doll shoes, socks, dress patterns, doll books, doll stands, reproduction bodies, hands and feet. Doll molds by American Beauty Ceramics, paints. Catalog $.50. (Wholesale and retail. Shop and mail order.)

9918 Lorain Avenue
Cleveland, OH 44102
(216) 961-3545

Anili Dolls Designed

by Elena Scavini - who was known as Madame Lenci.

Except for the few that tourists bring home from abroad, every Anili Doll that arrives in America comes first to The Pittsburgh Doll Company, signed and dated. Supplies of these fine dolls are very limited -- only about 400 a year are available to American collectors. Several of the finer doll shops and dealers carry various models and we always have some on hand. Of course, you can order whatever doll you choose from our illustrated list. There are five types and about 50 different models, including some great clowns. Prices from $175. SASE for information and prices. $1.00 and LSASE for information, prices and illustrated descriptive list of entire line.

THE PITTSBURGH
DOLL COMPANY

Shirley Buchholz
2814 Herron Lane
Glenshaw, PA 15116
(412) 486-4978

Joyce Kintner
4 Old Timber Trail
Pittsburgh, PA 15238
(412) 963-7881

Mandeville's Antiques and Collectibles

The finest in collectible dolls in mint condition bought and sold. Always interested in purchasing quality dolls. Selling premium collectibles by mail and at better shows. (Mail order and shows.)

380 Dartmouth Court
Bensalem, PA 19020
(215) 638-2561

Gigi's Dolls

Antique to modern dolls for sale. Norman Rockwell, Effanbee, Suzanne Gibson and Sasha. Dolls bought and repaired. Write wants.

Route 30 and Route 59
Plainfield, IL 60544
(815) 436-6488
(312) 729-0187

Yesterday's Children

We buy and sell antique and collectible dolls. Our color Madame Alexander post cards are available, 12 cards for $3.00. Postage and insurance additional. List subscription (issued five times a year) $5.00. Current list $1.25 (Wholesale and retail. Mail order only.)

P.O. Box 233
Buffalo, NY 14226

New Hampshire's miniature fairytale land.

The Little Red Doll House

A fantasy world of collectors' dolls and miniatures from all over the world. Featuring local artists and craftsmen. Open daily 10 a.m. - 5 p.m. Sundays 12 noon - 4 p.m. Prepare to be enchanted. Send SASE for brochure. (Shop and mail order.)

**141 Union Street
Manchester, NH 03103
(603) 624-4898**

22in (55.9cm) Bru Jne.

Maxine Berv

Love your investment - antique bisque character babies, French, German, Schoenhuts, Fulpers, large and small. Excellent quality and values, beautifully dressed. Return privileges, layaways. Postage and insurance additional. SASE for free list. (Mail order and shows.)

**Box 341
Oceanside, NY 11572
(516) 764-0158**

Plain & Fancy Doll Shoppe

Antiques, collectibles bought and sold. General repairs, custom dressing. Lay-a-way terms. Night appointments for your convenience. Will answer letters on "wants." (Shop and mail order.)

**13505 Spriggs Road
Manassas, VA 22111
(703) 791-3364**

Jane Miller

Mint-in-box Sun Spell - Moon Mystic Goddesses, Barbies, vinyl, small foreign dressed, advertising dolls and modern dolls. Also make doll clothes. Send LSASE for free list. (Mail order. Lay-a-way plan.)

**10347 Southwest East Ridge
Portland, OR 97225**

Dollie Dear

Beautifully handmade dolls from Mainland China. Three different styles available: Girl with Yo Yo, Sleeping Girl on Pumpkin, Girl Pulling Pumpkin, 5½in (14.0cm) high, $4.50 each + $2.50 postage. Send SASE for printed list. (Mail order only.)

**P.O. Box 2383
North Canton, OH 44720
(216) 494-7322**

Gerweck's Small World of Dolls

Complete line of doll making supplies to aid you in reproducing dolls from masters of times gone by. Also doll houses, miniatures, stands and kilns. Catalog $2.50. (Wholesale and retail. Shop and mail order.)

**6299 Dixon Road
Monroe, MI 48161
(313) 269-2536**

Trenholm's Treasures

160 Sedalia Court
Alpharetta, GA 30201
(404) 475-3379

HOSPITAL TRAINING
MANNEKINS

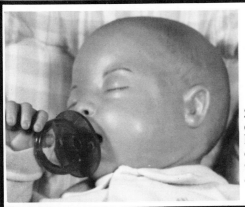

Baby Susie

(Resusci Baby)

22in (55.9cm) long, vinyl; molded closed eyes/beautifully painted eyelashes and eyebrows. Ball jointed; can be taken apart; sexed. Comes wearing shorts, packed in a suitcase. $225.

CANDY

Candy

20in (50.8cm) long, 6¼ pounds, not sexed. Fully-jointed like a doll rather than a mannekin. All vinyl, rosy-pink coloring. Auburn painted hair, super-quality blue sleep eyes. $80.

Anthony & Amy

Cuddly newborns made of silky soft vinyl, 21½in (54.6cm) long, 7¼ pounds. Anthony is a sexed boy; Amy is a sexed girl. Brown painted eyes and deeply molded, painted brown hair. Ball-jointed, very detailed bodies. Anthony - $165.; Amy - $140.

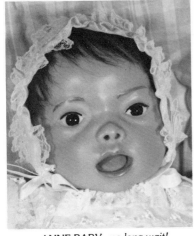

ANNE BABY - no long wait!

Anne Baby

21in (53.3cm) long, 6½ pounds, vinyl. She drinks, wets, messes her pants. Ball-jointed body; sexed. Choice of original or new blue, brown or green eyes. Comes in hospital clothes and covered bathtub. With original eyes - $155.; with new eyes - $160.

SEXED BILLY & KEVIN

Sexed Billy & Kevin

23in (58.4cm) long, 11 pounds, 12 ounces, 6 months old, vinyl, unjointed, sexed boys. Eyes molded closed; add $10. for painted eyelashes and eyebrows. Kevin has black features/molded afro. $135. each.

Nathan

Beautiful, unsexed boy mannekin. Made of good quality vinyl, fully-jointed, body strung. 22in (55.9cm) long, weighs almost 6 pounds. Painted eyes, painted, brush-stroked hair. $130.

NATHAN

Delivery times vary; some items in stock; shipped free in US. All babies come with a birth certificate. Prefer certified check or money order. Lay-a-way and COD available. Many other dolls and related items available. Send $1.00 for catalog.

Doll Dealers

41

Bisque limited edition Gerber Baby.

Ronelle Sales

New limited edition bisque Gerber Baby. Each doll is numbered and comes with certificate. Also black vinyl new Gerber Baby. Send $1.50 for catalog and information featuring modern collectible dolls. (Mail order only.)

**1841 Stanley Drive
Merrick, NY 11566**

Memory's Doll Hospital & Shop

Old and modern dolls. Bisque, celluloid, compo, papier-mâché, wood, vinyl and cloth. Old Ginnys, old Alexanders also. Wanted: nude 8" Alexander walkers, 42" Penny Alexander and bisque, Alexander hard plastic 21" girl dolls and 21" compo Alexander girl dolls. (Mail order only.)

**P.O. Box 684
Temple City, CA 91780**

Grace Ochsner Doll House

Antique dolls for sale, characters, black, doll furniture, babies, collectors' dolls. Shop open six days, closed Thursdays, or by appointment. Inquiries welcome by mail or phone. Printed list $.50, Photographs $1.00 each. (Shop and mail order.)

**R. R. 1
Niota, IL 62358
(217) 755-4362**

Dollie Dear

Discontinued Vogue dolls: Sleepy Eye 8in (20.3cm) Ginny; 18in (45.7cm) Baby Dear, brown hair; 25in (63.5cm) Baby Dear, blonde hair; 22in (55.9cm) Hug-a-Bye; 16in (40.6cm) Brickett, red or blonde hair; Miss Debutante. Send $5.00 for catalog or SASE for printed list. (Mail order only.)

**P.O. Box 2383
North Canton, OH 44720
(216) 494-7322**

Small Wonders Antiques

From bisque to plastic, we carry a varied selection of dolls and antiques. Quality handmade teddies. Phone ahead before visiting. LSASE for doll list or teddy information. (Dolls retail only. Teddies wholesale and retail. Shop and mail order.)

**131 Church Street
New Windsor, MD 21776
(301) 875-2850**

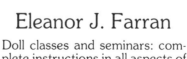

Eleanor J. Farran

Doll classes and seminars: complete instructions in all aspects of doll making including pouring, cleaning, china painting, stringing, setting eyes, wig making, costuming and much more!

**33 Fieldview Drive
Fort Salonga, L. I., NY 11768**

Some dolls from my more than 150 molds.

Doll Dealers

Barnard Originals

Original porcelain doll heads on porcelain bodies (by leading doll mold companies) available either undressed or dressed. Glass eyes and finest quality synthetic wigs are used. Price range $75. - $115. (Mail order only.)

3065 Sumter Drive
Dallas, TX 75220

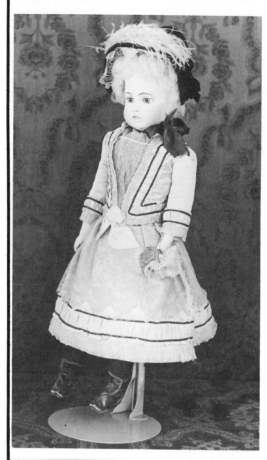

The Antique Shop of Elizabeth Winsor McIntyre

Largest collection of antique dolls in an open shop in New England. Open daily 11-5. (Wholesale and retail. Shop, shows and mail order.)

Riverton (Hitchcocksville), CT 06065
(203) 379-4726

Angie's Doll Boutique

The most unique shop in Old Town offers you a fine selection of dolls, antique, Alexander, Effanbee, Sasha, Vogue (Ginny) and bears. We buy and sell dolls. Printed list $1.00. (Retail only. Shop. Mail order MIB dolls only.)

1114 King Street, Old Town
Alexandria, VA 22314
(703) 683-2807

Afternoon tea party. Dolls illustrated are for sale.

New 1982 Sasha.

The Doll's Nest

Complete line of modern dolls. Sasha dolls are just one of the many lines available. Sasha catalog and price list $.50 postpaid. For list of old and antique dolls send SASE. (Retail only. Shop and mail order.)

1020 Kenmore Boulevard, Dept. D
Akron, OH 44314
(216) 753-2464
New 1982 Sasha.

Dianne's Dolls

Alexanders, Vogue, Effanbee, Barbies. We specialize in TV personalities, movie stars and discontinued dolls. Always a large selection. Open by chance or appointment. LSASE for printed list. (Shop and mail order.)

521 Caudle
Springdale, AR 72764

(501) 756-3573

Winter, Katia and Spring by Anili (Lenci's daughter).

Stefanie's Treasures

Weekly telephone specials. Every order is promptly acknowledged. Lines include: Anili, Lenci, Corolle, Sasha, Effanbee, Hummel, BJY, Rockwell, Kruse, Steiff, Hermann, North American Bears and many others too numerous to list. We have porcelain, bisque, vinyl, wax and the Lenci and Anili felt. Artist originals and reproductions. You will love Stefanie's Treasures and her prices! Send $2.50 (U.S. funds) for any of the following catalogs: Marjorie Spangler, Suzanne Gibson, Effanbee or Sasha. (Mail order only.) Visa/Master Charge/Interbank/Bank America Card.

**P.O. Box 904
Sunnyside, WA 98944
(509) 837-4302**

Empire Antiques & Dolls

Dolls - bisque, china, composition, hard plastic and vinyl. Doll accessories - shoes, stockings, excellent lines of clothes, wigs. Doll artist, Paul Crees' dolls - Dietrich, Garbo, Garland, Harlow, Crawford. Write for information. Photographs $1.00 each. (Retail only. Shop and mail order.)

**6740 Empire Way South
Seattle, WA 98118
(206) 722-9906**

Sasha and Effanbee dolls.

Dusty's Doll Hospital & Supply

We carry a complete line of Effanbee, Royal, Kehagias, Gorham and Applause (introducing "Annie") dolls. Due to our volume buying, customer's individual orders may take additional time in shipping. Free estimates for repairs. (Shop and mail order.)

**4855 Highway 78
Lilburn, GA 30247
(404) 972-5626**

"From yesterday through tomorrow."

Kay's Doll House

Picture shows one doll of each manufacture. We have complete line of Sasha and Effanbee dolls. Sasha catalog $1.50, Effanbee catalog $2.50. (Retail only. Shop and mail order.)

**P.O. Box 367, 222 East Vine
Ellettsville, IN 47429
(812) 876-2237**

Barbara Jo Dolls

Specializing in rare and hard-to-find Madame Alexander dolls. Always a beautiful selection to choose from. We buy and sell Madame Alexander, Ginny and Shirley Temple collectible dolls and books. No catalog or list. (Mail order and shows only.)

Barbara Jo McKeon
P.O. Box 1481—T.D.C.
Brockton, MA 02402
(617) 586-1279

Heubach Baby Stuart pincushion head.

Zelda H. Cushner

I sell antique dolls, modern artists' dolls (featuring NIADA), collectible dolls occasionally and many small all-bisque and bisque-head dolls, also some replicas. Printed list $.50 + LSASE (4 ounces.) (Home and mail order.)

12 Drumlin Road
Marblehead, MA 01945
(617) 631-5819

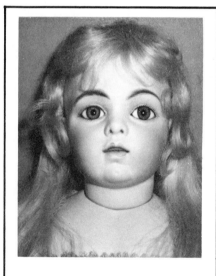

Billie Nelson Tyrrell's Dolls

Always a large selection of fine antique and collector's dolls. Two printed lists available; one for antique dolls, one for personality dolls. Send 4 stamps. (Mail order, conventions, and shows only. Retail only.)

P.O. Box 1000
Studio City, CA 91604

The Unicorn

Collect the heartland of America. Fall in love with these limited edition Norman Rockwell character dolls, handcrafted of German porcelain with removable clothing. Send $2.50 for our brochure. Also available Effanbee, Hagara collectibles, Seeley Doll plates.

Suite 1946
28 North Dryden
Arlington Hts., IL 60004
(312) 253-1280

Hobby Center Toys — Where Doll Collections Begin

"Hobby Center Toys is the Leader in Doll Collections in Ohio, Michigan and Indiana with over 20 stores to meet your needs. In stock is a large variety of original doll artist dolls and collectable dolls. Manufacturers featured include:

Madame Alexander	Heidi Ott
Alresford	Louis Nicole
Joanne McCracken	Faith Wick
Gerber	Classic Doll Creations
Sasha	Kendall
Effanbee	Kathe Kruse
Marjorie Spangler	Lenci
Suzanne Gibson	Marcello
Peggy Nisbet	Doulton-Nisbet Dolls
Furga	Doll-Lain Originals
Dolls by Pauline	Ann Parker Dolls
The Gorham Doll Collection	Zapf Dolls
Dolls by Jerri	Armand Marseille

Official Babyland General Adoption Center

In addition, Hobby Center Toys carries a large selection of Steiff Animals and unusual Teddy Bears such as Herman, Lemon Bear, Trupa, Bialosky Bear and North American Bear.

Hobby Center Toys is glad to accept special orders on many items. Mail orders, and lay-away terms are available. Master Card, Visa and American Express are accepted.

As part of Hobby Center Toys' continuing commitment to Doll Collectors, the Fourth Annual International Doll Show and Sale will take place September 30 through October 3, 1982 at the Franklin Park Mall, Toledo, Ohio. The show will feature representatives from leading doll manufacturers, appraisals of private collections, as well as special guests who will visit during the show.

AKRON, OHIO
Chapel Hill
Summit Mall

CANTON, OHIO
Belden Village Mall

CINCINNATI, OHIO
Beechmont Mall

CLEVELAND, OHIO
Randall Park Mall

DAYTON, OHIO
Dayton Mall

ELYRIA-LORIAN, OHIO
Midway Mall

FINDLAY, OHIO
Findlay Village Mall

FREMONT, OHIO
Potter Village

LIMA, OHIO
Lima Mall

NEW PHILADELPHIA, OHIO
Monroe Mall

TIFFIN, OHIO
Tiffin Mall

TOLEDO, OHIO
Franklin Park Mall
North Towne Square Mall
Southland
Southwyck Mall
Westgate
Woodville Mall

ANN ARBOR, MICHIGAN
Briarwood Shopping Center

DEARBORN, MICHIGAN
Fairlane Town Center

ROCHESTER, MICHIGAN
The Toy Store
Great Oaks Mall

SOUTH BEND, INDIANA
Scottsdale Mall

HOBBY CENTER TOYS
CRAFTS MODELS TRAINS

Franklin Park Mall
Toledo, Ohio
Thursday, September 30 - Saturday, October 2 - 10 A.M. to 9:30 P.M.
Sunday, October 3 - 12 P.M. to 5 P.M.

Doll Dealers

26in (66.0cm) Handwerck - Halbig.

Maribeth Doll Clinic

Varied selection of dolls from 1860 to 1960. Also furniture, toys, accessories. Accent on authentic costuming. Expert composition restoration. SASE for free estimate, list. Photograph $1.00. Visa, Mastercard. Price range $25. - $1,000. (Shop and mail order.)

3 Bicknell Street
Norwood, NY 13668
(315) 353-2437

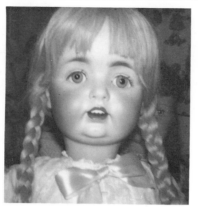

42in (106.6cm) K★R #260 character child.

Barbara DeVault's Dolls

Always a nice selection of dolls from bisque to composition; some vinyls, too. Selling from my collection. Photographs $1.00 each. (Shop and mail order.)

Box 138
New Springfield, OH 44443
(216) 542-2096

Royal Wedding Pair.

Dolls International

Peggy Nisbet dolls, authentic national dolls and artists' dolls. Color leaflets and price lists available. (Mail order only.)

412 Southwood Drive
Kingston, Ontario, Canada K7M 5P6

Yesterdears Doll Shop

Antique dolls, quality contemporary dolls and accessories. Printed list $1.00. Photographs $1.00. (Retail only. Shop and mail order.)

2410 West Broadway
Council Bluffs, IA 51501
(712) 328-1100

Tom Sawyer and Becky, Dolls by Jerri, 1982.

Olde Towne Doll Shoppe

Dolls by Alexander, Effanbee, Gibson, Sasha, Lenci, Heidi Ott, Jerri, Norman Rockwell, Marjorie Spangler, Royal Doulton, choice collectible dolls from England, France, Germany and Italy. Steiff teddy bears. Printed list available. (Retail shop and mail order.)

217 Main Street
Wethersfield, CT 06109

Handel & Associates

Porcelain dolls; greenware bisque (blanks); kits painted, unpainted, dressed and undressed. Dolls dressed just for you. One outfit or more. We now carry two new companies for doll clothes patterns: Paule's Dolly Patterns; Unique Antique Doll Clothes Patterns. $1.00 + SASE for list. (Wholesale and retail. Shop and mail order.)

1010 Westmoreland Avenue
Waukegan, IL 60085
(312) 336-1010-1051

Marcelle's Doll Shoppe & Hospital

Hand fashioned clothing new, antique, reproductions, repair, restore if possible, wigs, related doll findings. Shirley Temple, Effanbee clowns, many old collectible dolls, Soft animals, Mother Tooth fairy, customer ideas? Special mail requested information. (Retail only. Shop and mail order.)

**170 West Main Street
Wytheville, VA 24382
(703) 228-3210**

Marcelles favorite restoration.

The Doll Shop

New dolls include Effanbee, Sasha, Ideal, Royal, Lenci, Gibson, Hummel and Zapf. Steiff and Russ animals plus name teddy bears. Antique and collectible dolls. Stands, books, clothing, shoes, stockings, wigs. Catalog $1.50. Printed list $1.00. (Wholesale and retail. Shop and mail order.)

**903 South A Street
Richmond, IN 47374
(317) 962-5365**

Beautiful storybook reproduction doll is bisque, ours alone for $65. each. Mail order available. Visa/Mastercard accepted.

Doll Faire Miniatures

Beautiful reproduction dolls by the finest artists. Vinyl collectors' dolls by Effanbee, Marjorie Spangler, Jerri, Suzanne Gibson. Imported dolls by Sasha, Götz, Zaph and Corvele. Official Little Person Adoption Agency. Complete selection of patterns, clothes, accessories. Write for information. (Retail only. Shop and mail order.) Daily 10:00 am - 5:30 pm. OPEN SUNDAYS 12:00 - 5:00 pm.
**1270-A Newell Avenue
Walnut Creek, CA 94596
(415) 933-3655**

Bru-11

Dunham Porcelain Art

Artist originals and antique replicas. You will find these dolls to be the answer to a collector's dream and a child's prayer. Range: $20. -$600. + postage. Printed list: $1.00. (Wholesale, retail and mail order.)

36429 Row River Road
Cottage Grove, OR 97424

25in (63.5cm) Téte Jumeau.

Doll Carousel

Specializing in antique French and German dolls. Return privileges. Lay-a-ways. Interested in buying quality dolls. (Mail order and shows.)

P. O. Box 1377
Princeton, NJ 08540
(609) 924-6295

Sheri's Doll Shoppe

Extra large and rare dolls. Delicate coloring of lashes and brows. 5in to 42in (12.7cm to 106.6cm). Retail price: $25. - $350. Postage and insurance additional. SASE for printed lists. Photographs available. (Wholesale and retail. Shop and mail order.)

2256 South Mayfair
Springfield, MO 65804
(417) 883-1450

30in (76.2cm) Téte Jumeau,

Lola's Doll Shoppe

Antique dolls, reproduction dolls, doll making supplies, all doll accessories, repairs, costuming, greenware. Doll making seminars, wig classes, hat classes. Seeley's distributor. Hours 10 a.m. - 5 p.m. weekdays. Saturdays 10 a.m. - 2 p.m. Closed Wednesdays. (Retail only. Shop and mail order.)

1930 Gull Road
Kalamazoo, MI 49001
(616) 344-2539

Undressed doll bodies wired for positioning as shown.

Dolls by Penny

Doll house dolls come bodied and wigged, ready to dress. Bodies are wired for positioning (see illustration). Only sold with purchase of one of my patterns (see listing in pattern section). Price $37. postpaid. LSASE for list. (Retail only.)

414 Cessna Avenue
Charleston, SC 29407
(803) 571-0376

Heirloom Dolls by the DeAngelos

Quality antique doll reproductions. Great care given to assure exactness to original. Large selection of Steiner, Brus, Jumeaus, A.T.s, German character dolls, miniatures, all-bisque. Large SASE for price list. (Wholesale and retail. Shop and mail order.)

5003 Tahoe Trail
Austin, TX 78745
(512) 444-2323

Selection of over 100 dolls.

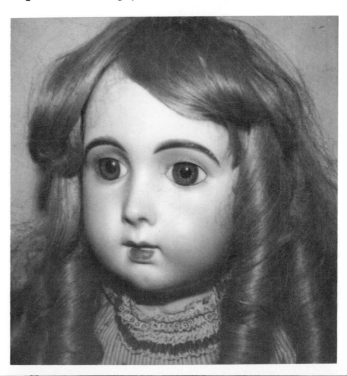

Joyce's Dolls

We carry lines by Effanbee, Horsman, Sasha, Suzanna Gibson, Peggy Nisbet, Furga, Dolls by Jerri, Heidi Ott, Royal Doulton, GTC German, Ideal, Yesteryear and modern collectibles. Catalog, pictures and prices available. (Shop and mail order.)

6435 Knowlesville Road
Oakfield, NY 14125
(716) 948-5519

Alexander's 1968 Godey Portrette.

Cherib

Collectible modern dolls from the leading (and trailing) makers. Books and accessories. We search for dolls and sometimes even find one! LSASE for printed list. (Retail only. Mail order only.)

738 East Palmaire Avenue
Phoenix, AZ 85020

Baby Gloria, reproduction by Sarah Burton.

Doll Depot

Reproduction porcelain dolls finished and kits. Original porcelain dolls, Seeley distributor, IMSCO dealer, Effanbees, stands, shoes, socks, hats, wigs, clothes. Porcelain greenware and bisque. Classes and seminars. Printed list $.50. (Wholesale and retail. Shop and mail order.)

560 Locust Street
Middletown, IN 47356
(317) 354-4885

Mella's Doll Shelf

Largest selection of German and French dolls, Bru fashion 235, 236, 237, Jumeaus, characters, compositions, Dionnes, excellent Bye-Los, nursing Bru, largest size Jumeaus, composition Shirley Temples, creche, M.A.S. Lay-aways. Printed list $1.00, photographs $2.00. (Wholesale and Retail.)

Box 751
Melville, Long Island, NY 11747

Oh you beautiful Dollies.

Once Upon a Time Doll Shop

Antique and collectible dolls. A shop for dollies and their friends. Open Tuesday through Saturday 10:30 a.m. - 5:30 p.m. (Retail only. Shop and mail order.)

8942 Tampa Avenue
Northridge, CA 91324
(213) 701-5937

Marilyn Harris

Barbies and other modern collectible dolls. LSASE for list. (Retail only. Mail order and shows only.)

**1833 Cripple Creek
Garland, TX 75041**

Doll note paper, "The Tea Party."

Jean's 20th Century Dolls and Decorated Eggs

Chittenango R#2, NY 13037

New and Older Collectible Dolls. Books - Paper Dolls - Supplies. Doll Note paper - cocktail napkins. Decorated Lg. Goose Eggs with doll pictures, etc. Doll pictured placques (several styles). Strawberry Shortcake soft doll + more. Teddy Bears. Doll clothing and sweater sets. Doll Swing. "Lots more."(Sell hand made items on consignment.) Write: Beverly Jean Smith Misc. List $1.00 - Doll - book etc. List $.75.

"Remember Me" in The Grainery

Connie Kaffel

Collector dolls and old time toys. Send SASE for list. (Retail only. Shop and mail order.)

**Oak and Elwood Street
Frankfort, IL 60423
(815) 469-6399**

*Michelle, 23in (58.4cm) marked: S * H — Hanna.*

Kelley's Doll Porch

Midwest's most complete selection of collectors dolls, TV and modern day dolls and accessories. Alexanders, Effanbee, Nisbet, Sasha, Faith Wick, Jerri, Spangler, Gibson, Lenci. Send your wants - - we special order. SASE - a must, two stamps. (Wholesale and retail. Shop and mail order.)
**25 West Main Street
Marshalltown, IA 50158
(515) 752-4960**

Ageless Treasures

Barbie, Madame Alexander, Ideal, Vogue and other collectible dolls and paper dolls. Current dolls including Berjusa's Minene, Wishniks, Jesmar, Royal Doll Co., Kehagias. Doll related cards, notes and gift items. Printed list $.75. (Wholesale and retail. Mail order only.)

**403 Kingsbury Drive
Arlington, IL 60004
(312) 870-8162**

Jesmar's Mency Mama sings in Spanish as she rocks her baby.

54   Doll Dealers

Dorvey's Antiques

29 INVERNESS AVENUE WEST
Hamilton, Ontario, Canada L9C 1A1
Telephone: (416) 388-9835
Wanted to Buy: Mme Alex Quints, French Bisque & German Bisque

We stock beautiful antique dolls. We buy collections. We ship dolls all over the world. We appraise collector's dolls. We repair dolls. Always Something Rare. Always Something Reasonable. Always Terms Available.

Chargex or Master Charge.

Doll Emporium

We have one of the largest selections of old dolls and old parts in the country. (Retail only. Shop and shows only.)

13035 Ventura Boulevard
Studio City, CA 91604

Barbara Jo McKeon

Rare and Hard to Find Madame Alexander Collector's Dolls
by Barbara Jo McKeon
A must for doll lovers! Over 80 dolls never seen in reference books before. 300 full color pages, over 600 dolls. Single copy $24.95. New Price Guide II $3.95 plus $.75 postage and handling. Write for quantity discounts.

Madame Alexander Scarletts Calendar 1983
by Barbara Jo McKeon
Full color calendar, 9 x 10″. Photographs of Scarlett dolls from the past to the current are truly beautiful. Each month has a different 5 x 7″ color photograph of a Scarlett giving year, type and value of each doll. First 500 numbered and signed. $17.50 postpaid.

P. O. Box 1481-T.D.C.
Brockton, MA 02402
(617) 586-1279

The Prairie Miss.

Linda MacLennan

Earliest American doll. Handcrafted reproductions and adaptations of mid 19th century favorites including peddlers. Sawdust stuffed kid and/or cloth bodies. Price range $35. - $150. Catalog $1.50. (Wholesale and retail.)

**183 Glasgow Street
Clyde, NY 14433
(315) 923-3531**

The Doll Shoppe in the Park

Alexanders, specializing rare and hard-to-find: rare Dionne MIB, Jenny Lind, Janie-faced Lucinda, Lissys, Jacqueline, Prince Charles, Tinkerbelle, Maggie-face Japan, Coco. All currents available. Please specify wants. Send LSASE for list. (Shop and mail order.)

**8000 Crow Canyon Road
Castro Valley, CA 94546
(415) 582-5553**

Left to right: (rare) White Wendykin Ballerina, B/K Laurie and Wendy Walks her Dog.

5½in (14.0cm) 19th century china head sisters.

Betty's Doll Haven

I have a fine selection of antique, unusual and collectible dolls, something for every collector's taste and budget. Come by and visit when passing through. Large SASE for free list. Photograph $1.00. Always interested in buying dolls. (Retail only. Shop and mail order.)

**1020 California Southeast
Albuquerque, NM 87108
(505) 265-2548**

Doralee Burger

Noted appraiser, author, lecturer, auction - cataloguist, antique doll restorer. Old dolls bought and sold. Postage and insurance additional. Photographed antique doll list available for long SASE. Satisfaction guaranteed. (Shows and mail order.)

**37-E Colburn Drive
Poughkeepsie, NY 12603
(914) 462-6688**

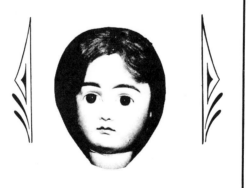

John Wayne - the 3rd of Effanbee's Legend Series.

Rocky & His Friends

A fun place to visit! Lovely old shop in quaint historic village. One of the area's leading doll centers including antiques, collectible, complete line of Effanbee dolls, doll houses and miniatures. (Shop and mail order.)

**18 North Main Street
Medford, NJ 08055
(609) 654-8558**

C & W Enterprises

Mary Ann Cook

Antique, collectible and modern dolls including Alexander, Effanbee, Nisbet, Sasha, Vogue, Heidi Ott, Wicket Originals, Babyland "Little People," stands, Kewpie and teddy bear greeting cards, Steiff. Printed list $.75 + LSASE. (Wholesale and retail. Mail order and shows.)

**2700 Titleist Drive
Salem, VA 24153
(703) 389-2615**

© Arabelle Creations 1982.

Doll Dealers

Stoeckel's Antique Clocks & Dolls

We carry a good line of antique and collectible dolls. We are open most days from 9 to 5. Other times by chance and appointment. Postage and insurance additional. (Wholesale and retail.)

615 Northwest Third Street
Faribault, MN 55021
(507) 334-7772

German closed-mouth marked 8.

Main Street Emporium

French and German antique dolls from fashion to baby dolls. Hundreds to choose from, many rare and unusual. Printed list, photo each $1.00. (Wholesale and retail. Shop and mail order.)

41 Main Street
Brockport, NY 14420
(716) 637-5400

Georgianne's Dollhouse Dolls By Georgianne

Finest antique reproduction porcelain dolls 80 different ones, retail price range $22. - $250.; miniatures; unusual gifts. Doll making classes. Complete doll repair. Supplies and beautiful handcrafted clothes and accessories. Printed list $1.00; photographs available. Monday through Saturday 10 a.m. - 5 p.m. LSASE $.50. (Wholesale and retail. Shop and mail order.)

73-981 Highway 111
Palm Desert, CA 92260
(714) 346-3641

Arline Schuetz

Specializing in Madame Alexander dolls, Shirley Temples. Printed list $1.00 or call (314) 239-3380. (Mail order only.)

P. O. Box 363
Washington, MO 63090
(314) 239-3380

The Santa Cause

Unusual Santas for Santaphiles, gifts and happiness! Variety paper items including dolls, German "scrap." Article--"Mother of the Sunbonnet Babies" $2.25. Sunbonnet pictures for framing--4 different $5.50. SASE for information. Brochure $1.00. (Wholesale and retail. Mail order and shop by appointment.)

174 West Pinewood Drive
Slidell, LA 70458

Quality Gifts & Imports

Dolls: Käthe Kruse, Heidi Ott, Lenci, Baitz, Berliner. Originals by Filis Coit and Helen Kish. Musical Gorham porcelain dolls. Suzanne Gibson. Stuffed animals: Steiff & Kruse. SASE for list. (Shop and mail order.)

6850 North Academy Boulevard
Colorado Springs, CO 80918
(303) 599-5080

Doll Dealers

Kitzler's Kollectables

Limited edition collector dolls, plates, figurines, lithographs, thimbles and bells. Specialization in appraisals. Headquarter store for Seeley doll plates and limited collectibles along with full line Jan Hagara collectibles. Newsletter at no cost upon request. (Shop and mail order.)

**29516 Gratiot
Roseville, MI 48066
(313) 775-4664**

Museum of Collectible Dolls & Doll Shop

Vintage dolls, collectibles of 20th century, Alexanders, Effanbees, 500 Ginnys, movie star and character dolls, internationals, male dolls, etc. Doll hospital offers complete costuming, restoration, repairs and doll appraisals. SASE for printed list. Museum displays over 2,000 dolls. (Retail only. Shop and mail order.)

**1117 South Florida Avenue
Lakeland, FL 33803
(813) 687-8015 or 682-8484**

Corolle - soft vinyl dolls from France.

The Heather & the Holly

We carry vinyl, bisque and cloth dolls including Effanbee, Royal House, Kahegias, Sasha, GTC, Corolle, Gorham, Royal Doulton, Spun Fancy Delights, Faith Wick, Doll-Lain, etc. and many teddy bears. Price range $6.50 - $1,600. (Retail only. Shop only.)

**6017 Sunrise Boulevard
Citrus Heights, CA 95610
(916) 966-2942**

Dolls, miniatures and small surprises.

**Harborplace #98
201 East Pratt Street
Baltimore, MD 21202
(301) 332-0711**

A Little Something Ltd.

Dolls by Effanbee, Sasha, Suzanne Gibson, Dolls by Pauline, Royal and more. Porcelain reproductions and originals. Doll house furnishings and accessories. Beatrix Potter and Anette Petersen miniatures. No catalog. (Retail only. Shop and mail order.)

EXQUISITE!

20in (50.8cm) F 11 G Reproduction by Connie Walser Derek.

Museum Quality Reproductions by

Connie Walser Derek

Finally...quality reproduction dolls as serious investments for the discriminating collector or for those simply looking for a beautiful doll to enjoy and cherish. Each doll is a work of art meticulously crafted with quality materials, insuring you the finest authentic reproductions available. Write for information — Long SASE would be appreciated.

Connie's DOLLS & CO 421 S.E. 6th St., Grants Pass, Oregon 97526 · (503) 474-3030

Reproductions · Antiques · **Seminars** **Effanbee** **Steiff** **Lenci** Accessories Fabrics Lace

Girl in the Park, 1887.

Arnot Art Museum Shop

Original limited edition porcelain doll, created by River House Shoppe artists, Binghamton, New York, from painting "Girl in the Park," George Waters, 1887, in the museum's collection. $250. postpaid. Picture postcard $.25. (Retail only. Shop and mail order.)

**235 Lake Street
Elmira, NY 14901
(607) 734-3697**

Servant's

Victorian designed doll furniture. Display up to 24in (61.0cm) dolls in elegance at a reasonable price. Each piece individually handcrafted in fine wood. Price range $75.-$100. Catalog $2.00. (Wholesale and retail.)

**2124 Stow Street
Simi Valley, CA 93063**

Margot Owles, Imports from England

Reproduction doll sheets: Peggie and Teddie (1912), Teddy Bear Sheet (1905), Mignonne (ca. 1900), also 1918 printed rag toys. All sheets in full color with printed instructions. Write for lists of these and other items, stating whether retailer or collector.

**P.O. Box 135
Ewan, NJ 08025**

It's worth the trip!

Marcy Street Doll Co.

A wonderland for all to enjoy. It is well worth the trip to this special place of dolls, bears, patterns, stuffed animals, books, paper dolls and much more. Catalog $2.00. (Shop and mail order.)

**60 Marcy Street
Portsmouth, NH 03801
(603) 436-2863**

Heubach children reproductions.

Greta's Doll Nook

A complete supply source. Seeley distributor. Karen Ann, Lyn's, Frankie's patterns, wigs, shoes, eyes, composition bodies, greenware, blanks. Classes in cloth and porcelain doll making. Handcrafted collectible and play dolls. (Retail only. Shop only.)

**1918 East Prince Road
Tucson, AZ 85719
(602) 323-1523**

Rare incised Depose Jumeau.

The Stetson House

Antique dolls only. Accent on French, character dolls, fashions, early primitives; no compositions. Send LSASE for free pictured list. (Wholesale and retail. Shop and mail order.)

**Box 235, 234 South Main Street
Waynesville, OH 45068
(513) 897-2720 or 897-1747**

Mexico

USA

Scotland

Brazil

Great Britian

LIMITED EDITION
DOLLS OF ALL NATIONS

- 7½" tall handpainted bisque face, hand and feet of a lovely young lady with soft cloth body
- Each has hat and dressed in detail costume of the nation it represents
- Set of 12 nations, others not in picture are: Holland, Norway, Poland, Greece, Romania, Czechoslovakia, Yugoslavia
- $8.50 each, a great collection value
- $99.95 for set of 12 shipping free
- Matching stand $1.00 each
- Shipping $1.50 for one, $2.50 for 2, $3.00 for 3
- MAIL ORDER AND WHOLESALE
- Bisque clowns and other Dolls also
- Send $1.00 for color cataloge credit to your first order.

Touch of Rainbow

P.O. Box 1034
10345 Lakewood Boulevard
Downey, CA 90640

The Doll Carriage

Collector dolls and accessories. Buy, sell and trade.

Highway 158
Camden, NC 27921
(919) 338-1160

Margaret Hydrick Bridgman

Alexanders, Shirley Temples, Ginnys, Barbies, Nancy Ann Storybooks, Kewpies, many others. Send SASE for reply.
2824 Norbridge Avenue
Castro Valley, CA 94546
(415) 886-3980

Shoppe Full of Dolls

Madame Alexander, Effanbee, American artists' dolls, unique European dolls and much, much more. Discontinued dolls at discount prices. Plan a family or doll club trip to historical New Hope, PA. We are waiting to greet you! Can't visit? We are ready to serve your doll needs through our excellent mail order service. LSASE and 2 stamps for our latest edition.

39 North Main Street
New Hope, PA 18938
(215) 862-5524

Unusual new and old collectible dolls. Dolls from Spain and Italy plus the United States. Doll stands, shoes and accessories. My Baby Girl from Spain, life size $60. plus $3. shipping. Printed list $1.00. (Wholesale and retail. Shop and mail order.)

**819 South Tustin
Orange, CA 92666
(714) 997-8290**

My Baby Girl.

Willoughby's Dolls & Things

Antique and collector dolls and teddy bears bought and sold. Doll restoration supplies, accessories and related items.

**300 Water Street
St. Charles, MO 63301
(314) 946-0471**

Left to right: Amanda, Amy, baby doll, Susan, Ming Yi.

Highlander House, Inc.

We directly import the best quality bisque porcelain dolls and doll stands. They are priced for the average collector. We allow low minimum orders for dealers. Color catalog is available. (Wholesale and retail. Shop and mail order.)

**70 Main Street
Melrose, MA 02176
(617) 665-3581**

The Doll House

Antique and collectible dolls at reasonable prices. Free lists spring and fall for LSASE. Photographs available. Return privilege. Have been supplying satisfied doll lovers for 20 years. (Shop and mail order.)

**6195 Willow Drive
Williamson, NY 14589
(315) 589-8192**

DOLL SHOP
3562 METAMORA ROAD
METAMORA MI.48455

1-800-521-0367 Toll Free Outside Michigan

1-313-678-3470 Michigan

We are located in picturesque, Metamora, Michigan, about 50 miles north of Detroit. Our doll shop not only offers a very large selection of antique dolls, but also modern collectibles, teddy bears, vinyl and bisque, and many other country related items.

For your convenience we have a toll free number, free guaranteed and insured delivery anywhere in the Continental U.S.A. Lay-a-ways, Visa/Mastercharge are accepted. (Shop and Mail order.)

WE WOULD LIKE TO KNOW IF YOU HAVE DOLLS OR DOLL COLLECTIONS FOR SALE.

IF SO, PLEASE WRITE TO US AND LET US KNOW.

Meyer's Collectible Doll Corner

Meet Delores Sears, Judy Gogoly, Harold Shapiro and Lee Tomori.

Meyer's has been in business 68 years. Our reputation for quality and dependability is well known, so shop with the assurance of being pleased.

We have expanded our doll department to accomodate our collector customers, bringing new doll artists and companies into our store for your consideration.

In addition to our beautiful porcelain reproductions (in limited editions), we have;

Madame Alexander, Effanbee, Peggy Nisbet, Suzanne Gibson, Minene, Dolls by Anne, Gerber babies, Goebel, Zaph, Heidi Ott, Sasha, Furga, Zanni & Zambelli, Sebino, Dolls by Jerri, Segeguchhi, Little People from Babyland General, Dolls by Maria Lee, Royal Dolls, Corolle, Faith Wick, Dolls by Pauline, Louis Nichole, Ideal's Shirley Temple, Mattel's Barbie and most current dolls.

YESTERDAY DOLLS at YESTERDAY'S PRICES
DISCONTINUED EFFANBEE DOLLS
(while quantities last)

595 HIGHWAY 18, EAST BRUNSWICK, NJ 08816
(201) 257-8800

SHOP and MAIL
ORDER
SEND $1.00 for
BROCHURE

MEYER'S
PLAYTHINGS
AWARD WINNER
OUTSTANDING
DOLL
DEPARTMENT

meyer's *Since 1914*

16in (40.6cm) Lenci new for 1982.

Janet G. Aston

Complete line of Lenci and Heidi Ott dolls. Plush featuring teddy bears from Lenci, Nisbet Childhood Classics and Merrythought of England--much more. Little People TM born at Babyland General TM Hospital, are ready for adoption. Catalog $2.50. (Retail only. Mail order only.)

1236 Buckhorn Drive
Suffolk, VA 23437

Doll Dealers

67

Lord Fauntleroy by Madame Alexander, 1981. *Photograph by John Axe.*

DOLL MANUFACTURERS

All Prices Listed Are Subject To Change Without Notice.

"Oh You Beautiful Baby,"... The 1982 Gerber Bisque Baby, that is.

The whole world loves a baby and the newest Gerber Baby will soon be welcomed with loving arms by doll collectors all over the globe. The life-like Collector Doll debuts during the 1982 Toy Fair at the showroom of Atlanta Novelty.

The face has been admired by millions for over 50 years; yet the baby's "spanking" new. The appealing Gerber Baby, world-famous trademark of the Gerber Products Company, has again been immortalized as a magnificent bisque, limited edition, collector doll by Atlanta Novelty. The brand new 12-inch bisque doll, which will be produced only in 1982, joins the 1981 limited edition doll as a most sought after collectors' item.

THE GERBER BABY: MAGNIFICENT COLLECTIBLE—BORN 1982

Atlanta Novelty DIVISION OF **Gerber Products Company**   200 5th Ave., Suite 1372, NY 10010
General Offices: 47-34 33rd St., Long Island City, NY 11101

Introducing . . .

Little David

Meet Little David, born in 1982 at the studios of master dollmaker Jerri Mc-Cloud. The hustle and bustle of the world interests him, and he watches it with bright eyes. But when things settle down at the end of the day, Little David does what all good babies do — he goes quietly to sleep!

Little David has a bright future, too — although he might not be aware of just how interesting it's going to be. Jerri Mc-Cloud has already begun to plan for his first faltering steps, the days when he will run and jump and play with other children, and even go to school! Watch as Little David grows up in future editions of the Dolls by Jerri catalogs of fine porcelain bisque collector's dolls. But begin your collection now — editions will be limited to 1,000 dolls.

#829: Little David. *Porcelain bisque two-faced head, glass eyes on "awake" side, porcelain hands, fabric body. Costumed in white gown, bonnet. Pillow included.*

Exact specifications of costumes or accessories are subject to change or modification
due to availability of fabrics and other materials.

Dolls by Jerri

Post Office Box 21097
Charlotte, North Carolina 28206
704/333-3211

The Mark Twain Collection

The three beloved children from the fertile mind and prolific pen of Mark Twain hold a very special place in American hearts. Who has not — after reading of their adventures — wanted to emulate their carefree lifestyle . . . much to the distress — or envy — of most grown-ups!

From the studio of master dollmaker Jerri McCloud, here are America's favorite folk heroes — handmade in fine porcelain bisque and exquisitely costumed in authentic 19th-century American styles. Tom wears a tweed suit with matching cap, the detested cravat tied snugly beneath his brave chin. Huck has a tattered straw hat perched atop his tangled hair. And Becky is turned out in all of the ruffles and bows that any Midwestern lass of her time would have worn.

Dolls by Jerri is proud to add Tom Sawyer, Huckleberry Finn, and Becky Thatcher to its catalog of fine porcelain collector dolls — all made in limited editions of 1,000. You'll want to have the whole set — so see your dealer soon!

#828: Huckleberry Finn. *Porcelain bisque head and 5-piece body, human hair, glass eyes. Total height about 19 inches. Costumed in shirt, cut-off jeans with suspenders, moccasins, straw hat. Bag of marbles included.*

#827: Becky Thatcher. *Porcelain bisque head and 5-piece body, human hair, glass eyes. Total height about 19 inches. Costumed in ruffled dress, bonnet, shoes, appropriate undergarments.*

#825: Tom Sawyer. *Porcelain bisque head and 5-piece body, human hair, glass eyes. Total height about 19 inches. Costumed in tweed suit with suspenders, shirt, cravat, cap, shoes. Slingshot included.*

Dolls by Jerri

Post Office Box 21097
Charlotte, North Carolina 28206
704/333-3211

#821: Katie. *Porcelain bisque head and 5-piece body, human hair, glass eyes. Total height about 20 inches. Costumed in velvet coat with acrylic fur trim and matching hat over white dress with blue dots, knitted mittens, boots, appropriate undergarments.*

Dolls by Jerri

Post Office Box 21097
Charlotte, North Carolina 28206
704/333-3211

Introducing . . .

Katie

Presenting . . .

Little Red Riding Hood

Here's Katie, all decked out in her best winter togs and on her way to make social calls—when everybody knows she'd rather be curled up in a warm corner with a favorite book! Katie might be inclined to pout about it a little — but she is so proud of her blue velvet coat with fur trim and matching hat that most people won't even notice!

Red Riding Hood is, of course, the heroine of one of the world's best-known fairy tales. She is costumed in the scarlet cape you always *knew* she'd be wearing when you finally met her, basket in hand, on the path through the scary woods that leads to Grandmother's house.

Katie and Red Riding Hood are just two of the many fine porcelain collector dolls from the catalog of Dolls by Jerri, both produced in limited editions of only 1,000. See them at your dealer.

#822: Little Red Riding Hood. *Porcelain bisque head and 5-piece body, human hair, glass eyes. Total height about 19 inches. Costumed in dress, hooded cloak, shoes, appropriate undergarments. Basket included.*

Walt Disney's
Cinderella

Dolls by Jerri

presents

The Walt Disney Collection

Dolls by Jerri proudly introduces Cinderella and Prince Charming, the first in a new series of collector dolls based on the wonderful characters given life through the magic animation of Walt Disney.

Lovingly created in fine porcelain bisque and beautifully costumed by master dollmaker Jerri McCloud under license from Walt Disney Productions, the Walt Disney Collection is offered in registered limited editions of 1,500. Watch for other Disney dolls in the future; collectors everywhere will want to own them.

Dolls by Jerri's 1982 collection also includes subjects from fact and fiction such as Tom Sawyer, Huckleberry Finn, and Becky Thatcher; Little Red Riding Hood; and two lovable "people" named Katie and Little David.

Cinderella, Prince Charming and all the other Jerri Dolls are available only thru fine doll shops, toy stores, gift shops and department stores.

Dolls by Jerri

Post Office Box 21097
Charlotte, North Carolina 28206
704/333-3211

© 1982, 1949 W.D. Productions

Cinderella and Prince Charming

Glamour Gals™
COLLECTION

Glamour Gals are high-fashion models, movie stars, beautiful career women, anything a modern-day woman might choose to be.

Each 4 inch doll wears a different outfit, and their long rooted hair can be combed and styled. Their shoulders, hips and knees move for added realism.

Exciting accessories almost bring these little dolls to life, and make collecting them even more enjoyable.

Kenner Products
1014 Vine Street
Cincinnati, OH 45202

Here's the Exciting World of Fashion, Romance, Adventure and More in 42 Collectable Glamour Gals!

Glamour Gals TM Ocean Queen TM Cruise Ship.

Glamour Gals TM Party Place TM Set.

Glamour Gals TM Beauty Salon TM Playset.

Glamour Gals TM Showplace Collector's Case.

Glamour Gals TM Dateline TM Sets.

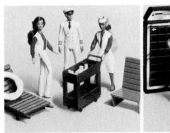

Glamour Gals TM Party Line TM Sets.

Glamour Gals TM Fancy Firebird.

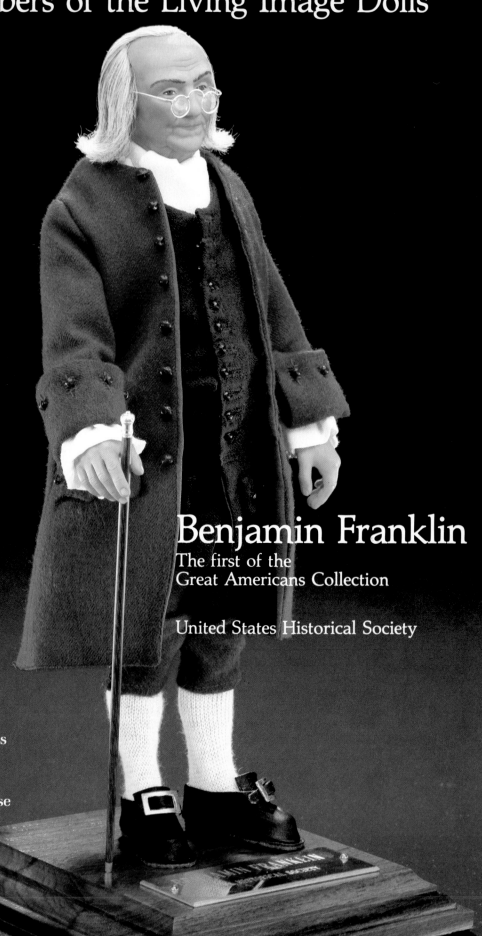

"I congratulate the
United States Historical Society
for pioneering such life-like
and accurate dolls.
The quality is unsurpassed—
altogether a unique collection."

Gary Ruddell
The Doll Reader

Lenci ®
Dolls from Italy

Pictured on these pages is the complete current line of fine LENCI dolls available on the American market. The Classic Dolls are listed by year, size, number and name. Each is produced in strictly limited numbers of 999 world wide. They are numbered on the back of the head, and come complete with a signed and numbered certificate of authenticity. These are the absolute guarantee of the genuine LENCI doll produced only in Turin in the LENCI craftsman workshops. Please note that the 1978 and 1979 dolls are nearing the end of their subscription.

The head and legs of the Classic Dolls are fully jointed. Each doll comes in an attractive box covered with a dark blue design. The box opens in the middle, showing a lining of white artificial silk and forming a simulated shadow box which frames and enhances the appearance of the doll.

HISTORY OF LENCI

Beginnings:

The company that eventually would bear the world famous LENCI name was begun in Turin, Italy in 1919 as a craft industry. Dolls were designed by well known Italian artists and crafted in pressed felt, a material indigenous to Turin. Wonderfully expressive and lifelike faces were painted on the shaped heads of the dolls, and

continued

1978

Susanna—20"
203

Clo Clo—20"
201

1978

Melania—27"
312

Rossella—27"
311

1979

Corinne — 20"
105

Colette—20"
106

1980

Liviana—20"
103

Vanessa—20"
207

1979

Matelda—20"
204

Samantha—27"
313

1980

Debora—20"
206

Stefania—20"
104

1981

Mario—20''
208

Patrizia—20''
209

1982

Brunilde—20''
210

Belinda—20''
102

1981

Violetta—20''
107

Cristina — 27''
314

1982

Amanda—20''
101

Fedora—27''
315

Doll Manufacturers

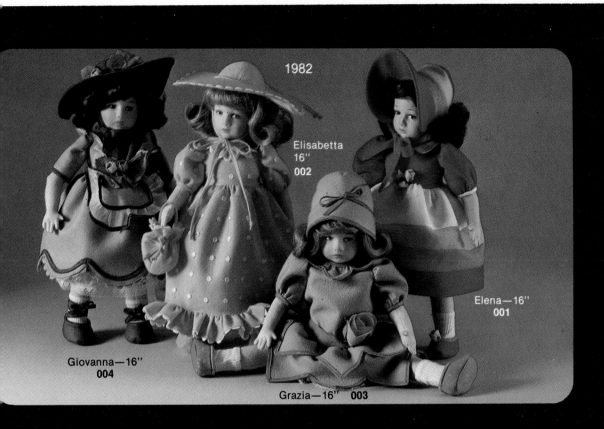

1982

Elisabetta
16"
002

Elena—16"
001

Giovanna—16"
004

Grazia—16" 003

finally they were dressed in clothes reflecting the styles of the period.

The trademark registered was "Ludus Est Nobis Constantes Industria," (To Play Is Our Constant Work) and was written in a circle around a child's spinning top, with the first letter of each word capitalized.

Development:

By 1922, the dolls produced by the LENCI factory had achieved worldwide recognition, and were especially sought after in the United States. It was at this time that the initials of the Latin motto were first used to create the "LENCI" name.

During the 1920's, dolls available on the market had either flat rag heads which could not recreate the beauty of the human face, or had heads of porcelain which were too fragile for a child's play. The patented LENCI process, however, produced dolls using a material that was both beautiful and unbreakable.

The advent of depression and then war brought this success to a close. The LENCI factory diversified and continued to supply the Italian market with plush, Italian historical dolls, ceramic figurines and other items.

Revival of the Classic Dolls:

Original LENCI dolls from the 1920's have become highly sought after collector's items, but good examples are scarce. The original moulds, catalogs, original models, the colors and the patterns for the doll's clothes all were preserved, however. Thus, influenced by a glorious tradition and stimulated by a remarkable increase in demand, LENCI has revived the production of these world famous dolls using the original equipment and methods from the 1920's.

Today, as in the 1920's, there is no doll the world over that can match the superb coloring, the beauty of expression, and the magnificent costuming of the LENCI.

Royal Doulton presents the fairest of them all.
Our original collection of Heirloom Dolls.

"Vera," from the Kate Greenaway Collection.

Royal Doulton is proud to present an exquisite series of Heirloom Dolls, each one as graceful and charming as the era it recalls. The delicate English ivory bone china head and hands are modelled by Eric Griffiths, the Royal Doulton Art Director of Sculpture. Each expression is hand painted by master figure painters.

The dolls' authentic costumes are of the finest fabrics, designed and hand-sewn by England's House of Nisbet, the premier creators of collector dolls. The first series is comprised of seven Birthday Dolls, one for each day of the week, as in the Victorian poem, "Monday's child is fair of face..." The second is a limited edition of ten Portrait Dolls based on paintings by the famous 19th century artist, Kate Greenaway. Each is limited to 5000 worldwide and collectors have recognized the beauty and value of these sought-after Heirloom Dolls.

Each doll bears the Royal Doulton backstamp, comes with a wrist leaflet, and is displayed in a presentation case. For complete details, please write to Royal Doulton, Dept. DRC, 700 Cottontail Lane, Somerset, NJ 08873.

Royal Doulton®
Since 1815, the gift of imagination.

Our "Firstborn" is not just a doll,
but an heirloom.

The newest and sweetest addition to Royal Doulton's exquisite family of Heirloom Dolls is a rosy-cheeked baby. "Firstborn" is 12¼" long, with delicately pink-tinted bone china head, hands, and feet modelled by Eric Griffiths, the Royal Doulton Art Director of Sculpture.

The doll's beautiful features have been lovingly hand painted by master figure painters and the renowned House of Nisbet has created "Firstborn's" lacy white christening gown and bonnet. Our bundle of joy arrives nestled in a fully fitted, English cane baby basket. Each doll bears the Royal

Doulton backstamp. For complete details, please write to Royal Doulton, Dept. DRC, 700 Cottontail Lane, Somerset, NJ 08873.

Royal Doulton®
Since 1815, the gift of imagination.

DOLL-LAIN

Porcelain Originals
P.O. Box 910
308 West 4th Avenue
Milan, IL 61264

Presently, Doll-Lain porcelain originals are becoming more advanced and prestigious in the collectable world. Porcelain and doll lovers from coast to coast are seeking out these miniature humanistic figures. Catalog $3.00. (Wholesale only. Shop only.)

St. Nicholas, *a limited edition of 200, sculptor Maureen Nalevanko. Porcelain head; mohair wig and beard; glass eyes; height 17in (43.2cm); carries a leather bag of miniature toys; made in U.S.A. $600.*

Littlest Angel Karrissa, Gloria, Michael, *a limited edition of 200 each, sculptor Dianna Effner. Porelain head, hands and feet; human hair wig; glass eyes; height 13½in (34.3cm). made in U.S.A. $340; Karrissa Sold-Out $415.*

King's Fool, Jester, *a limited edition of 350, sculptor Maureen Nalevanko, Porcelain head and hands; glass eyes; height 15½in (39.4cm); carries porcelain bauble; made in U.S.A. $600.*

1646-1716 French Royal Court, King Louis XIV, *a limited edition of 350, sculptor Maureen Nalevanko. Porcelain head and hands; mohair wig; glass eyes; height 20in (50.8cm) holds miniature grapes; mounted on walnut and velvet throne; made in U.S.A. $900.*

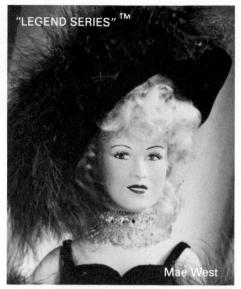

"JUST FRIENDS" ™
Dutch Treat Boy & Girl

"LEGEND SERIES" ™

Mae West

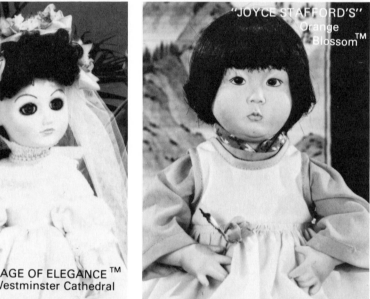

"JOYCE STAFFORD'S"
Orange
Blossom ™

AGE OF ELEGANCE ™
Westminster Cathedral

BOBBSEY TWINS ®

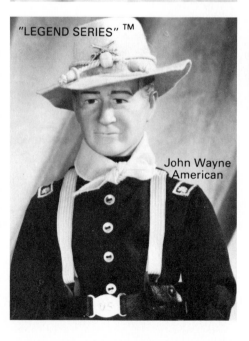

"LEGEND SERIES" ™

John Wayne
American

1982 LIMITED EDITION

Diana, Princess of Wales

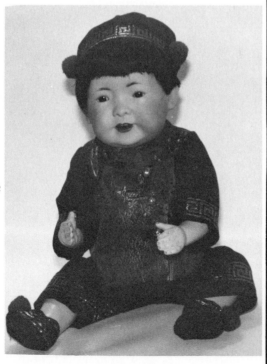

THE GOOD OLD DAYS

are still with us through the

GERDA DOLLS.

In small workshops in Nuremberg these dolls are still made completely by hand. Skilled artisans produce about 50 styles of which we show you here Snowwhite and the Seven Dwarfs.

If you would like to know more about the GERDA Dolls, please send $1.00 for a color catalog. State whether you are a retailer or individual.

Staufen Studio

8564 Mulberry Road
Chesterland, OH 44026
(216) 729-7863

Doll Manufacturers

Two J.D.K. *Hildas* and a 243 Oriental baby. *Mary Lou Rubright Collection.* From page 4, *Kestner: King of Dollmakers* by Jan Foulke.

A 20in (50.8cm) long baby, one of the finest examples of mold number 211 by Kestner. *Richard Wright Collection.* From page 136, *Kestner: King of Dollmakers* by Jan Foulke.

The Original ARMAND MARSEILLE
Porcelain Bisque Dolls Are Again Being Produced

Through extraordinary circumstances the original *Armand Marseille* molds have been made available exclusively to our associate company Zapf Creations of Rodental, Germany.

The dolls are being produced according to the original production methods: heads, arms, and feet are bisque; bodies are either cloth, leather, or papier mache; eyes are hand blown glass; hair is human hair. Clothes closely follow original designs.

Initially seven (7) dolls are being produced for 1982. Worldwide production has been limited to 1000 dolls of each style. Only 500 of each have been allocated to the United States. Each doll has the original A.M. markings and, each doll of the new production is numbered. A signed registration certificate will be issued with each doll. The following dolls are available at selected quality doll retailers beginning May 1982.

#06800 *Anne. A.M. 20 DEP, approximately 13", papier mache body.*
#06798 *Fanny. 2461/A6M, papier mache body, approximately 22".*
#06799 *Sandrine. 3200 AM 8/0 DEP, leather body, approximately 12".*
#06797 *Adelaide. 390N DRGM A6M, leather body, approximately 24".*
#06803 *Caroline. A.M. 351/3, cloth body, baby with bonnet approximately 12".*
#06802 *Samy. A 33 M, cloth body, black baby, approximately 13".*
#06801 *Cyrille. AM 382/3, cloth body approximately 12".*

Imported and Distributed exclusively by:

FNR International Corp.

300 CANAL STREET • LAWRENCE, MA 01840 • (617) 682-6621

DEALER INQUIRIES ONLY

Suzanne Gibson Dolls

Suzanne Gibson dolls are designed by one of America's outstanding designers, who has been producing dolls since 1961.

For her outstanding efforts in the field of doll making, she has been elected to the National Institute of Doll Artists. Her famous Kalico Kids are being reintroduced this year, and for the collectors, a signed and numbered edition of Mother Goose and her goose is being offered. Together with the limited edition Mother Goose, a series of Nursery Rhyme dolls has also been introduced this year.

Reeves International

1107 Broadway
New York, NY 10010

Available at your nearest Department Store, Fine Doll or Toy Store.

The Heidi Ott dolls from Switzerland originated from her molding and sewing of dolls for her daughter. Her career began at a trade fair in Bern, Switzerland, where she was the hit of the show, and soon became recognized by serious collectors.

Her dolls are soft bodied and have faces that reflect warmth and friendship. Each doll is signed and dated to show when it was made. Only a limited quantity can be produced each year, as a great portion of the face is still hand decorated by Heidi Ott. Prices range from $190. to $300.

Steiff, long recognized as the premier stuffed toy in the world, has a range of teddy bears and other animals for young and old.

A series of limited edition bears have been offered for the past two years, as is being offered again this year. The quality and life-like reproduction have always been associated with the "Button In Ear" brand of Steiff.

The House of Peggy Nisbet Limited, from England, specializes in dolls with traditional historical costumes. Some of the many dolls included are European historical figures, American Presidents and their wives, as well as movie stars.

Also for the collectors, they have signed and numbered limited edition sets of the Royal Couple's Wedding, and for 1982, a Christening Set which is to include the Royal Couple and child.

Approximately 106 molded body dolls are available and prices range from $29.95 to $69.95.

Reeves International

**Distributors of Suzanne Gibson Dolls
Peggy Nisbet Dolls, Heidi Ott Dolls
and Steiff Animals**

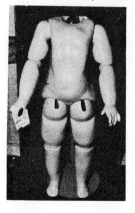

The Legend Lives On
The 1982 Limited Edition Sasha....

Kimberly® in her Hanten® skating outfit by Tomy.

In the tradition of
Sasha Morganthaler's original "one of a kind" dolls.

She wears a fine white pintucked cotton dress over a lace trimmed petticoat. Dark green velvet shoes and white anklet socks. Her fair hair is real, wigged rather than rooted, and graced with a flower and barrette. Eyes are painted brown.

Production is limited to 6000 dolls, each engraved

with its individual registration number. A signed and numbered certificate accompanies each doll.

Available nationally through your doll dealer.

Send for the "Sasha Story" and catalogue of the complete family of Sasha dolls. Available free of charge.

An exclusive of
™ INTERNATIONAL PLAYTHINGS, INC.
151 Forest Street, Montclair, New Jersey 07042

Tomy Corporation

Kimberly® is a doll who is a lot like the little girl that owns her. She has long hip length hair that can be washed, curled and styled. She comes in her sporty Hangten® skating outfit and has four other outfits for any occasion. 17in (43.2cm) retails for approximately $25. Catalog and photograph available. (Wholesale and retail.)

**901 East 233rd Street
Carson, CA 90749
(213) 549-2721**

Milano's Creative Clay Cottage

Manufacturers and creators of choice china heads and parts. Some bald with bare feet, others with painted hair, boots, gloves and bonnets. Babies, children, women, men and clowns. Large orders accepted. $5. - $45. retail; $3.50 - $25. wholesale. Catalog $2.50. (Shop and mail order.)

**625 Rowe Avenue
Yuba City, CA 95991
(916) 673-2771**

TOY FAIR...
Guide to Collectible Manufacturer Dolls
of 1982

by EDITORIAL STAFF - DOLL READER

The job of researching the American Toy Fair to present the myriad of 1982 collector dolls by manufacturers was some experience! The manufacturers listened to the message collectors echoed in 1981 "keep those original doll designs made expressly for doll collectors!" There was such an extensive array of beautiful new doll models presented. Collectors in 1982 are in for a "feast and famine" situation. The feast is for the hundreds of new dolls to choose from whether they be porcelain, vinyl, cloth, wood or resin. The famine is sure to follow after the grocery money is spent on updating one's collection.

Effanbee Doll Corporation again silenced those who said "How can Effanbee top its' 1981 dolls?" The nostalgia and authenticity of "the Legend Series" sees two new blockbusters that will only be produced in 1982. A younger version of the Duke (No. 2981) as a frontier U.S. Cavalry soldier in blue with pistol, suspenders and hat is *John Wayne* "Guardian of the West." This 18in (45.7cm) doll is 1in (2.5cm) taller than last year's edition. This is the third "Legend" doll and the second and final version of this popular American hero. *Mae West,* the fourth "Legend" series doll, is as one remembers her - - sassy and voluptuous. The

shapely 18in (45.7cm) Miss West (1982) is costumed in a tightly fitted black taffeta gown with lace flounces. Her black hat with brim is trimmed with grey marabou and is finished with elaborate jewelry, white gloves, marabou feather boa, and a ribbon wrapped cane.

The "Craftsmen's Corner Collection" welcomes Joyce Stafford with her Effanbee debut of *Orange Blossom* (No. 7501). This 13in (33.0cm) Chinese tot is dressed in an orange peasant dress with green embroidered apron. You will not be able to forget her winsome expression. Faith Wick has two new entries. One doll is the 18in (45.7cm) old-fashioned *Nast Santa* (No. 7201). Her other new vinyl doll is a 16in (40.6cm) *Billy Bum* (No. 7007).

Among the 60 new models from Effanbee for 1982, collectors should note: "Storybook Collection" *Mary Poppins* (No. 1198), *Hans Brinker* (No. 1172), *Rapunzel* (No. 1199); 13in (33.0cm) "Absolutely Abigail Collection" of turn-of-the-century era with *Cousin Jeremy* (No. 3310), *Sunday Best* (No. 3311), *Recital Time* (No. 3312), *Strolling in the Park* (No. 3313), and *Afternoon Tea* (No. 3314); "Grande Dames Collection" with 15in (38.1cm) *Guinevere* (No. 1551), *Olivia* (No. 1552), *Claudette* (No. 1554), *Hester* (No. 1553) plus 11in (27.9cm) *Eliza-*

Illustration 1. *Mae West,* Effanbee's 4th "The Legends Series". *Photograph courtesy Effanbee Doll Company.*

beth (No. 1151), *Amanda* (No. 1152), *Katherine* (No. 1153), and *Robyn* (No. 1154); 18in (48.7cm) "Age of Elegance Collection" with *Buckingham Palace* (No. 7851), *Versailles* (No. 7852), *Victoria Station* (No. 7853) and *Westminster Cathedral* (No. 7854); and, 11in (27.9cm) *Bobbsey Twins, Flossie* (No. 1202) and *Freddie* (No. 1201) with outfits of clothes Winter Wonderland (No. 1221 boy and No. 1222 girl), At the Seashore (No. 1223 boy and No. 1224 girl), Out West (No. 1225 boy and No. 1226 girl) and Go A' Sailing (No. 1227 boy and No. 1228 girl). The new *1982 Effanbee Doll Catalog* in color is available for $2.50 from Hobby House Press, Inc.

Madame Alexander doll collectors can add some new treasures to their collections in 1982. First and foremost is the third set of six 14in

Illustration 2. Third six "First Ladies" by Madame Alexander. Left to right: *Martha Johnson Patterson, Jane Pierce, Harriet Lane, Abigail Fillmore, Mary Todd Lincoln,* and *Julia Grant.* Photograph courtesy of Alexander Doll Company.

Illustration 3. *John Wayne II, third "the Legend Series." Photograph courtesy of Effanbee Doll Company.*

(35.6cm) "First Ladies." *Abigail Fillmore* (No. 1514), 1850 to 1853, a brunette, wears a pink brocaded gown with pink taffeta ruffled overskirt. Her gown is trimmed with multiple bows and braid and a knit shawl. *Jane Pierce* (No. 1515), 1853 to 1857, a blonde, wears a black jewel-tone net gown lined with black taffeta, over a pink taffeta petticoat and pantaloons, with a matching jewel-tone net shawl. The third First Lady, *Harriet Lane* (No. 1516), 1857 to 1861, with black hair, served as the hostess for her bachelor uncle, James Buchanan. She wears a white satin moire gown. A sweeping skirt has a pleated ruffle and braid trim over a white taffeta petticoat and pantaloons. In addition, *Harriet* wears a beige lace shawl. The famous *Mary Todd Lincoln* (No. 1517), 1861 to 1865 has brown hair pulled to one side in a long curl, adorned by flowers.

Mrs. Lincoln wears a purple cotton velveteen gown trimmed with cream color voille sleeves with a black shawl. The skirt is taffeta lined. Her petticoat and pantaloons are taffeta. The fifth First Lady, *Martha Johnson Patterson* (No. 1518) 1865 to 1869, has blonde hair and served as official hostess in the absence of her sick mother. She wears a pink, blue and gold brocaded gown trimmed with silver at waist and neck. Her full length crepe cape and hood is edged with gold lace and has tassels. Her petticoat and pantaloons are of white taffeta. The last First Lady of this third set is *Julia Grant* (No. 1519), 1869 to 1877, with blonde hair, wears a white and silver brocaded coat style gown with lace shawl, peach satin underskirt with white taffeta ruffled petticoat and panties.

The 21in (53.3cm) "Portrait Dolls" have two new additions. *Goya* (No. 2235) is a dark haired, brown eyed beauty wearing a black point d'esprit dress with a V-neck and puffed sleeves. The full skirt has wide black lace trim along the bottom. A black lace mantilla, black fan, and flowers and decorative comb complete her toilet. The second new "Portrait Doll" was inspired by *Manet* (No. 2225). This blonde lady doll looks as through she just stepped out of a painting with her double ruffled striped spice colored satin gown floating over her bouffant petticoat and pantaloons. The gown has long sleeves with lacy ruffles and a lace collar around the neck. Her hat and purse are of velveteen. The other new Alexander doll is a 17in (43.2cm) *Bridesmaid* (No. 1655). New fashions are sported by 14in (35.6cm) Cinderella Ball Gown (No. 1548), 20in (50.8cm) Victoria (No. 5748), 20in (50.8cm) Mommies Pet (No. 7136), and for the three sizes of *Pussy Cat* (14in [35.6cm] No. 3224, 20in [50.8cm] No. 5228, 24in [61.0cm] No. 6246.)

Mattel's newest *Barbie* is *Magic Curl Barbie* (No. 3856) and *Black Magic Curl Barbie* (No. 3989) with hair you can curl, straighten, and curl again. A *Pink & Pretty Barbie* (No. 3554) comes in a glamorous six-piece mix-and-match wardrobe with accessories. *Barbie* now has her own electronic toy baby grand piano that really works, a luxury bath, and both she and *Ken* have their own fashion signature jeans.

Athletic *All Star Ken* (No. 3553) actually flexes his muscles, has bendable wrists, and a bending, twisting waist. Joining the *Barbie* family is the "Sunsational Malibu" series in beach attire: *Skipper* (No. 1069), *Barbie* (No. 1062), *Ken* (No. 1088),

P.J. (No. 1187), *Christie* (No. 7745), and *Ken* (black) (No. 3849).

Dazzle (No 5286) and her eight friends are introduced this year as 4½in (11.5cm) fashion dolls. With names such as *Glimmer* (No. 5292), *Rhinestone* (No. 5293), *Glissen* (No. 5295), *Glossy* (No. 5288), *Diamond* (No. 5289), *Crystal* (No. 5290), and *Spangle* (No. 5291). These little beauties have additional fashions, a horse, and their own city with change-around room.

Vogue Dolls, a division of Lesney, presents a new 8in (20.3cm) *Ginny* with a poseable body and new face painting. In addition to *Ginny* and her Sasson designer fashions, a new series is introduced: a magnificent collection of *Ginny* dolls dressed in traditional bridal costumes from 12 countries around the world. Packaged individually in window display boxes, these dolls will retail for between $10.00 and $12.00 each.

Spain, Greece and Japan have been added to the "Far-Away Lands" series.

"Glitter Girls," 5½in (14.0cm) miniature fashion dolls, have been added to the Vogue line. Named after precious jewels, these six different dolls have a Take-Along Fashion Penthouse and additional "Glitter" fashions. *Sapphire, Ruby, Crysta' Jade, Amber,* and *Pearl* each have totally poseable bodies and long silky hair that can be combed.

Sixteen-year-old Brooke Shields and her manager-mother Teri wanted the *Brooke Shields* doll to look as much like Brooke as possible. They aided designer Karyn Weiss in arriving at the final version of the doll, which looks exactly like the young star.

The *Brooke Shields* doll is all-vinyl and fully-jointed and is an 11½in (29.2cm) "fashion doll" that has 16 costumes. The sculpture for the head of the doll was done by Ken Sheller, a New York sculptor. Karyn Weiss traveled to Hong Kong twice to personally supervise the manufacture of the doll. Packaged with each *Brooke Shields* doll will be a star-shaped ring containing strawberry flavored lip gloss and a picture of Brooke signed "with love, Brooke Shields."

Brooke Shields appeared on the Johnny Carson Show on February 9 to display the doll likeness. *Time* magazine (February 8) reported that Brooke received one million dollars from L.J.N. Toys for the privilege of manufacturing the doll.

Shirley Temple, first introduced as a doll by Ideal in 1934, reappears this year in two sizes: 8in (20.3cm) and 12in (30.5cm). There are six dolls in each size dressed in costumes from the child star's most popular movies. These include: *Heidi, Stand Up and Cheer, The Little Colonel, Stowaway, Captain January,* and *The Littlest Rebel.*

Two other "classic" dolls are being revived by Ideal this year. They are: 15in (38.1cm) *Beautiful Crissy* and *Country Fashion Crissy* with growing hair; *Tiny Tears* in three 14in (35.6cm) drink and wet versions; and *Thumbelina* in four sizes.

"The Sophisticated Ladies" came to town and made a splash! Marcy, Dollspart's designer, is credited with this nostalgic and chic group of four 24in (61.0cm) dolls. Marcy has designed and selected elegant and exquisite characteristics and attire reflecting high society life throughout the years. Each doll has a soft-stuffed cloth body with a uniquely hand-painted porcelain face and poseable porcelain arms and legs. The models are *Lauren* (No. MB421), *Josephine* (No. MB242), *Clara* (No. MB243), and *Kim* (No. MB244).

Shader's China Doll Inc. has five new musical dolls with porcelain heads and soft sculpted bodies. *Angel* (No. SS-1), dressed in all white, plays "Silent Night." The *Ballet Dancer* (No. SS-2), dressed in an elaborate white satin costume trimmed in lavender and wearing satin ballet slippers, has a fanciful white feathered headdress and plays "Music Box Dancer." The exotic *Belly Dancer* (No. SS-3) wears an appropriate costume of red and blue enhanced with glitter. She has a flowing black hairdo. The artistically costumed *Saloon Girl* (No. SS-5) plays "Deep in the Heart of Texas." Shader's *Mermaid* (No. SS-4), which plays "Ebb Tide," has an exaggerated hairdo. She is wearing a pink costume with a brilliant green tail.

Shader also has a new group of beautifully costumed dolls that are reproductions of antique classics.

The porcelain original Dolls by Jerri have several unique models for 1982. The "Mark Twain Series" includes three 18in (45.7cm) characters, *Tom Sawyer* (No. 825), *Huck* (No. 828) and *Becky* (No. 827) dressed in typical clothing from the Twain stories. These are limited editions of 1000 dolls each.

In the Walt Disney collection are two authentic doll renditions based on characters from the movie *Cinderella.* *Cinderella* (No. WD1-1) is 21in (53.3cm) tall in her blue ball gown. *Prince Charming* (No. WD1-2) is wearing red trousers and an off-white jacket with gold trim. The set also includes a satin pillow decorated

Illustration 4. *Shirley Temple* by Ideal in two sizes, 8in (20.3cm) and 12in (30.5cm). Six costumes. *Photograph courtesy of Ideal Toy Corporation.*

with gold tassels holding *Cinderella's* blown glass slipper. Each doll is marked with the catalog number of the doll and "JERRI//Walt Disney Productions © //1982." These dolls are limited to 1500 each.

Little David (No. 829) is an 18in (45.7cm) two-faced baby in a christening dress and lying on a pillow. This edition is also limited to 1000.

A new company - Doll Classics by Al Trattner - launches its 1982 line by presenting four models in porcelain that are inspired by classical 17th century and 18th century paintings of children.

The children are *The Infanta Margarita,* the Spanish princess who married Louis XIV of France, from the painting by Diego Velazquez in 1654; *The Artist's Daughter* by Cornelis de Vos from the Low Countries, 1627; the child from *Nurse and Child* by Dutch artist Frans Hals, about 1620; and the cousin of the Infanta Margarita, *Don Manuel Osorio de Zuniga* ("the Red Boy") by Francisco Goya, 1786.

The dolls were sculpted by Howard Kalish and are made in Delaware. Only 1500 dolls of each design will be made for 1982 and they will retail for $200 each. Each doll is a faithful representation of the child in the original painting. The dolls have brown glass eyes. They are "breathers" with pierced nostrils. *Margarita* has a light blonde wig; *Don Manuel* has a brown wig; the other girls have light red wigs. All of the clothing is made from authentic materials and is faithful to the designs from the famous masterpieces of European art.

Tiderider Incorporated is introducing several new items in the Lenci line from Italy.

For the first time another classic Lenci face - the fourth one that has been used by the successor of the original Lenci dolls - will be utilized. The doll is a 16in (40.6cm) girl of felt with felt clothing. The models are *Elena* (No. 001) in red and white; *Elisabetta* (No. 002) in salmon pink; *Grazia* (No. 003) in light blue; and *Giovanna* (No. 004) in light green

Illustration 5. *Don Manuel Osorio de Zuniga "the Red Boy" by Francisco Goya by Doll Classics by Al Trattner. Photograph courtesy of Doll Classics by Al Trattner.*

and white. These dolls more closely resemble the traditional Lenci dolls from the 1920s and the 1930s than previous models do. The wigs on the dolls are a synthetic fiber, but they have the look and feel of human hair. The number marked on each tag matches the number marked on the neck of each doll.

A Pinocchio doll that in 1981 won an award in a contest in Italy for the best design to be used for the 100th Anniversary of Pinocchio is available in felt in 12in (30.5cm). A Pinocchio hanging ornament is also new.

Lenci also has a line of six new plush teddy bears. Four of the models are sitting and two are standing.

The Sasha Limited Edition doll for 1982 will be produced as 6000 examples. She has a fair colored natural hair wig and brown eyes. Her dress is white pintucked cotton worn over a lace trimmed petticoat. The shoes are dark green velvet. Each doll will be marked with her individual number and she will be accompanied with a signed certificate of authenticity.

Sasha introduced *Gregor Red-head* (No. 312), a new 16in (40.6cm) doll who wears a T-shirt, blue trousers and jacket, and white shoes. A 16in (40.6cm) girl, *Sasha Blonde* (No. 112) with a short hairdo, is attired in a white belted sweater, beige skirt, white knee-socks and white shoes.

Little *Baby Bear* (No. 512), 12in (30.5cm) has a dress, turned-up brimmed hat and panties all of white piqué. Her shoes are red, and she is holding a little white bear decorated with a red ribbon. Separate new clothes from Sasha include the costumes worn by these three dolls. In addition there is a blue mackintosh and red beret; and, also their holiday ensemble which consists of a T-shirt, shorts, hat striped swimsuit, socks, shoulder bag and training shoes.

Steiff "Teddy Bear Picnic." 1982 Limited Edition of 10,000 numbered with certificate. Four bears the size of "baby bear" from 1981 will be produced in four colors: brown, carmel, honey and white. Comes with "table" replete with tiny tea set with Steiff mark on tablewear.

Effanbee Limited Edition Doll Club announced their 1982 selection is "A Royal Bride Diana, Princess of Wales." This 18in (45.7cm) vinyl doll wears the candlelight ecru English Royal wedding gown made of silk-like fabric. The doll is complimented by a magnificent trailing train and carries a huge bouquet of flowers. Members who bought last years "Girl with the Watering Can" are first in line for the 4220 total pieces to be made. To be put on the waiting list and for a free brochure write to Effanbee Limited Edition Doll Club at 200 Fifth Avenue, New York, NY, 10010.

Atlanta Novelty is presenting another limited edition of the *Gerber Baby* who has been so popular for more than 50 years. A brand-new 12in (30.5cm) bisque doll will be produced only during 1982, and like the 1981 limited edition doll, will have all molds destroyed at the end of a

Illustration 6. Limited Edition Sasha new for 1982. *Photograph courtesy of International Playthings.*

year's production. The new doll was sculpted by Neil Estern of New York. Mr. Estern has won many awards for his work in sculpture, the best known of which is a memorial to President Kennedy in Brooklyn, New York. He worked from the original charcoal sketch of the *Gerber Baby* done in 1928 by artist Dorothy Hope Smith. Each 1982 limited edition of the lifelike *Gerber Baby* will be marked, dated and numbered and she will be dressed in an elegant turn-of-the-century gown.

Pierrot was one type of doll that was seen in many different styles and designs from an unusually large number of different doll manufacturers. The Cardinal China Co. has a classic example in porcelain with hand-painted features and Charles Zadeh, Inc., has a very attractive musical *Pierrot* by Sankyo in three exquisitely costumed sizes. One of the most artistically conceived of all the Pierrots is *Piá* from Bradley Dolls. *Piá* is 21in (53.3cm) and has a hard plastic head, hands and feet on a cloth body which contains a music box that plays "Send in the Clowns." This doll has meticulous facial detail, was hand-painted in Korea and comes in four styles.

An Ohio-based importing firm, Kathy Ann Dolls, offers many different styles and designs of quality European-made dolls. Kathy Ann Dolls concentrates on beautiful play dolls from Germany by Hans Goetz and Engel that have realistically sculpted features and soft, life-like bodies. A line of original porcelain dolls, which are appealing-looking children and are based on old molds from Sonneberg in Germany, rounds out the extensive and well-researched merchandising program of Kathy Ann Dolls.

The House of Nisbet (Peggy Nisbet) from England showed many new dolls from 1982. Among the new celebrity dolls are *The Princess of Wales* in her wedding dress, *The Archbishop of Canterbury*, *President Anwar Sadat*, *The Empress of Austria*, *Nancy Reagan* and *Ronald Reagan* dressed as a cowboy. Two rather unique dolls represent the *Statue of Liberty* and *Britannia*, the symbol of the British Empire. *Liberty* is all green and *Britannia* is all bronze in color. One of the best of Nisbet's new dolls is a jolly, fat *Santa Claus* dressed in red and trimmed with white fur. From "the marriage of Royal Doulton and the House of Nisbet" there will be a special doll called *Firstborn*. *Firstborn* has a pink bone china head, hands and legs created and painted by Royal Doulton artists;

Firstborn's christening gown is trimmed with satin ribbons and is an exclusive design of the House of Nisbet. This baby is 12¼in (31.2cm) tall.

Several other doll companies, each of whom has its own distinctive and identifiable line of dolls for collectors, showed new editions for 1982. Among them, the following are worthy of special note: Rumble-Seat Press, Inc., will have *Polly*, Number 9 in a series of 20 dolls. *Polly* is a plump little French peasant girl in wooden shoes from the Norman Rockwell illustration in which she is teaching a World War I Doughboy how to speak French. Beginning in June 1982, there will be a *Dr. Crisfield* to go with *Mimi*, who needed her doll checked by the doctor. Suzanne Gibson Dolls will feature several new storybook characters, among which will be *Mary Mary Quite Contrary, Little Girl With a Curl, Little Miss Muffet, Little Bo Peep, Mary Had a Little Lamb*, and perhaps the most interesting of the group, a limited

edition *Mother Goose*. Among the new dolls by Heidi Ott of Switzerland are *Mit Kissen*, soft-bodied babies that are filled with plastic pellets. Palo Imports is offering a more economically priced version of the Heidi Ott dolls. This group of dolls is made in Germany under a Heidi Ott license. There are also fashions for Heidi Ott dolls and authentic Heidi Ott shoes from Palo Imports. The Heidi Ott dolls are all made from contemporary materials - vinyl and cloth - and are one of the most appealing renditions of babies and children that are being made. Heidi Ott dolls are not produced in large quantities and each doll is a high quality item.

Several well-known doll and toy manufacturers who concentrate mainly on the retail market for children have presented dolls in their 1982 lines that will be of special interest to collectors. Most of these dolls are reasonably priced items and their appeal is sometimes nostalgic and sometimes that of a more contemporary nature, yet they are going

Illustration 7. Jerri and Jim McCloud of Dolls by Jerri, holding Cinderella's glass slipper on a satin cushion. In the background in front of the movie poster is *Cinderella* by Dolls by Jerri. *Cinderella* is a porcelain original based on the character from the Walt Disney film. She is 21in (53.3cm) tall and is dressed in a blue ball gown.

Illustration 8. Jack Wilson, the Director of the House of Nisbet, Ltd. with Peggy Nisbet dolls. To the left of Mr. Wilson's head are the 1982 *Britannia* and *Statue of Liberty* dolls. Below them are the two versions of *Ronald Reagan*. The one dressed as a cowboy is the 1982 edition.

Illustration 9. Al Trattner with Doll Classics by Al Trattner. The porcelain limited edition dolls are 12in (30.5cm) tall and they are based on classical 17th and 18th century paintings. On the top shelf are *Don Manuel Osorio de Zuniga*, the "Red Boy," and *The Infanta Margarita* from the paintings by Spanish artists Goya and Velazquez. On the lower shelf are the *Child* from *Nurse and Child* by Frans Hals and *The Artist's Daughter* by Cornelis de Vos.

to be among the most collectible dolls of the very near future. The following manufacturers do not respond directly to collectors, but collectors are going to respond to their 1982 dolls because they are so interesting.

Hasbro. The 11½in (29.2cm) *G. I. Joe* dolls from Hasbro, produced from 1964 through the mid 1970s, have been receiving deserved attention from collectors recently. Hasbro ended production of these popular dolls for boys because of negative public reaction to combat dolls at the end of the Vietnam Era. *G. I. Joe* is back again in 1982. This time the dolls are 3¾in (9.6cm) and they come in nine different *G. I. Joe* figures with two figures from the "enemy arm of COBRA Command." The figures have snap-on helmets, battle packs and special weapons plus motorcycles, jeeps, tanks and all sorts of modern artillery weapons. About 20 different companies have already applied for licenses to use the name and image of *G. I. Joe.*

Kenner. Kenner has several different lines of dolls and figures that will be of interest to collectors. From *Star Wars: The Empire Strikes Back* there are nine new figures, now making a total of 47 different *Star Wars* figures. (Two have been discontinued.) For 1982 there is also a series of 57 different die cast metal figures in the "Star Wars Micro Collection." In Kenner's 4in (10.2cm) *Glamour Gals* collection there are 27 new dolls, making a total of 42 different *Glamour Gals* dressed in 42 differ-

ent fashions. Glamour Gals play sets include six different boyfriends for the "gals." Kenner's latest smash hit is a series of dolls from the popular film *Raiders of the Lost Ark.* They are about 4in (10.2cm) each. These include *Indiana Jones* in two different versions, *Toht, Marion Ravenwood, The Cairo Swordsman* and *Belloq.* These dolls also have extra play sets that are reconstructions of scenes from the film. The *Strawberry Short-cake* line, now a classic, has been expanded to add four new characters, including *Sour Grapes* with *Dregs, the Snake.* Each of the scented *Kids* from *Strawberry Shortcake* comes with his own pet animal.

Knickerbocker. This company has been prominent for years with its line of traditional *Raggedy Ann* and *Andy* dolls. For 1982 Knickerbocker introduced a complete line of *Snoopy* and *Belle* fashion dolls. *Snoopy* and *Belle* are brother and sister dogs as dolls from the *Peanuts* comic character family. They have "Fun Fashions" and "Fancy Fashions" for every occasion with clothing that ranges from bathrobes to rock star costumes. There is a large line of plush animals including *Bonzo,* the chimp with whom Ronald Reagan attended college in the 1952 film *Bonzo Goes to College.*

In the Knickerbocker show rooms on Fifth Avenue in New York an entire room was dedicated to displaying one of the most exciting lines of dolls and toys at the 1982 American Toy Fair. This is "The World of Annie," which is so extensive that

the merchandise requires a separate catalog. *Annie,* based on the adventures of Little Orphan Annie, from the comics and the Broadway play, will be released as a musical film in the summer of 1982. It is the most expensive musical production ever produced by Columbia Pictures. Dolls of characters from the film come in sizes of 6in (15.2cm) and 7in (17.8cm) and will be more reasonably priced than comparable quality dolls from other companies. They are Aileen Quinn as *Annie* and Toni Ann Gisondi as *Molly* in the smaller size and Albert Finney as *Daddy Warbucks,* Geoffrey Holder as *Punjab* and Carol Burnett as *Miss Hannigan* in the larger size. There are also "Annie Fashion Assortments;" an "Annie Limousine" (a 1929 Dusenburg); an "Annie Mansion," an 18½in (47.0cm) high doll house; *Annie* cloth dolls; *Sandy,* Annie's dog; 12 miniature figures of characters from the film; and various other items that are sure to become highly collectible.

Mego Corp. Among all the dolls offered by Mego Corp. there are three distinct lines that are sure to appeal to collectors.

The first of these is the *Jordache* 11½in (29.2cm) *Fashion Doll* who comes in white and black versions. For 1982 there is now a *Jordache Cheerleader Doll* with "Pom-Pom Action." The basic doll in blue jeans now has 20 different fashion ensembles to wear. She also has a companion. He is 12in (30.5cm) *Jordache Jordan, Male Fashion Doll. Jordan* is "devilishly good looking." He has six extra fashion assortments that include sports outfits. For both dolls there is *Sundance,* a horse made of a soft foam material, with rooted mane and tail.

Mego has an extensive line of dolls from popular television shows. From "The Dukes of Hazzard" *Daisy* in the 8in (20.3cm) size has a new head mold. There are eight characters in the new 3¾in (9.6cm) size, including *Bo, Luke, Daisy, Boss Hogg, Sheriff Rosco Coltrane, Cooter, Uncle Jesse* and *Cletus.* The first five of these also have their own vehicles and *Cooter* has a garage play set. There are six small dolls from "The Love Boat." These include *Captain Stubing,* his daughter *Vicki, Gopher, Isaac, Julie* and *Doc.* For these figures there is a *Love Boat* with six rooms and scale furniture. From the new adventure show "The Greatest American Hero" there are three 8in (20.3cm) dolls and two 3¾in (9.6cm) dolls. These are William Katt as *Ralph* and Robert Culp as *Bill* in both sizes and Connie Sellecca as *Pam* in the larger size.

Another new line from Mego is the *Eagle Force.* This is a series of 18 different die cast metal figures that are fully-articulated and are painted in gold and other colors. They are 1/25th scale, making them each about 2¾in (7.1cm) tall. They represent 12 different military specialists and eight enemy villains. The *Eagle Force* has play sets that include military equipment.

Mego is also marketing small drum-shaped stands to hold the *Eagle Force* figures and another set of stands to hold any 3¾in (9.6cm) dolls and figures.

Illustration 11. Grouping of 16in (40.6cm) Lenci dolls for 1982. From left to right: *Giovanna* (004) in light green and white, *Elisabetta* (002) in salmon pink, *Grazia* (003) in light blue and *Elena* (001) in red and white. Tiderider is the United States distributor.

Illustration 10. From "The World of Annie" by Knickerbocker. 6in (15.2cm) *Annie* is seated in the 1929 Dusenburg, her "Limousine." *Daddy Warbucks* is standing near the car; *Punjab* is in front of the "Annie Mansion." These dolls are 7in (17.8cm). Each doll is fully-jointed and is made of vinyl and has painted eyes. Annie has bright red rooted hair.

Illustration 12. A lovely Avigail Brahms doll distributed by the Thomas Boland Company.

Hi! I'm McCoy.

Playhouse Designs, Inc.

Our 19in (48.3cm) McCoy is quality made of bright, assorted color fabric. He is cut, sewed, filled with 100% polyester and hand finished here in our factory. He is completely washable. Retail price $14.95. Five different rag dolls available. Retail price range: $14.95 - $175. Wholesale price range: $7.50 - $85. Catalog or printed list $.50. (Wholesale only.)

920 North Main Street
Corsicana, TX 75110

13in (33.0cm) Alex by Heidi Ott, 1981. Made in Switzerland. Distributed in the United States by Reeves International. Photograph by John Axe.

DOLL and CLOTHING PATTERNS

All Prices Listed Are Subject To Change Without Notice.

Dotty, 18in (45.7cm) clown doll.

Kurly Kuddly Kids

Forty-five doll kits and patterns at affordable prices. Dolls feature "washable stay in curls. Ours alone." Order Dotty (shown) pattern $3.75 postpaid. Kit $12.95 + $1.50 UPS in USA. Free pattern in catalog $1.25. Brochure $.35. Price range $1.15 - $14.95. (Mail order only.)

**1921 Juliet Avenue
St. Paul, MN 55105**

Elegant.

Celinda's Doll Shoppe

Complete costuming, head to toe. Excellent execution; velvets, satins, silks, cottons with lace, trims, silk flowers, etc. Patterns adapted to period, your picture, etc. Wigs, shoes and other accessories. SASE. (Shop and mail order.)

**4626 Northeast 4th Street
Minneapolis, MN 55421
(612) 572-1633**

Judi's Dolls

Original doll patterns for detailed cloth dolls and clothes. Shirley Temple and movie wardrobes in two sizes. Dionnes and wardrobe, Cupie, Bi-Lo, Terri Lee, Patsy Ruth and lots of characters. Over 40 patterns. Price range $2.50 - $4.50. Catalog $1.50; printed list. (Wholesale and retail. Mail order only.)

**P. O. Box 607
Port Orchard, WA 98366**

18in (45.7cm) and 27in (68.6cm) Shirley Temples in cloth.

Beverly Powers

Patterns! Send $2.00 for illustrated catalog of over 1000 patterns. Antique and modern doll wardrobes. Cloth dolls and animals. Doll related items. Price range $1. - $4.50. (Retail only. Mail order only.)

**Box 13
South Lyon, MI 48178**

Lyn Alexander

Lyn's Doll House

Original dress, underwear, hat and shoe patterns for antique or reproduction dolls adapted from period fashion magazines. New patterns developed regularly. Catalog $1.50. Dress $2.50, Underwear $2., Shoe $1.25, Hat $.75. (Wholesale and retail. Mail order only.)

**P. O. Box 8341 C
Denver, CO 80201**

Peggy Trauger,
Dolls Patterns Costumes

Dress and pinafore pattern for all 17in (43.2cm) Shirley Temples (with or without embroidery) $1.75 plus $.50 postage. About 150 patterns available from $.50 - $3. Send $1.00 for illustrated catalog of other costume and wardrobe patterns. (Wholesale and retail. Mail order only.)

**20 Wendover Road
Rochester, NY 14610**

Kahler Kraft

Doll clothes patterns reprinted. Lettie Lane's Daisy Vacation & Wedding Clothes; various 1880-1930 girl, lady and rag dolls, teddy bears. Releasing soon Book of seven patterns miscellaneous crochet costumes, 1900s.

Lettie Lane's Daisy 1911 18"

99	Bathing suit	$1.25
100	Dress with front panel	1.10
102	Apron (really a dress)	1.10
103	Empire dress	1.10
104	Tucked Dress & Guimpe	1.10
105	Langerie hat	.75
106	Sunbonnet	.75
107	Apron	1.00
108	Bag	.50

Wedding Set

112	Empire dress	$1.10
113	Afternoon dress	1.10
114	Apron	.75
115	Wedding dress	1.10
116	Evening dress	1.10
117	Morning dress	1.10

Other Patterns Available

101 Mercer Girl 1860 18" Day dress with underwear for fashion or china $1.10

109 Minaret Lady 1907 18" Lady doll tunic dress $1.10
110 Butterick reprint 18" Underwear and nightgown $1.10
111 McCall Reprint 14" Dress with center opening $1.00
118 Dress with revers 14" $1.10
119 Middy Dress 14" Pleated skirt and blouse $1.35
120 Butterick Reprint 1870 12-16" complete set of underwear $1.10
121 Butterick Reprint 1880 12-16" night dress and night cap $1.10
122 Butterick Reprint 1882 18" Rag doll $1.35
123 Butterick Reprint 1884 12-16" lady doll street costume $1.10
124 Butterick Reprint 1885 20" girl nightdress, chemise and drawers $1.35
125 Butterick Reprint 1885 12-16" doll house costume and tedora vest $1.35
126 Butterick Reprint 1885 12-16" lady doll walking skirt, basque and muff $1.10
127 Butterick Reprint 1886 16" lady doll wrapper and fancy work apron $1.50
128 Butterick Reprint 1886 12-16" baby doll cloak, cap and slippers $1.50

129 Butterick Reprint 1886 12-16" lady doll wrap and trained costume $1.50
130 Butterick Reprint 1886 12-16" lady doll coat and cap $1.50
131 Butterick Reprint 1886 12-16" girl doll cloak and bonnet $1.50
132 Butterick Reprint 1887 12" baby doll dress, skirt and sack $1.35
133 Butterick Reprint 1879 12" stuffed cloth rabbit $1.10
134 Butterick Reprint 1879 10" stuffed cloth horse $1.35
135 Butterick Reprint 1864 8" stuffed cloth bear $1.10
136 Excella Reprint 1930's 20" frock, hat, slip and panties $1.50
137 Jointed Teddy Bear 1900's Pattern taken from Art Fabric Mills $1.50
138 Butterick Reprint 1900's 26" Girl doll dress and underwear $2.00
139 McCall Reprint 1900's 22" basque dress, cape and Scotch dap $1.50
140 Butterick Reprint 1920's 22" dress, bloomers and hat $1.35
141 McCalls Reprint 1900's 22" Red Riding Hood set, dress and cape $1.50
142 McCalls Reprint 1900's 22" coat, hat and dress $1.50
143 Harper's Bazar 1870 5 costumes in 16, 18, 19 and 20" sizes set $3.00
Soon to be released - Reprint of 7 clothing patterns and misc. crochet patterns from 1900 Germany, accompanied by charming child's story and directions.

***Lettie Lane "Sheila" series 18" doll 1909 fashions available October 1982.

**9605 Northeast 26th
Bellevue, WA 98004**

Shirley, KA-8013, 16in (40.6cm) Pattern $4.00.

Agnes, KA-8014, 30in (76.2cm) Pattern $4.50.

Twirp, KA-7912, 12in (30.5cm) Pattern $3.50.

Karen Ann's Doll Patterns

Dress your valuable antique or reproduction dolls in the most stylish clothing imaginable. All patterns are professionally designed so that you can easily follow the step by step instructions. 8x10 photo included with each pattern. Order any of the four patterns shown or send $1.00 for complete pattern catalog. (Catalog free with order.) Postage: add $.50 per pattern.

**9941 Guatemala Avenue, Dept. C-82
Downey, CA 90240**

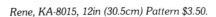

Rene, KA-8015, 12in (30.5cm) Pattern $3.50.

Pioneer doll.

Terian

Pattern for 15in (38.1cm) Pioneer doll and her wardrobe. Other doll and wardrobe patterns also available. Retail price range $3. - $5. SASE for catalog. (Wholesale and retail. Mail order only.)

**Box 318
Albuquerque, NM 87106**

Little Women doll clothes pattern.

Tinker's Corner

Authentic, extensive wardrobes for the collectible dolls of the 1940s and 1950s -- Ginny, Alexander, Ideal, Sweet Sue, etc. Sizes 8in (20.3cm), 14in (35.6cm), 18in (45.7cm) 20-21in (50.8-53.3cm), 22-24in (55.9-61.0cm). Retail price range $2. - $6. Full-size patterns. Catalog $1.00. (Wholesale and retail. Mail order only.)

129 South Whitcomb (Dept. DB)
Fort Collins, CO 80521

House Beautiful of Texas, Inc.

Barbie and Ken size dolls. American and European historical costumes, patterns, wig kits. Also available, dolls dressed in costume - retail $50. each. Thirty-six full-size patterns available retail $3. each. Brochure $1.00. (Wholesale and retail. Mail order only.)

13017G Clarewood
Houston, TX 77072

Barbie and Ken size dolls in historical costumes.

Angie's Doll Boutique

Try our new "Prairie Ensemble." Your doll will love the headband, blouse, very full skirt and slip. Will fit 15in (38.1cm) to 18in (45.7cm) doll. $15. + $1.50 for shipping. Catalog $1.00. (Retail only. Shop and mail order.)

1114 King Street, Old Town
Alexandria, VA 22314
(703) 683-2807

Hard plastic doll in "Prairie Ensemble" made by Leola Field.

The Doll's Nest

Patterns available for cloth bodies, leather bodies (jointed and gusseted styles 11in [27.9cm] to 28in [71.1cm]). Finished leather bodies also available. Original fabric dolls and antique to modern clothing patterns. Retail price range of 75 patterns $.50 and up. Catalog $.75. (Wholesale and retail. Shop and mail order.)

1020 Kenmore Boulevard, Dept. P
Akron, OH 44314
(216) 753-2464

26in (66.0cm) Jumeau style - Catalog B #128.

Wonderland World of Dolls©Ⓣ

Exquisitely detailed costume patterns. Two catalogs list over 775 patterns and accessories for all size antique to modern dolls. Period, modern, foreign, First Ladies, movie characters, historical. Also reprints. Price $5.50. (Retail only. Mail order only.)

3755 Ruth Drive, Dept. DC82
Brunswick, OH 44212

House Beautiful of Texas, Inc.

Barbie and Ken size dolls. Western and Eastern European folk costumes. Also available, dolls dressed in costume - retail $45. each. Thirty-eight full-size patterns available retail $3. each. Brochure $1.00. (Wholesale and retail. Mail order only.)

13017J Clarewood
Houston, TX 77072

Barbie and Ken size dolls in folk costumes.

Polly's Guides To Costuming Antique Dolls:

Booklet #1 - *Fitting and Costuming An Antique Doll*
for those who would like to be finished by lunch

Designed for those who have never dressed a doll,
or have tried and been unhappy with the results.

Booklet #2 - *Fitting and Costuming Babies and Toddlers.*

Booklet #3 - *Fancy French and German Dresses.*

All three for $12.95

Each booklet contains many drawings and illustrations to help
you with pattern-making, fitting, designing, etc.
Complete construction details are given. All
booklets may be used individually or as a
complement to each other.

32 pages, cardstock cover.
$5. each ppd. Order from:
Peak Doll Enterprises, Polly Ford
P.O. Box 757
Colorado Springs, CO 80901
Shop address: **117 South Main**
Fountain, CO 80817
(303) 382-8750

Dress patterns in many sizes designed with easy instructions to
accompany *Polly's Guides* and to fit **our** bodies.

Milano's Creative Clay Cottage

Geri Milano original doll patterns
(300), full size, ready to use with
complete instructions and line drawings for antique or reproduction
dolls. Adapted from fashion magazines and books. $1.50 - $3.50
retail; $.90 - $2.10 wholesale. Catalog $2.50. (Shop and mail order.)
625 Rowe Avenue
Yuba City, CA 95991
(916) 673-2771

LuAnn and little Lulu.

Bettina's Doll Designs (ODACA)

Adorable LuAnn, 20in (50.8cm)
toddler with jointed arms and legs.
Her dolly, Lulu, is 8in (20.3cm).
There is also a pattern for fur-
trimmed coat, hat, boots and muff
- $2.50. Eighteen patterns available,
retail price range $3. - $5. Catalog
$1.50. (Primarily mail order.)
6120 North Orange Tree Lane
Tucson, AZ 85704

Dolls Dolls by Penny

Doll house doll patterns. Authentically correct period styles from
Colonial to late Victorian patterns,
two in a package with photograph
on envelope. Patterns full size.
$2.45 per package postpaid.
LSASE for list. (Wholesale and
retail.) **414 Cessna Avenue**
Charleston, SC 29407
(803) 571-0376

*French Fashion Pattern No. 7, Nanny &
Baby Pattern No. 8 and 9.*

Bird's Nest Doll Fashion Patterns
Leah Ann Bird

All new revised Catalog No. IV.
Handmade leather doll shoes. Patterns $3. each. Shoe patterns.
Authentic styles from old pictures
and clothes. New patterns for
French fashions. 70 patterns from
$3. - $10.50 retail. Catalog $2.00
(refundable with minimum purchase). (Wholesale and retail. Mail
order only.)
4866 West 131st Street, Dept. DC
Hawthorne, CA 90250

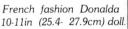

*French fashion Donalda
10-11in (25.4- 27.9cm) doll.*

Sam Molds

261 West Commercial Street
Pomona, California 91768
(714) 629-9011

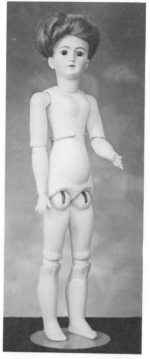

*Faith Gibson Girl
S&H 1159
Available in 2 sizes
Sam Head Mold 118A - $50.00
H.C 9½" Fits Lady Body 118BCDEF

*Sam Head Mold 119A - $40.00
HC 8" Fits Lady Body 100BCDEF - $120.00

*Faith Gibson Girl
Body Makes 22" Doll
Sam Body Mold 118BCDEF - $179.50

Sam Body Mold 100BCDEF $120.00
Makes 16" Doll

Shirley Has Created 2 Patterns for Gibson Girl in 2 Sizes

SA - 181 Lady Shoes $5.50.

SA175 Faith. 22" Doll Lady Body
175 - 22" $5.95
175 - 16" $4.95
Pattern includes
Hat-Jacket-Skirt-Slip-Drawers

SA176 - 22" $6.50
176 - 16" $4.95

Patterns plus .40 Ea postage
Our catalog is 2.50 USA
5.00 Foreign

Put Your Doll in the Finest, A Shirley Pattern
*All measurements, fired porcelain

Miss Marybeth, pattern $5.

Tiffany, Tina and Tim, pattern $4.75.

Jolly Stitchkin's

Create beautiful cloth dolls with our detailed, illustrated patterns complete with cover photo. Special body fabric, yarn and other doll making supplies plus complete kits for Tiffany, Tina and Tim also available. Fourteen different doll and clothing patterns all in one and full-size. Price range $3.50 - $6. Catalog $1.50. (Retail only. Mail order and doll shows.)

22492 Forest Hill
El Toro, CA 92630

Girl's western outfit from More Little Friend.

Living Doll Fashions

Patterns for sewing and crocheting doll clothes for many of the small modern dolls. Baby dolls to fashion dolls. Designs by Janice Rose Rader plus crochet patterns by Susan Leishman. Price range $1.25 - $3.50. Catalog $1.00. (Retail only. Mail order only.)

Box 399
Alliance, NE 69301

Our Sunday Best!

Marcy Street Doll Co.

A variety of patterns (50 in all) for the 13in (33.0cm) and 16in (40.6cm) doll. New needlepoint-face 23in (58.4cm) rag doll kit named Gretel. Fairyland rag doll patterns, clown, animal bean bags. Catalog $2.00. (Shop and mail order.)

60 Marcy Street
Portsmouth, NH 03801
(603) 436-2863

9159
Front View.

9159
Back View.

GIRLS' COSTUME, (PATENT APPLIED FOR).

Ulseth-Shannon

Costumes for child dolls (1880-1890) in varied sizes include underwear and hats. Patterns include Father Christmas and Mercer Fashion, both 16in (40.6cm) and children's underwear, 6-22in (15.2-55.9cm). Newly published *Handbook for Doll Collectors*. Most patterns (2 sizes in each) $4. Printed list. (Wholesale and retail. Mail order only.)

4515 Greilick Road
Traverse City, MI 49684
(616) 946-5379

Doll Clothing Patterns

Doll Clothing Patterns

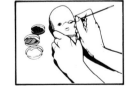

HAPPY HANDS ORIGINALS

P. O. BOX 314

ROSEMOUNT, MN 55068

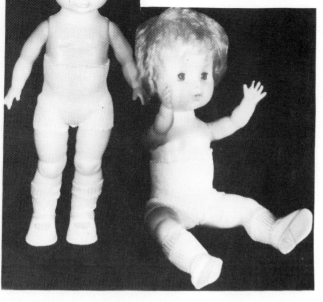

513–13" Toddler   # 512–12" Baby
Moving arms, legs & eyes. $4.00 each

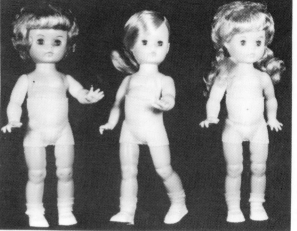

#116   #216   #316
All 16" dolls with moving arms, legs &
eyes. $5.00 each

#1400   #1401   #1402
14" molded hair   14" Poodle hair   14" Pixie hair
$4.00 $4.50 $4.50

All have moving arms, legs & eyes.

#619   #819
19" Toddler   19" Toddler
Moving arms, legs & eyes
$6.50

"DRESS ME UP DOLLS"

Dress them up with your knitted, crocheted or sew them some outfits. Get ready for Christmas, bazaars etc.

All dolls include panties, socks and shoes. Choice of blonde or brunette hair.

TABLE OF COSTS FOR SHIPPING HANDLING AND INSURANCE

For quicker handling of your order figure the total amount for merchandise ordered. Find this amount on chart to right - add the amount indicated which includes shipping, handling & insured delivery and enclose with your order.

to 7.00	1.50
7.01 to 10.00	1.85
10.01 to 15.00	2.10
15.01 to 20.00	2.45
20.01 to 30.00	2.80
30.01 to 40.00	3.20
40.01 & Over	3.50

Original soft sculpture doll patterns.

Miss Martha Originals

Two of the most lovable dolls you'll ever make. Full-size patterns with illustrated step-by-step instructions. Order by pattern name. 26in (66.0cm) Collette $4.50 ppd. 20in (50.8cm) Preshus $4.50 ppd. SASE for brochure. (Wholesale and retail. Mail order only.)

P.O. Box 5313
Glencoe, AL 35905

Hazel Pearson Handicrafts

PD4 Wedding Ensemble.
PD6 Victorian Peddler
PD8 Victorian Cleaning Lady
Printed list/sales sheet. (Wholesale and retail. Mail order.)
16125 East Valley Boulevard
City of Industry, CA 91744

Full color on fabric
No sewing involved!

COLONIAL LITTLE LINGERIE
designed by Elspeth

"Exciting New Concept in 1in to 1ft (2.5cm to 30.5cm) Scale Doll House Doll Dressing"

Fabric sheet containing ladies' clothing fashions of the period in miniature, from the inside out. Each set of Little Lingerie is coordinated with a set of the Little Linens series to completely accessorize a room of that period.

Designed to fit a standard doll house doll or use the appropriately scaled cloth doll that is included as part of every set. The clothing need not be used to dress miniature dolls. Instead, consider placing it about the doll house room in a realistic casual manner. Dealer Inquiries Invited.

Handprinted in America

Authentic period designs reproduced in multi-color on fabric as bed linens and curtains. Also set includes pattern for very simple four-poster bed. Separate instructions included.
No hemming needed.
COLONIAL LITTLE LINENS
Multi-color. Also includes bed canopy plus side and back panels plus pattern to make a simple four-poster bed. Available in rose accent color, blue accent color, gold accent color.   **$9.95**
DESIGNER COLONIAL LITTLE LINENS
Design only in one color for embroidery, or other finishing. **$7.**
VICTORIAN LITTLE LINENS
22 x 36in (55.9cm x 91.4cm) fabric. Available in rose accent color, blue accent color, gold accent color.   **$9.95**
20TH CENTURY LITTLE LINENS
22 x 36in (55.9cm x 91.4cm) fabric. Available in rose accent color, blue accent color, gold accent color.   **$9.95**

Dollhouse 1in to 1ft (2.5 to 30.5cm) scale designs

14 cloth clothes items
ROSE Colonial Little Lingerie $9.95
BLUE Colonial Little Lingerie $9.95
GOLD Colonial Little Lingerie $9.95

LITTLE LINENS
by Elspeth

20th Century Little Linens by Elspeth

Hobby House Press, Inc.

900 Frederick Street
Cumberland, MD 21502
Dealer Inquiries Invited
(301) 759-3770

MADAME ALEXANDER DOLL CLOTHING PATTERNS

Designed by Patricia Gardner. Full-size patterns with detailed descriptions of dolls and instructions.

GA 0800	Cowboy & Cowgirl Pattern	$2.00
GA 0801	Indian Boy & Girl Pattern	$2.00
GA 0802	*Little Genius* Pattern	$2.00
GA 1300	*McGuffey Ana - Flora McFlimsey*	$2.00

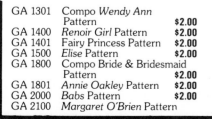

GA 1301	Compo *Wendy Ann* Pattern	$2.00
GA 1400	*Renoir Girl* Pattern	$2.00
GA 1401	Fairy Princess Pattern	$2.00
GA 1500	*Elise* Pattern	$2.00
GA 1800	Compo Bride & Bridesmaid Pattern	$2.00
GA 1801	*Annie Oakley* Pattern	$2.00
GA 2000	*Babs* Pattern	$2.00
GA 2100	*Margaret O'Brien* Pattern	

HH 206 GIRL DOLLS CLOTHES PATTERNS

14in (35.6cm). Three pattern groups. *Butterick* Pattern No. 259 from 1902, frock pattern, *Butterick* No. 313 from 1907, coat and guimpe (no dress pattern). *McCall* Pattern from 1916, dress combination. Price: $2.50.

HH 207 GIRL DRESS PATTERNS

23-24in (58.4-61.0cm) (without head) bisque doll. Two pattern sets, *Harper's Bazar* of 1877 and 1883. One set has a dress with skirt, overskirt and waist. Dress of 1883 has layered hem. Instructions and storage envelope. Price: $1.75.

HH 302 LADY DOLL PATTERNS

24in (61.0cm) (without head) bisque doll. Three pattern sets for elegant doll clothes include six different costumes. *Butterick* Patterns of 1879 includes: fancy wrap, panier polonaise trimmed walking skirt and long coat with hood. *Harper's Bazar* 1868 promenade dress. Instructions for this grand set of patterns for large dolls. Price: $4.50.

HH 203 YOUNG GIRL DOLL PATTERNS

26in (66.0cm) bisque doll. Reprint of three *Harper's Bazar* patterns from 1896/1897. One set has frock with cemise, drawers and hat. Another set has cloak and bonnet. Last set has frock with puffy sleeves. Instructions and storage envelope. Price: $3.

HH202 GIRL DOLL CLOTHES PATTERN

12-13in (30.5-33.0cm) (without head) bisque dolls. *Harper's Bazar* 1879/1883. Suit pattern with waist/skirt. Another suit pattern has knitted leggings and hat. Instructions and storage envelope. Price $1.50.

Pattern Catalog free upon request
Dealer Inquiries Invited

Hobby House Press, Inc.

900 Frederick Street
Cumberland, MD 21502
(301) 759-3770

Doll Clothing Patterns

Further patterns continued on pages 124 and 125.

DOLL MUSEUMS

Doll Museums and Exhibits
by Evelyn Jane Coleman

Fortunately museums are now becoming aware of the importance of their doll collections and are treating them as treasures. Many museums are endeavouring to make their doll collections more available to the viewing public and are actively acquiring dolls. Please note the larger selection of museums listed in this publication than previously listed, thus indicating this growth of interest.

The year 1982 is an important one for the opening of museums which have outstanding collections of dolls. This is the year of the long awaited opening of the *Strong Museum* in Rochester, New York, here in the United States. Representatives of museums from all over the world are planning to attend this important event. The *Strong Museum* will house probably the largest collection of dolls made in the period from about 1800 to around 1930 which was ever brought together. Hopefully, in time this collection will become more available for scholarly research as well as be the delight of the casual visitor or the focal point for gatherings of groups of doll collectors.

In addition, in Europe there are several museums with doll collections which have recently opened or are planning to open within this year. Many European museums include not only collections of finished dolls which were originally used as playthings but also include some of the molds, machinery and tools which were required to make the dolls. They also feature slide pro-grams showing pictures of the actual workers making the dolls. Such exhibits are very important for our understanding of how the dolls that we collect were made. Such displays give one a better understanding of the multiplicity of steps and materials required for the dolls' manufacture and distribution and thus give the modern collector a far better appreciation of the creation of the dolls.

As one travels from one museum to another, one soon realizes that museums have different reasons for creating their collections of dolls. Many were started because one or two collectors kindly donated their dolls to a musuem, thus forming the nucleus. Therefore, the collection represents the taste of that individual collector or pair of collectors. For this reason many of the museums have collections of the earlier dolls such as the woodens, waxes, papier-mâchés, china and the so-called "parians;" these were the types of dolls which interested the majority of collectors in the past. Some collections have been developed as part of the general museum collection. In the case of a costume museum, the clothes on the dolls would be all important. In the case of a . historical society or a museum developed to show the past of a certain region, one would find a collection of the kinds of dolls that were played with in that region and/or the collection would focus on the representation of the folk tradition of the region. Some museums have been developed to show the industrial aspects of making dolls. One tends to find this in areas where the dolls were originally manufactured. Of course, most museums have items which reflect all of the above mentioned aspects of collecting.

As mentioned in the 2nd Edition of **The Doll Catalog,** it is always advisable to confirm that the museum will be open on the given day that you wish to visit and that there will be a sufficient variety of dolls available for you to view in order to make your trip worthwhile. Many museums with fine collections of dolls may only bring the dolls out for Christmas or some other special occasion such as when a doll group will be gathering in a particular area. If and when you first start to plan to have a convention, it is always advisable to contact the local museum to let them know of the forthcoming event for they may be able to bring out some of their dolls from storage and set up a special exhibit for your group. Many museums are willing to do this if sufficient time is given for their preparations.

The editor of this publication would appreciate hearing about any museums which contain a fine collection of dolls for possible inclusion in the next edition of **The Doll Catalog.**

Geographical General Museum Listing

ARKANSAS

Geuther's Doll Museum
188 North Main Street
Eureka Springs, Arkansas 72632

CALIFORNIA

Hobby City Doll & Toy Museum
1238 South Beach Boulevard
Anaheim, California 92804
(714) 527-2323
Every day 10am - 6pm. Admission: adults -$1.00, children and Senior citizen $.50. On permanent display are 2 or 3000 plus antique toys with 1500 antique dolls, 500 collectible dolls and 200 or more modern dolls. Doll from pyramids of Egypt 3,000 to 5,000 years old (proof). Dolls made by N.I.A.D.A. artist. Madame Alexander old dolls and presidents' wives. 5' x 10' Korto Palace and All of the Family, 1870. For further listing see information on page 128.

Kern County Museum and Pioneer Village
3801 Chester Avenue
(805) 861-2132
Bakersfield, California 93301
Weekdays 8am - 5pm (Museum). Saturday, Sunday, Holidays 10am - 5pm (Museum). Pioneer Village -- ticket sale for admission to the village closes at 3:30pm daily allowing 1½ hours to tour the exhibits. Admission: Museum - Free. -- Pioneer Village - $1.00. No permanent display (changing exhibits); Available for seasonal Christmas display are 10 antique dolls, 35 collectible dolls and 15 modern dolls.

Pittsburg Historical Museum
40 Civic Avenue
P.O. Box 1816
Pittsburg, California 94565
(415) 439-9783
Sundays 1-5 pm. Special Tours by appointment. Voluntary contributions. On permanent display are 3 dolls with 1 antique doll and 2 collectible dolls.

Santa Barbara Museum of Art
1130 State Street
Santa Barbara, California 93101
(805) 963-4364
Tuesday through Saturday, 11am - 5pm. Sundays 12noon - 5pm. Closed Mondays. Admission: - free. Donations accepted. On permanent display are 550 dolls with 525 antique dolls and 25 collectible dolls. Queen Anne; French mechanical, Pierotti, Sheppard, Motschmann-type, Munnier, Bru, Juneau, Walker, Huret, etc., along with an excellent selection of papier-mâché, china and Parian.

Bulah Hawkins Doll Museum
1437 6th Street
Santa Monica, California 90401
(213) 394-2981
Phone museum for current days and hours. Admission: adults - $2.50, children - $1.50, group discounts. 1800 Victorian style building containing approximately 3500 dolls from around the world. A 150 year old English doll house estate, miniatures, doll furniture and more. Doll restoration done. Dolls, clothes, wigs and accessories for sale.

Cupid's Bow Doll Museum
117 South Murphy Avenue
Sunnyvale, California 94088
(408) 773-1577
Monday through Saturday 10:30am-5pm. Sundays 1-4pm. Admission: $1.00 (children under 5 free). On permanent display are 2,000 antique and contemporary dolls. Museum in Old Town Historical Sunnyvale in building built in 1894, site of Murphy Station - non profit organization. Museum includes shop, schoolroom in doll making classes, library (free reading), laboratory and research department, new doll artist dolls on display each month.

continued on page 128

Exterior of museum, one-half scale of Washington, D.C. White House.

Hobby City Doll & Toy Museum

Fifty-nine years of collecting 2,000 to 3,000 dolls and toys including bisque, chinas, Parians, fashions, wooden, wax and many more. An education for young and old. Open seven days a week, 10 a.m. - 6 p.m. Admission: Adults $1., children $.50, senior citizens $.50. Dolls and doll-related items for sale.

1238 South Beach Boulevard
Anaheim, CA 92804
(714) 527-2323

Museum displays old, odd and original dolls.

Geuther's Doll Museum

Geuther's Doll Museum featured in February/March 1982 *Doll Reader* is moving to 188 North Main Street, Eureka Springs, Arkansas. Opening in new location summer 1982. Brochure for SASE.

188 North Main Street
Eureka Springs, AR 72632

Cupid's Bow Doll Museum

Antique, contemporary, artists' dolls, to create nostalgia in the young and old alike. Dolls made in a wide array of materials. Each month a guest artist displays their art in the front showroom apart from the museum. For sale shop. Descriptive literature available. Open Monday through Saturday 10:30 a.m. - 5 p.m. Sundays 1 - 4 p.m. Admission: $1., children under 5 free.

117 South Murphy Avenue
Sunnyvale, CA 94086
(408) 773-1577

continued from page 127

COLORADO

Cameron's Doll & Carriage Museum

218 Becker's Lane
Manitou Springs, Colorado 80829
(303) 685-9486

Memorial Day - Labor Day daily except Sunday, 9am - 5pm. May and September by chance or appointment. Admission: adults - $2.00, children - $.50. On permanent display are 300 antique dolls, 300 collectible dolls, 300 modern dolls, 125 ethnic dolls, 30 wooden dolls and 30 cloth dolls. There are 1,500 dolls - plus 150 baby and doll carriages. For further information see listing on page 129.

CONNECTICUT

New Britain Youth Museum

30 High Street
New Britain, Connecticut 06053
(203) 225-3020

Monday through Friday 1pm - 5pm. Admission: Free. On partial display and available for seasonal Christmas display are 20+ antique dolls, 20 collectible dolls and 100+ foreign dolls.

Lyman Allyn Museum

625 Williams Street
New London, Connecticut 06320
(203) 443-2545

Tuesday through Saturday 1-5pm. Sundays 2-5pm. Closed Mondays and holidays. Admission: Free. On permanent display and available for seasonal Christmas display are 60 dolls with 113 antique dolls, 4 collectible dolls and 4 modern dolls.

DISTRICT OF COLUMBIA

DAR Museum

1776 "D" Street, NW
Washington, DC 20008

National Museum of History & Technology

14th St. & Constitution Ave., NW
Washington, DC 20560

Washington Dolls' House & Toy Museum

5236 44th Street, NW
Chevy Chase, Washington, DC 20015
Near Lord-&-Taylor and Neiman-Marcus
(202) 244-0024

Tuesday through Saturday, 10am - 5pm. Sunday, Noon - 5pm. Admission: adults - $2.00, children under 14 - $1.00. A carefully researched collection of Antique dolls, Dolls' Houses, Toys & Games on display. For further information see listing on page 129.

FLORIDA

Deland Museum

449 East New York Avenue
Deland, Florida 32720
(904) 734-4371

Monday through Friday 9am - 5pm. Sundays 2-4pm. Admission: Contribution suggested - $1.00. Available for rotating permanent display are 115 dolls with 40 antique dolls, 35 collectible dolls and 40 modern dolls. Several very early 19th century American dolls and dolls with an international flavor.

Cameron's Doll & Carriage Museum

1500 dolls on display, antique to modern. All kinds and sizes. 150 doll and baby carriages - the best carriage collection in the U.S. Open Memorial Day to Labor Day Mon. - Sat. 9 a.m. - 5 p.m. May and Sept. by appointment or chance. Doll related items for sale. Adults $2.00. Children $.50.

218 Becker's Lane
Manitou Springs, CO 80829

The Children's Museum of Indianapolis

Over 100 dolls from 1830 to 1930 are displayed. Dolls are viewed as mirrors of their times, each showing how its era viewed the world and the roles of children and women. Free admission. Open Tuesday through Saturday 10 a.m. - 5 p.m. Sunday 12 noon - 5 p.m. Closed Mondays. Shop on premises. Descriptive literature available.

3000 North Meridian Street
Indianapolis, IN 46201
(317) 924-5431

Homosassa Doll Museum

Route 2, Box 6
Homosassa, Florida 32646
(904) 628-2390
Daily 7am - 3pm. Admission: adults - $1.00. Available for display are 1,700 dolls with many antique dolls, many collectible dolls and a few modern dolls.

Jacksonville Museum of Arts and Sciences

1025 Gulf Life Drive
Jacksonville, Florida 32207
(904) 396-7062
Tuesday through Friday, 9am - 5pm. Saturdays 11am - 5pm. Sundays 1-5pm. Admission: adults - $2.00, children over 4 - $1.00. Available for permanent display are 95 dolls with 30 antique dolls, 50 collectible dolls and 15 modern dolls.

Museum of Collectible Dolls

1117 South Florida Avenue
Lakeland, Florida 33803
(813) 687-8015 or 682-8484
Available for display are 2,000 dolls.

Florida's Silver Springs Antique Car Collection

State Road 40
P.O. Box 370
Silver Springs, Florida 32688
(904) 236-2121
9am - 5pm year round (to 6pm summer months). Admission: adults - $7.50, children (3-11— - $5.50, children under 3 - free. On permanent display are 300 dolls with 300 collectible dolls (Collection probably includes some dolls made before 1910, but it is not known exactly how many.) Only surviving doll from Sara Bernhardt's col-

lection of 28 dolls. Amos and Andy dolls and Bye-Lo dolls.

Museum of Old Dolls & Toys

1530 Sixth Street, NW
Winter Haven, Florida 33880
(813) 299-1830
Museum located one mile North of downtown Winter Haven on U.S. 17. Monday through Saturday 10am - 5pm. Sundays and major holidays 12 noon - 5pm. Admission: adults - $2.00, juniors 8 through 15 - $1.00, under 8 with parent - no charge. On permanent display is a major collection with dolls spanning three centuries, doll houses, toys and miniatures.

GEORGIA

The Toy Museum of Atlanta

2800 Peachtree Road, NE
Atlanta, Georgia 30305

Museum of Antique Dolls

505 East President
Savannah, Georgia 31401
(912) 233-5296
Tuesday through Saturday 10am - 5pm. Closed major holidays. Admission: $1.50. On permanent display are 375 dolls with 225 antique dolls, 100 collectible dolls and 50 modern dolls. Greiner doll and tea set formerly owned by the Greiner family; excellent groupings of wax, papier-mâché and rag dolls bearing famous makers' names; permanent Christmas display; Devereux's Queen Victoria; early 19th century Samurai doll; numerous NIADA dolls; many doll accessories (houses, furniture, costumes, toys, silver, china, etc.); fully representative dolls of all media.

continued on page 130

WASHINGTON DOLLS' HOUSE & TOY MUSEUM

In the Museum:
A carefully researched collection of Antique dolls, Dolls' Houses, Toys & Games on display.

In the Museum Shop:
Dolls' Houses, Furnishings, Toys, Books, Postcards, Building & Wiring Supplies and old dolls and toys in the Antiques Consignment Corner.

Special Arrangements for Birthday Parties in the "Edwardian Tea Room."

Shown above:

Three French children - a "nursing Bru held by her older Bru sister, and a "long-faced Jumeau", are part of the Nancy Petrikin Menoni collection in the museum.

Set of 12 full-color postcards, please specify style, $2.00 postpaid:
(a) "Three French Children" (shown)
(b) "A Shoeless Beauty by Jumeau"
(c) "A Rare Pair of Bisque Ice Skaters"
(d) Assortment of above

Box of 20 full-color notecards and envelopes, "Two Jumeaus Share a Pot of Tea", $6. postpaid.

5236 44th STREET, N.W.
Chevy Chase
WASHINGTON, D.C. 20015

PHONE: (202) 244-0024

Near Lord & Taylor and Neiman-Marcus

Open Tuesday through Saturday 10 to 5
Sunday noon to 5
Children under 14 - $1 • Adults - $2

Flora Gill Jacobs, Director

Windy Acres Doll Museum

Mother Goose Scenes created by Magge Head. Display of antique dolls and doll houses. Presidents and First Ladies sculptured by Magge Head and Bill Tharp. Adults: $1., Children: $.50. By appointment. Call.

**R.R. 1 (Carlos)
Lynn, IN 47355
(317) 874-2302**

22in (55.9cm) Tigure Au 14 - Paris Parisien.

Fairhaven Doll Museum

300 bisque head dolls, German characters, French fashions, Jumeaus, chinas, babies, Noah's Ark with Noah and all animals hand carved. Open Tuesday through Saturday 10 a.m. - 4 p.m. Admission: Adults $1., Children $.50. Dolls and related items for sale.

**384 Alden Road
Fairhaven, MA 02719**

continued from page 129

ILLINOIS

Klehm's Pink Peony Doll & Mini Museum
2 East Algonquin Road
Arlington Heights, Illinois 60005
(312) 437-2880
Daily 10am - 5pm. Admission: adults - $1.00, children $.50. On permanent display is a large collection of dolls.

Chicago Historical Society
Clarke Street and North Avenue
Chicago, Illinois 60614

Vermilion County Museum
116 North Gilbert Street
Danville, Illinois 61832
(217) 442-2922
Tuesday through Saturday 10am - 5pm. Sundays 1-5 pm. Admission: adult - $1.00, children ages 6 to 14 - $.50. On permanent display are 85 dolls with 10 antique dolls, 55 collectible dolls and 20 modern dolls.

University Historical Museum
200 Block S. School
Illinois State University, Williams Hall
Normal, Illinois 61761
(309) 436-8341 or 829-6331
Tuesday through Friday 10am-4:30pm. When school is in session Saturdays and Sundays 1-5pm. Closed holidays. Guided tours by reservation, requested for groups of ten or more. Admission: Free. On permanent display, partial display and seasonal Christmas display are 350+ dolls with 100 antique dolls, 200 collectible dolls and 25 modern dolls.

INDIANA

The Children's Museum of Indianapolis
3000 North Meridian Street
Indianapolis, Indiana 46201
(317) 924-5431
Tuesday through Saturday 10am-5pm, Sunday 12noon-5pm, closed Mondays. Admission: Free.

Wayne County Historical Museum
1150 North A
Richmond, Indiana 47374
(317) 962-5756
Tuesday through Sunday 1-5pm. Admission: adults - $2.00, children and students - $1.00, under 6 years - free. On permanent display and available for seasonal Christmas display are 150 dolls with 19th & 20th century dolls of all kinds, 50-75 antique dolls, 50 collectible dolls and 30 modern dolls. Many doll accessories and an elegant doll house of 1870s-1880s period.

Windy Acres Doll Museum
R.R. 1 (Carlos)
Lynn, Indiana 47355
(317) 874-2302
By appointment only. Admission: adults -$1.00, children - $.50. Display antique dolls and doll houses. For further information see listing on page 130.

KANSAS

Thomas County Museum
1525 West 4th Street
Colby, Kansas 67701
(913) 462-6972
Monday through Friday 9am-5pm, Saturdays and Sundays 1-5pm. Closed Mondays and holidays. Admission: adults - $1.00, children - $.50. On permanent display are 240 dolls with 167 antique dolls and 73 collectible dolls. Mechanical Jumeau French doll made in 1852-1870. French fashion doll signed by Rocharde, dated 1875. Doll has necklace of magnified pictures of paintings and Parisian scenes.

Riley County Historical Museum
2309 Claflin Road
Manhattan, Kansas 66502
(913) 537-2210
Tuesday through Saturday 8:30-5pm. Sundays 2-5pm. Closed Mondays and national holidays. Admission: Free. Available for partial display and seasonal Christmas display are varies types of dolls throughout the year.

Poe Museum
Peabody, Kansas 66866

MAINE

Shore Village Museum
104 Limerock Street
Rockland, Maine 04841
(207) 594-4950
June 1 through September 30 daily 10am-4pm. Open by appointment throughout the year. No admission. Donations welcome. On permanent display is the Llewella Mills Doll Collection shows 34 contemporary dolls dressed in costumes dating from 1399 to the Gay 90's.

MARYLAND

Historical Society of Carroll County
210 East Main Street
Westminster, Maryland 21157
(301) 848-6494
On permanent display are 200 antique dolls.

MASSACHUSETTS

Children's Museum
300 Congress Street
Boston, Massachusetts 02210

Fairhaven Doll Museum
384 Alden Road
Fairhaven, Massachusetts 02719
(617) 994-4050
Tuesday through Saturday 10am-4pm. Admission: adults $1.00, children $.50. On permanent display are 300 types of dolls with antique French, Ger Bisque, China. Papier mâché etc. As stated above, French fashions, characters. We sell also Madame Alex. compos, hard plastics, Saucy Walkers and celebrities.

Manchester Historical Society
10 Union Street
Manchester, Massachusetts 01944
(617) 526-7230
July and August Tuesday through Friday 2-5pm. All other times by request. Admission: adults - $1.00, children - $.50. On permanent display are 36 antique dolls and 10 collectible dolls.

Essex Institute
132 Essex Street
Salem, Massachusetts 01970-3773
(617) 744-3390
June 1st through Labor Day Monday through Saturday 9am-6pm, Sundays and holidays 1-6pm. Open Mondays after Labor Day through November 1. Closed Thanksgiving, Christmas and New Year's Day. Admission: adults - $2.00, children (6-16 years) - $1.00, senior citizens - $1.50, children under 6 free. On permanent display are approximately 150 types of dolls (Many French and German, late 19th century. A charming variety of "folk dolls."), very few collectible dolls.` We have two outstanding doll houses, one 1876 one circa 1855.

Yesteryears Museum

Main and River Streets
Sandwich,
Cape Cod, Massachusetts 02563
(617) 888-1711, May through October:
Winter: 1 (617) 563-6673
Open: 1 May through 31 October 1982.
Monday through Saturday 10am-5pm.
Sundays 1-5pm. Other times, for groups
only, by appointment. (Located on two
floors of the historic First Parish Meeting
House 1638.) Admission: adults - $2.00,
children - $1.00, under 12, senior citizens
-$1.50. On permanent display are thousands
of antique dolls; doll houses; miniature
shops; kitchens; room; etc. Thousands of
fine French, English, German, US, Japanese, Chinese and miscellaneous dolls.
95% of the collection are antique dolls, 5%
collectible dolls and about 10 modern
dolls. Many dolls made for royalty!
Beidermeier furniture made for Frans
Joseph's daughter; dolls and toys for
several of Japan's royal families; 17th
Century fashion doll of Princess of Wurtem-
burg; dolls presented to US Ambassador
to France by Napoleon III (1840's) and
President Franklin Pierce (1851); Court
Dolls of Louis XIV.

Wenham Doll Museum

132 Main Street
Wenham, Massachusetts 01984

Wenham Historical Association & Museum, Inc.

132 Main Street, Route 1A
Wenham, Massachusetts 01984
Monday through Friday 1-4pm. (Summer
hours 11am-4pm). Sundays 2-5pm. Closed
Saturdays, holidays and February. Ad-
mission: adults - $1.00, children - $.25.
Dolls' houses, rooms, dolls from 1500 BC
to present.

Worcester Historical Society

Worcester, Massachusetts 010601

MICHIGAN

Children's Museum/Detroit Public Schools

67 East Kirby
Detroit, Michigan 48202
(313) 494-1210
Monday through Friday 1-4pm; Saturdays
9am - 4pm. (October through May) Closed
Sundays and holidays. Available for partial
display are 242 dolls with 10 antique dolls,
100 collectible dolls and 132 modern dolls.
Miss Akita Japanese friendship doll.

Greenfield Village & H. Ford Museum

Oakwood Boulevard
Dearborn, MI 48121

Rose Hawley Museum

305 East Filer Street
Ludington, Michigan 49431
(616) 843-2001
Summer. Monday through Saturday, 11am-
5pm. Off season, Tuesdays and Thursdays,
1-5pm. Other times by appointment.
Admission: $.50 contribution suggested.
On permanent display are 50 dolls with 35
antique dolls, 10 collectible dolls and 5
modern dolls.

MINNESOTA

Pope County Historical Museum

SHighway 104
Glenwood, Minnesota 56334
(612) 634-3293
Monday through Friday, 9am - 4:30pm.
May through September Saturdays and
Sundays, 1-5pm. Admission: adults - $1.00,
children under 12 - $.25. On permanent
display are 25 dolls with 7 antique dolls, 10
collectible dolls and 8 modern dolls.

continued on page 132

Doll Museums

Eight room Victorian doll house.

Wenham Historical Association & Museum, Inc.

Dolls' houses, rooms, dolls from 1500BC to present, bisque, wax, cloth, wood, papier-mâché, ethnic; 17th century house with period furnishings; special changing exhibits. Open Monday through Friday 1 - 4 p.m. (summer hours 11 a.m. - 4 p.m.) Closed Saturdays, holidays and February. Admission: Adults $1., Children $.25. Miniatures and publications for sale.

132 Main Street, Route 1A
Wenham, MA 01984
(617) 468-2377

17th century wooden Spanish fashion doll.

Dolly Wares Doll Museum

2500+ dolls of all shapes and sizes, old ones, new ones and many in between. The most complete doll museum on the Pacific coast. Hours 10 a.m. - 5 p.m. Summer -Tuesday through Sunday; Winter - Wednesday through Sunday. Admission: Adults $3.50, Children $2.00. Dolls and related items for sale.

3620 Highway 101 North
Florence, OR 97439

continued from page 131

Hennepin County Historical Society

2303 Third Avenue South
Minneapolis, Minnesota 55404
(612) 870-1329
Tuesday through Friday 9am - 4:30pm. Sundays 1-5pm. Admission: Free. Contribution box. On permanent display are 125 dolls with 70 antique dolls, 50 collectible dolls and 5 modern dolls.

MISSOURI

Audrain County Historical Society Museum

501 South Muldrow Street
Mexico, Missouri 65265
(314) 581-3910
March through November Tuesday through Saturday 1-4pm, Sundays 2-5pm. Closed Mondays, holidays, month of January. Admission: adults - $1.00, children - $.25. On permanent display are approximately 400 dolls with 40 antique dolls and 200+ collectible dolls.

Eugene Field

House & Toy Museum

634 South Broadway
St. Louis, Missouri 63102
(314) 421-4689
Tuesday through Saturday 10am-4pm. Sundays 12noon-5pm. Closed Mondays and national holidays. Admission: adults -$1.00, children under 12 - $.50. On permanent display, available for partial display and seasonal Christmas display (special exhibits in February and October) are 350 dolls with 350 antique dolls, 1,250 collectible dolls and less than 100 modern dolls. Single pick-a-ninny sculpted from artist casting plaster, property of Eugene Field prior to 1882.

NEBRASKA

Old Brown House Doll Museum

1421 Avenue F
Gothenburg, Nebraska 69138
(308) 537-7596
May 1 through September 30, 9am-6pm. The rest of the year by appointment. Admission: adults - $1.00, children (ages 6 to 12) - $.50, under 6 - free. Maximum family charge - $2.50. Over 1,000 dolls displayed.

NEW JERSEY

Good Fairy Doll Museum & Hospital

205 Walnut Avenue
Cranford, New Jersey 07016
(201) 276-3815
Open by appointment or chance. Admission: $1.00. Miscellaneous old and new dolls; some designed by Noby. Dolls and doll related items for sale.

Raggedy Ann Antique Doll & Toy Museum

171 Main Street
Flemington, New Jersey 08822
(201) 782-1243
February and March weekends only; April through December Wednesday through Sunday 10am-5pm. Closed January. Admission: adults - $.75, children under 12 $.50, children under 5 - free. On permanent display are 6,000 dolls with 3,000 antique dolls & toys, 2,000 collectible dolls and 1,000 modern dolls. Doll museum made for Queen Elizabeth of her first grandchild, doll of Ethel Barrymore.

Morris Museum/ Arts & Sciences

Normandy Heights and Columbia
Morristown, New Jersey 07960

NEW MEXICO

Playhouse Museum of Old Dolls & Toys

1201 North 2nd Street
Las Cruces, New Mexico 88001
(505) 526-1207
Tuesday through Sunday 1-5pm. Closed Mondays. Admission: (Rates for groups of 10 or more.) Adults - $1.50, children 6 to 12 - $.75. On permanent display are about 1,000 dolls with mostly antique dolls and a few modern dolls. Dolls are displayed in scenes. We have carriages, doll furniture, dishes, doll houses, miniatures, Japanese Girl Doll Festival and miscellaneous too numerous to mention. Small shop.

Museum of International Folk Art

P. O. Box 2087
Santa Fe, New Mexico 87501

Tucumeari Historical Museum

416 South Adams Street
Tucumcari, New Mexico 88401
(505) 461-4201
June 2 through September 2 Monday through Saturday 9am-12noon, 1-8pm. Balance of year Tuesday through Saturday to 5pm. Sundays all year from 1-5pm. (Closed January 1st and December 25th.) Admission: adults - $2.00, children (6-16) -$.50, under 6 - free. On permanent display are 15+ dolls (various types).

NEW YORK

Adirondack Center Museum

Court Street
Elizabethtown, New York 12932
(518) 873-6466
May 14 through October 17 Monday through Saturday 9am-5pm, Sundays 1-5pm. October 18 through May 13 closed. Open by appointment. Brewster Memorial Library (museum's reference library) open Tuesdays and Thursdays 9:30am-3pm (except lunch hour) year-round or by appointment. Admission: adults - $1.50, children - $.50, under 5 - free. Tour rate -$1.00, by arrangement. On permanent display are 158 dolls with 25 antique dolls, 6 (plus 6 paper dolls) collectible dolls, 1 modern doll, 61 dolls in Regional Costumes (including 37 miniature figure in Chinese wedding procession), 14 Ethnic Dolls, 31 Bisque-head dolls, 13 wooden dolls and 7 cloth dolls. We also have dolls' houses, furniture and a variety of other toys. We have two doll houses, both locally made in the 19th century.

Margaret Woodbury Strong Museum

One Manhattan Square
Rochester, New York 14607
(716) 263-2700
Tuesday through Saturday 10am-5pm, Sundays 1-5pm. Closed Mondays, Thanksgiving, Christmas, New Year's Day. Admission: adults $1.50. On permanent display are approximately 20,000 dolls. The doll collection will be housed in a study collection area of 98 cases. Dolls of all descriptions displayed from 18th century woodens to modern dolls of th 1960s. Included are such dolls as: French fashion, automata, Schoenhut, early American, character dolls, Palmer Cox Brownies, Rose O'Neill Kewpies, shell and more.

Staten Island Historical Society

Richmondtown
Staten Island, New York 10314

Victorian Doll Museum

4332 Buffalo Road (Route 33)
North Chili, New York 14515
(716) 247-0130
Tuesday through Saturday 10am - 5pm.
Sundays 1-5pm. Closed Mondays and
holidays. Admission: adults - $1.00, children
under 12 - $.50. On permanent display are
1,000 dolls with 400 antique dolls, 200
collectible dolls and 400 modern dolls.

The Shaker Museum

149 Shaker Museum Road
Old Chatham, New York 12136
(518) 794-9100
May 1 through October 31, daily 10am-
5pm. Admission: adults - $3.00, senior
citizens and students 15-21 - $2.50, children
6-14 - $1.00, under 6 free. Available for
partial display are 10 antique dolls.

NORTH CAROLINA

Arts and Science Museum

Museum Road
Statesville, North Carolina 28677
(704) 873-4734
Daily, except Monday, 2-5pm. Mornings
by appointment. Admission: Free. On permanent display are 26 dolls with 14
(estimated age) antique dolls and 12 collectible dolls.

OHIO

The Western Reserve Historical Society

10825 East Boulevard, University Circle
Cleveland, Ohio 44106
(216) 721-5722
Tuesday through Saturday 10am-5pm.
Sundays 12noon-5pm. Closed Mondays
and major holidays. Admission: adults -
$2.00, children and senior citizens - $1.00.
Available for partial display are 950 (on
display and in storage) with 400 antique
dolls, 500 collectible dolls and 50 modern
dolls. The Bingham Doll house (8-room
Georgian manor); 1889 Edison phonograph
doll; 1926 Performo-Toy "Micky Mouse"
(predecessor to the Disney version); circa
1910 walking, talking and kissing doll by
Simon and Halbig; other makers include
Bru, Jumeau, Armand Marseille, Handwerck, Lenci, Joel Ellis, Heubach, Kimcraft,
Kämmer & Reinhardt, Kestner, etc.

Garst Museum

205 North Broadway
Greenville, Ohio 45331
(513) 548-5250
Tuesday through Sunday 1-5pm. Closed
January. Admission: donations accepted.
On permanent display are 230 dolls with
approximately 30 antique dolls and 200
foreign dolls.

Milan Historical Museum

10 Edison Drive
Milan, Ohio 44846
(419) 499-2968
April, May, September and October, 1-
5pm. June, July and August, 10am-5pm.
Admission: donation box. Over 350 doll
collection on permanent display including
antique and collectible dolls, dolls in
regional costumes, ethnic, bisque-head,
wooden and cloth dolls. Also features doll
related objects such as doll houses, carts,
hats, buggies. The 350 dolls in the Museum's Coulton Room probably rate among
the nations finest collections, which started
with the Coulton family dolls and was
added to over a twenty-five year period, by
the late Mildred Smith Coulton of Cleveland. For further information see listing on
page 133.

Milan Historical Museum

Display includes 350 dolls representing 25 years of collecting by
the late Mildred Smith Coulton in
papier-mâché, bisque, wooden,
wax, china and Parian. Date 1790
to 1860. April, May, Sept., Oct. 1
to 5 p.m. - June, July, Aug. 10 a.m.
to 5 p.m. Closed Mondays.
10 Edison Drive
Milan, OH 44846
(419) 499-2968

*Oldest covered-wagon doll, 1790, leather
and homespun.*

McCurdy Historical Doll Museum

Over 2,500 dolls displayed including antique, story book, historical, Lewis Sorensen wax dolls,
Emma Clear dolls and Laura
Alleman kid leather dolls. Forty-
seven rooms of doll house miniatures. Open Tuesday through
Saturday 12 noon - 6 p.m. Admission: Adults $2., Children $1.00.
Brochures available. Dolls and related items for sale.
246 North 100 East
Provo, UT 84601
(801) 377-9935

Blair Museum of
Lithophanes and Carved Waxes

2032 Robinwood Avenue
Toledo, Ohio 43620
(419) 243-4115
By appointment only. Admission: $3.00
contribution or more. On permanent display are 50 wax dolls or statues. All before
1910. Portraits of famous people.

The Old Rectory -
Worthington Historical Society

50 West New England Avenue
Worthington, Ohio 43085
(614) 885-7632 or 885-1247
Open by appointment. Admission: $1.00.
On permanent display (many are per-
manently displayed, others rotate) are
200-300 (at any given time) with 400 antique
dolls and 100 collectible dolls. Many fine
accessories, a doll house, two large creche
figures circa 1700.

OREGON

Dolly Wares Doll Museum

3620 Hwy. 101 North
Florence, Oregon 97439
Summer: 10am-5pm (closed Monday).
Winter: 10am-5pm (closed Monday and
Tuesday). Admission: adults - $3.50, chil-
dren - $2.00. On permanent display are
2,500+ dolls with 100+/- antique dolls,
2,000+/- collectible dolls and 400+/- modern
dolls. Dolly Wares Doll Museum is known
for its variety of dolls dating from a pre-
Columbian figure of clay, 18th century
wooden dolls, 19th century wax, papier-
mâchés. The German & French bisc's,
there are modern dolls, compos-, international dolls, unusual dolls.

PENNSYLVANIA

Mary Merritt Doll Museum

RD 2
Douglasville, Pennsylvania 19518

Perelman Antique Toy Museum

270 South 2nd Street
Philadelphia, Pennsylvania 19106

Chester City Historical Society

225 North High Street
West Chester, Pennsylvania 19380

SOUTH DAKOTA

Camp McKen-z Doll Museum

Murdo, South Dakota 57559
(605) 669-2385
May 1 through October 1, 2-11pm. Other
times by appointment. Admission: adults
-$1.00, children - $.50. On permanent display
are 700 dolls with 100 antique dolls, 500
collectible dolls and 100 modern dolls.

TEXAS

Story Book Museum

Kerrville, Texas 78028
(512) 896-5448
By appointment only. Admission: Donation
appreciated. On permanent display and
available for seasonal Christmas display
are 20 antique dolls, 32 miniatures, 78
collectible dolls and 190 modern dolls. Big
display case full of doll & children's pressed
glass, china dishes (7 furnished doll houses
with correct doll house dolls.)

continued on page 134

Doll Museums

continued from page 133

Neill Museum

7th and Court
Fort Davis, Texas 79734
(915) 426-3969
June 1 through Labor Day, by appointment and by chance. Admission: adults - $1.00, children under 12 - $.50. On permanent display are 300 dolls with 100 antique dolls, 185 collectible dolls and 15 modern dolls. Antique toys, doll house, doll buggies, etc. Medallion House built 1898. Period furniture, five rooms open to public.

Museum of American Architecture and Decorative Arts

7502 Fondren Road
Houston, Texas 77074
(713) 774-7661 ext. 311
Tuesday, Wednesday, and Thursdays 10am-4pm, Sundays 2pm-4pm. Closed Mondays, Fridays, and Saturdays. Admission: Free (any contribution appreciated). On permanent display are 100+ dolls with 70 antique dolls, 20 collectible dolls and 10 modern dolls. Approximately 100 dolls kept on display at all times with various selections being made from our total collection of approximately 750 dolls.

UTAH

McCurdy Historical Doll Museum

246 North 100 East
Provo, Utah 84601
(801) 377-9935
Tuesday through Saturday 12-6pm year round. Admission: adults - $2.00, children under 12 - $1.00. On permanent display and available for seasonal Christmas display (our Christmas dolls are displayed in December only) are 2,500 dolls with 300 antique dolls, 2,000 collectible dolls and 200 modern dolls. Rosabell, Queen of the Dolls famous doll from the Cleao Heavener collections. 27 dolls from the Emma Clear collection. Patty Reed's doll, (replica made by Sherman Smith) famous Donner Party surviver.

VIRGINIA

The Valentine Museum

1015 East Caly Street
Richmond, Virginia 23219

VERMONT

Bennington Museum

West Main Street
Bennington, Vermont 05201

Kent Tavern Museum

Kents' Corner
Calais, Vermont 05648
(802) 223-5660 or 828-2291
July and August, Tuesday through Sunday, 12noon-5pm. Also open during Foliage Season (last three weekends before Columbus Day (Monday holiday), 12noon-5pm. Admission: adults - $1.50, children

- $.50. Available for partial display are 7 dolls with 5 antique dolls and 2 collectible dolls. Miniature rooms created by Louise Andrews Kent, "Mrs. Appleyard."

Springfield Art & Historical Society

Elm Hill
Herrick, Vermont 05156

Vermont Historical Society

109 State Street
Montpelier, Vermont 05602
(802) 828-2291
September through June-Mon.-Fri. July-August-Monday-Sunday. 8-4:30 - Monday-Friday, 10-5 - Saturday and Sunday. Admission: Free. No permanent display of dolls. Study collection of dolls available on special arrangement to serious students.

WASHINGTON

Cowlitz County Historical Museum

405 Allen Street
Kelso, Washington 98626
(206) 577-3119
Tuesday through Sunday 1-5pm. Admission: by donation only. On permanent display and available for partial display are 30 with 200 American and European dolls 19th-20th century bisque, parian, china, wood, rag, apple.

AUSTRIA

Spielzeugmuseum

Salzburg, Austria
Bürgerspitalgasse 1
47 560
Open 9am-5pm. 80 antique dolls, 82 collectible dolls and 2 modern dolls.

CANADA

Guelph Civic Museum

6 Dublin Street, South
Guelph, Ontario, Canada N1H 4L5

Yarmouth County Museum

22 Collins Street
(Postal address: Box 39)
Yarmouth, Nova Scotia, Canada B5A4B1
Winter 2-5pm (Tuesday through Saturday incl.) Summer 9am-5pm (Monday through Saturday incl.) (Sundays 1-5pm - July and August only.) Admission - $1.00, students $.50, children - $.25, family maximum - $2.50. On permanent display are 75 dolls with 45 antique dolls and 30 collectible dolls.

DENMARK

Legoland Museum

Billund, Denmark

EAST GERMANY

Museum of Folklore

Dresden, DDR, East Germany

ENGLAND

Woodspring Museum

Burlington Street
Weston-super-Mare,
Avon BS23 1PR, England
(0934) 21028
Throughout the year Monday through Saturday 10am-1pm, 2-5pm. July and August Monday through Friday 10am-6pm, Saturday 10am-5pm. Admission: Free. On permanent display are 36 dolls with 22 antique dolls, 14 collectible dolls and c100 modern dolls. Dolls' house (with dolls) made circa 1840 for the granddaughter of John Loudon McAdam, the famous road engineer. A collection of Peggy Nisbet dolls made in Weston-super-Mare.

Burrows Museum

Roman Bath Building
Bath, Avon, England

Museum of Costume

Assembly Rooms, Bennett Street
Bath, Avon BA1 2QE, England
(0225) 61111
April through October, Monday through Friday 9:30am-6pm. Sundays 10am-6pm. November through March Monday through Friday 10am-5pm. Sundays 11am-5pm. Admission £1. On permanent display are 159 dolls with 90 antique dolls, 59 collectible dolls and 10 modern dolls.

Museum of Art, Hove

19 New Church Road
Hove, East Sussex BN3 4AB, England
Brighton 779410
Tuesday through Friday 10am-1pm, 2-5pm. Saturdays 10am-1pm, 2-4:30pm. Closed Sundays, Mondays and bank holidays. Admission: Free. On permanent display are approximately 60 dolls with 46 plus approx. 12 in Dolls House, antique dolls (includes 3 eighteenth century dolls (wooden), also wax, wood, bisque, etc. of 19 century.) and 2 collectible dolls.

Blaise Castle House Museum

Henbury
Bristol, England

Playthings Past Museum

Beaconwood, Beacon Lane
Bromsgrove, England

Red House Museum & Art Gallery

Quay Road, Christ Church
Dorset, England

Saffron Walden Museum

Museum Street, Saffron Walden
Essex, England
(0799) 22494
April through September Monday through Saturday 11am-5pm, Sunday and bank holidays 2:30-5pm. October through March Monday through Saturday 11am-4pm, Sunday and bank holidays 2:30-5pm. Closed Good Friday, Christmas Eve and Christmas Day. Admission: Free. Suggested contribution: adults - 50p, children -20p. On permanent display are 35 dolls with 25 antique dolls and 10 collectible dolls.

Sudeley Castle

Gloucestershire, England

Museum of Childhood

Water Street, Menai Bridge
Gwynedd, England
(0248) 712498
Daily Easter through October 10am-6pm weekdays, 1-5pm Sundays. Admission: adults - $1.35, children - $.90. On permanent display are approximately 80 dolls with 35 antique dolls, 35 collectible dolls and 10 modern dolls.

Arreton Manor

Arreton
Isle of Wight, England

The Lilliput Museum of Antique Dolls

High Street, Brading
Isle of Wight, England
(0983)-72-231
Daily including weekends, winter 10am-5pm, summer 9:30am-10pm in height of season. Admission: adults - 45p, O.A.P.'s and children over 5 - 35p. On permanent display are approximately 1,000 dolls with all types, hundreds of antique dolls, hundreds of collectible dolls and one only donated by Nakita Kruschev, Premier of U.S.S.R. in 1961. Every doll or toy has been acquired from the original owner or descendant and is marked accordingly, many from famous people.

Cookworthy Museum

The Old Grammar School
108 Fore Street
Kingsbridge,
S. Devon TQ7 1AW, England
(0548) 3235
Easter to early October Monday through Saturday 10am-5pm (last admission 4:30 pm). Admission: adults - 40p, children 20p. On permanent display are 30 European dolls and approximately 200 miniature items. (Plus complete contents of dolls house circa 1910.

Tunbridge Wells
Municipal Museum

Civic Centre, Mount Pleasant
Tunbridge Wells,
Kent TN1 1RS, England
(0892) 26121 Ex. 171
Monday through Friday: 10am-5pm. Saturdays 9:30am-5pm. Sundays, bank holidays and Tuesdays after Spring and Summer closed. Admisssion: Free. On permanent display are 135 dolls with 120 antique dolls and 15 collectible dolls. Wax doll belonging to Princess Royal, daughter of Queen Victoria in original dress.

Museum of Social History

27 King Street
Kings Lynn PE30 1HA, England
Kings Lynn 5004
Tuesday through Saturday 10am-5pm. Closed Sundays, Mondays and bank holidays. Admission: summer 20p, winter 10p. On permanent display are 20-25 (About 55 in total collection) with 20-25 on show, 32 antique dolls, 17 collectible dolls and 5 modern dolls. Doll presented to local child by Queen Victoria.

Judges' Lodgings

Church Street, Lancaster
Lancashire, England

Abbey House Folk Museum

Abbey Road
Leeds LS5 3EH, England
(0532) 755821
Admission: adults - 50p, senior citizens - 15p, children under 5 - free. On permanent display are 30 antique dolls and 10 collectible dolls.

Usher Gallery

Lindum Road
Lincoln, England, LN2 1NN
(0522) 27980
Weekdays 10am-5:30pm. Sundays 2:30-5pm. Closed Good Friday, Christmas Day and Boxing Day. Admission: adults - 25p, children/students 10p. On permanent display are 13 dolls (approximately 30 dolls in reserve). Display changes to show others in collection) with 13 antique dolls. Wooden

Doll circa 1735 - country style clothes of circa 1820. Queen Anne Doll circa 1796 -wooden, dressed in elegant town garments. Late 19th century mechanical doll - 1873 hairstyle, pompadour style dress. Portrait doll of Jenny Lind circa 1864, porcelain (famous Swedish singer). Several Frozen Charlotte dolls - parian ware. Circa 1860. 6. several Armand Marseille dolls.

Llandudno Doll Museum
and Model Railway

Masonic Street
Llandudno Gwynedd LL30 2DU, England
Easter through end of September Monday through Saturday 10am-1pm and 2-5:30pm. Sunday 2-5:30pm. Admission: adults - 70p, children 30p. There are many rare and famous dolls in the collection from numerous centuries of the world, dating back as far as the 16th century. Someone is at hand all season for a talk around or to answer questions.

Bethnal Green Museum of Childhood

Cambridge Heath Road
London E2 9PA, England
(01) 980-2415
Monday through Thursday and Saturdays 10am-6pm, Sundays 2:30-6pm. Closed all day Friday. Admission: Free. On permanent display are 900 dolls with 300 antique dolls, 400 collectible dolls and 200 modern dolls. About 20 dolls formerly owned by Queen Mary. Several dolls, old and new which represent Royal Family persons.

The Museum of London

London Wall
London, England EC2Y 5HN

Pollock's Toy Museum

1 Scala Street
London W.1., England
(01) 636-3452
10am-5pm. Admission: adults - 30p, children 15p. On permanent display (display changes at least twice a year) are several hundred antique dolls, several hundred collectible dolls and several hundred modern dolls.

Gunnersbury Park Museum

Gunnersbury Park
London W3, England
(01) 992 1612
March through October Monday through Friday 1-5pm. Saturdays, Sundays, bank holidays 2-6pm. November through February Monday through Friday 1-4pm. Saturdays, Sundays, bank holidays 2-4pm. Admission: Free. Available for partial display are 74 antique dolls, 11 collectible dolls and 2 modern dolls (dolls displayed varies).

Luton Museum and Art Gallery

Wardown Park
Luton LU2 7HA, England
0582 36941
April through September weekdays 10am-6pm, Sundays 2-6pm. October through March weekdays 10am-5pm, Sundays 2-5pm. Closed Tuesdays. Admission: Free. On permanent display are 59 dolls with 31 antique dolls, 20 collectible dolls and 8 modern dolls. Small collection of doll's house furniture donated by Queen Mary.

Monks Hall Museum

42 Wellington Road, Eccles.
Manchester, M 30 ONP, England
061-789 4372
Monday through Friday 10am-6pm. Saturdays 10am-5pm. Closed New Year's Day, Good Friday, Christmas Eve, Christmas Day, Boxing Day. Admission: Free. On permanent display are 22 dolls with 18 antique dolls and 4 collectible dolls.

Stranger's Hall

Charing Cross
Norwich, England NR2 4AL

Museum of Costume & Textiles

51 Castle Gate
Nottingham, England
(0602) 411881
Daily 10am-5pm. Closed Christmas Day. Admission: Free. Available for partial display are 9 (but we hope to have more later this year) dolls with c.50 antique dolls and c.5 collectible dolls.

Grove House

Iffley Turn
Oxford, England

Harris Museum & Art Gallery

Market Square
Preston, Lancashire, England
0722/58248
Monday through Saturday 10am-5pm. On permanent display are 26 dolls with 25 antique dolls and 1 collectible doll.

Salisbury and South Wiltshire Museum

65 The Close
Salisbury, Wiltshire, SP1 2EN, England
(0722) 332151
Monday through Saturday 10:30am-5pm. Sundays in July and August only 2-5pm. Admission: 50p. Available for partial display are 10 antique dolls. Doll dressed by Marie Antoinette.

Penrhyn Castle

Bangor, Gwynedd
Wales, England

Warwick Doll Museum

Okens House, Castle Street
Warwick, England, CV34
Warwick 491600
Monday through Saturday 10am-6pm, Sundays 11am-6pm. Closed January and February. Admission: adults - 50p, children 25p. On permanent display are approximately 1,000 dolls with 600 (all types) wood, wax, bisque, toys and 400 collectible dolls. Several dolls belonging previously to Royal Persons.

Hereford and Worcester
County Museum

Hartlebury Castle, Hartlebury,
Nr. Kidderminster.
Worcestershire DY11 7XZ, England
(0299) 250416
March 1 through October 31 Monday through Friday 2-5pm. Sundays 2-6pm. Closed Saturdays. Admission: adults -40p. children & O.A.P. - 20p, family ticket - £1.00. 55 antique dolls.

Worthing Museum & Art Gallery

Chapel Road
Worthing, West Sussex,
BN11 1HQ, England
39999
October through March Monday through Saturday 10am-5pm. April through September 10am-6pm. Admission: Free. On permanent display are 20-60 dolls (variety -bisque, wax, wood, etc.) 300 antique dolls, 150 collectible dolls and 40 modern dolls.

York Castle Museum

Tower Street
York, England

continued on page 136

Doll Museums

continued from page 135

FRANCE

Musee Roybet-Fould

178 Boulevard Saint Denis
92400 Courbevoie, France
Wednesdays, Thursdays, Saturdays, Sundays and holidays 2-6pm. 150 displayed. 17th century wax; papier-mâché 1830-1850; Huret, Barrois, Jumeau, Steiner, Francois Gaultier S.F.B.J.; Fashion dolls; celluloid, Lenci with their accessories. Shop sells post cards, prints and bulletins of CERP (Centre d'Étude et Recherche sur les Poupées) Center for the study and research on dolls. Picture cannot be copied.

Musee Carnavalet

23, Rue de Sévigné
Paris 75003, France
272 21 13
Daily except Mondays 10am-5pm. Admission: 9FF.

Musee de l'Homme

Place du Trocadero
Paris, France 75016

Musee des Arts Decoratifs

107 rue de Rivoli
Paris, France 75001

Musee du Jouet

1 Enclos de l'Abbaye
Poissy, France 78300

Musee National des Techniques

C.N.A.M. 292, rue Saint-Martin
Paris 75003, France
Daily 1-5:15pm. Admission: adults - 8 F.F., children - 8 F.F.

IRELAND

Museum of Childhood

20 Palmerston Park 6
Dublin, Ireland

National Museum of Ireland

Kildare Street
Dublin 2, Ireland
(01) 765521
Tuesday through Saturday 10am-5pm. Sundays 2-5pm. Closed Mondays. Admission: Free. On permanent display are 29 dolls with 22 antique dolls and 7 collectible dolls.

MONACO

Princess Grace's Doll Museum

Musee National de Monaco
Monte Carlo, Monaco

NETHERLANDS

Nederlands Kostuummuseum

Lange Vijverberg 14-15
2513 AC The Hague, Netherlands
Monday through Saturday 10am-5pm, Sundays and holidays 1-5pm. Admissions: Free. Dolls in fashionable costume 18th century till the present time.

SCOTLAND

Museum of Childhood

38 High Street
Edinburgh, Scotland

SPAIN

Museo Romantico Provincial

12 Calle Montcada
Barcelona, Spain

SWEDEN

Lekaks Museum - The Toy Museum

Mariatorget 1
Stockholm, Sweden

SWITZERLAND

Kirschgarten

Elizabethstrasse 27
Basel, Switzerland
Tuesday through Sunday 10-12am, 2-5pm. Collection of early dolls and toys including paper dolls.

Spielzeug und Dormuseum Riehem

Baselstrasse 34
CH4125 Riehem, Switzerland
061-67-28-29

Doll Museum - Barengasse Zurich

Sasha Morgenthaler
Barengasse 20-22
8001 Zurich, Switzerland
Mondays 2-5pm, Tuesday through Sunday 10am-12noon, 2-5pm. Admission: Free. Museum devoted to the life and work of Sasha Morgenthaler including a film with her telling about her work.

Zurcher Spielzeng Museum

Fortunagasse 15/Rennweg
8001 Zurich, Switzerland
Monday through Friday 2-5pm. Collection of Feans Carl Weber.

WEST GERMANY

Neustadt Tract Museum

Neustadt near Coburg, West Germany

Dr. Lydia Bayer Museum

Theodorstrasse 7/11
85 Nurnberg, West Germany

Niederrheinisches Museum

fur Volkskunde und Kulturgeschichte
Haupt Str. 18
D 4178 Kevelaer, West Germany

H. G. Klein Collection

D 4155 Grefarth
Kreis Viersen, West Germany

AUCTION HOUSES

"The Doll Bazaar", from The Little Doings of Some Little Folks ca. 1889.

All Prices Listed Are Subject To Change Without Notice.

Doll collectors find more at Sotheby's.

No matter what type of antique dolls you collect, you will find a better selection at Sotheby's Collectors' Carrousel auctions, held regularly at our York Avenue Galleries in New York.

For more information about buying or selling dolls at Collectors' Carrousel auctions, call or write Pamela Brown Sherer, Sotheby Parke Bernet Inc., 1334 York Avenue, N.Y., N.Y. 10021, (212) 472-4783.

Sotheby's gives serious attention to dolls... and doll collectors.

Fine French bisque-head bébé, Bru Jeune et Cie, incised Bru Jne 8, sold at our New York Galleries on December 9, 1981.

SOTHEBY'S
Founded 1744

Rare and important French bisque-head "Oriental" fashion doll, height 17½ inches, sold at our New York Galleries on December 9, 1981.

Auction Center

Kenneth S. Hays & Associates, Inc.

We have professionally appraised and sold individual dolls, collections, as well as the contents of doll museums. Dolls and doll related items are included in beautifully illustrated catalogs and mailers advertising our sales. We always invite you to consign items to our future sales. Catalogs available one month prior to auctions. Catalog prices vary.

**4740 Bardstown Road
Louisville, KY 40218
(502) 499-8942**

Fain Auction Way

We specialize in dolls and other collectibles, also estates and others. Write and let us know what you need. Send a SASE for prompt reply..... and send $1.00 for our printed flyers.

**1420 Mimosa
Rosenberg, TX 77471**

Col. Kathryn Fain, Auctioneer.

Auction Houses

139

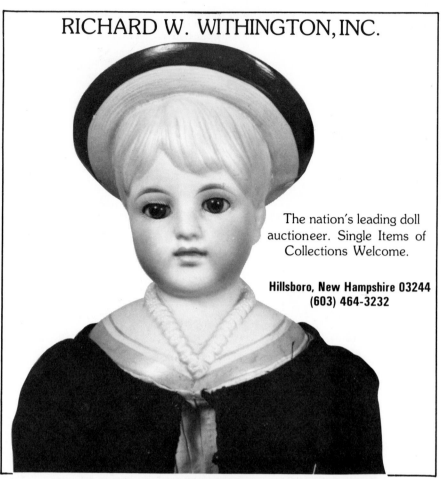

DOLL KITS

"I wanted to see the doll factory."   *From Our Darlings, ca. 1895.*

All Prices Listed Are Subject To Change Without Notice.

Crying Bye-Lo Baby, 10in (25.4cm). Kit $13.95, completed $49.95 ppd.

Audria's Crafts, Inc.

Exquisite heirlooms --- beautifully hand-painted on quality porcelain; each kit contains head, hands, feet (where needed) and instruc-'ions for cloth body and costume. Sixteen kits and same 16 completed dolls available. Retail price range of kits $11.95 - $72.95. SASE for complete line. (Wholesale and retail. Shop and mail order.)

913 East Seminary
Fort Worth, TX 76115
(817) 926-1191, 926-1451
Out-of-Texas--1-800-433-2918
(Toll Free)

Sheila Kwartler, (ODACA)

Put Some Mischief In Your Dollhouse

Peter & Penny are members of a 1"= 1' scale porcelain dollhouse family. All have natural flesh tones, swivel heads, and are wired for posing. Museum-quality originals. Available as: Pre-wired kits; finished undressed dolls; dressed dolls. For brochure & color photo of family send $1 (refundable with order) to:

10 Chadwick Road
Great Neck, NY 11023

Quality doll house doll kits.

Seaside Miniatures

Beautiful porcelain 1"-1' doll kits. French bisque or black flesh. Men, women, Gibson, children, pouties, babies, 2¼in (5.8cm) Bye-Los, maids, butlers. Doll house dolls dressed ($18.), kits ($7.). Other size dolls and kits available. Kits, retail $7. Catalog $1.00. $.25 + SASE for list. (Wholesale and retail. Mail order only.)

Route N, Box 44B
Peel, AR 72668

32in (81.3cm) Bru Jne 13.

Sheri's Doll Shoppe

Extra large and rare dolls reproduced in the finest porcelain from the most unusual antique originals. Delicate coloring and featherlight lashes and brows. Retail price: $40. - $175. SASE for printed lists Photographs available. (Wholesale and retail. Shop and mail order.)

2256 South Mayfair
Springfield, MO 65804

Bright eyes and sweet smiles.

DiAnn's Originals

Billy and Becky 20in (50.8cm) cloth dolls available in a mini kit which includes pre-painted face (permanent acrylic paints) and pale peach body fabric, ½ yard, plus pattern. $12. each doll kit. Does not include stuffing, clothes, fabric or yarn for hair. Specify eye color. Pattern only $3.50 each or $6. for both. Catalog of 12 dolls $.75. (Mail order only.)

P. O. Box 694, Dept. HH
Park Ridge, IL 60068-0694

Carolena's Precious Dolls

Reproduction dolls and kits. Carolena's TM Painting and Mixing Bisque Media $2.85 postpaid. Carolena's *Painting and Pouring Those Precious Dolls* booklet -32 pages. $4.00 postpaid; 12 vials matt doll paint kit $9.50 postpaid. Catalog $2.75.

5684 Sterling Road
Hamburg, NY 14075

MARIE LOUISE ORIGINALS

Nina, our Mexican Senorita - $19. postpaid.

25in (63.5cm) doll kits include pattern printed on body fabric, color heat transfer, button eyes, felt mouth, plastic plates for moveable arms and legs, clothes pattern. Nina's kit includes a heat transfer for blouse embroidery. Instruction book necessary with first kit only $7.25 postpaid. Catalog $1.00. (Wholesale and retail. Shop and mail order.)
16642 Robert Lane
Huntington Beach, CA 92647

Katrina, our Dutch Maid – $18. postpaid.

Past & present.

Rangely Arts & Crafts

Porcelain bisque kits - head, arms, body, legs, instructions. Barbie or Betty Boop $27. each. Hand china painted kits $55. each retail. Postage $2.50 per doll. Price list for other doll kits $1.50. (Wholesale and retail. Shop and mail order.)
P.O. Box 966
Rangely, CO 81648

Penny, 18in (45.7cm), one head turns to three faces. Kit $33.95, completed $66.95 ppd.

Audria's Crafts, Inc.

Exquisite heirlooms --- beautifully hand-painted on quality porcelain; each kit contains head, hands, feet (where needed) and instructions for cloth body and costume. Sixteen kits and same 16 completed dolls available. Retail price range of kits $11.95 - $72.95. SASE for complete line. (Wholesale and retail. Shop and mail order.)
913 East Seminary
Fort Worth, TX 76115
(817) 926-1191, 926-1451
Out-of-Texas--1-800-433-2918
(Toll Free)

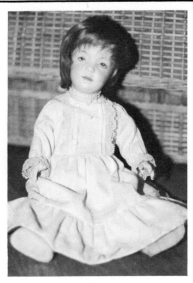

Little Sarah.

Sarah Beardshear

There is more to it...everything included to complete your doll. Sixty doll kits; price range $25. -$90. Printed list $.50 + SASE. (Retail only. Shop and mail order.)
P.O. Box 234
Homer, NE 68030
(402) 698-2261

Averill's Laughing Baby.

"The Doll Lady"

Averill's Laughing Baby, fine porcelain bisque. Kit contains china painted face, hands, legs, material for body and our own easy to make body pattern to make approx. 13in (33.0cm) doll. Special price with this ad $18.95 + $4.95 postage. Pattern for clothing $1.50. (N.Y. residents add tax.) Free catalog with purchase. For catalog and information (DISCOUNT) Doll Club, send $2.00.

P.O. Box 121-HHP-C
Homecrest Station
Brooklyn, NY 11229
(212) 743-5219

The Doll Corner

Approximately 250 kits available, also dressed dolls complete or will dress dolls to order. Catalog $3.50; refundable first $15. order. Kit prices range from $3. to $45. (Wholesale and retail. Shop and mail order.)

940 Richie
Lima, OH 45805

Angelic Sleeping Baby, handcrafted (USA) French bisque porcelain. China painted head, hands and soft body and legs. Complete with body and clothing patterns. A must for any collection. #316 10in (25.4cm) size $15.95; 15in (38.1cm) size $23.95, + $4.95 postage and ins. N.Y. residents add tax. Free catalog with purchase. For catalog and information (DISCOUNT) Doll Club, send $2.00.   **P.O. Box 121-HHP-C**
Homecrest Station
Brooklyn, NY 11229
(212) 743-5219

"The Doll Lady"

Sleeping Baby.

Milano's Creative Clay Cottage

Over 350 originals and reproductions, some bald, others with painted hair and bonnets. Patterns for bodies and complete costume drawn to enhance that particular doll head. Kits: $5. - $45. retail; $3.50 - $25. wholesale. Catalog $2.50. (Shop and mail order.)

625 Rowe Avenue
Yuba City, CA 95991
(916) 673-2771

"The Doll Lady"

Grace S. Putman's "Million Dollar Baby" (as the Bye-Lo was called) is reproduced by "The Doll Lady," in all its original charm and delicacy. Kit contains china painted head and hands, fabric for body, patterns for body and clothing, to make approximately 15in (38.1cm) doll. #318-W (white) or #318-B (black) $16.95 each kit + postage $4.95; add $2.00 for each additional kit. N.Y. residents add tax. Free catalog with purchase. For catalog and information (DISCOUNT) Doll Club, send $2.00. (Retail only. Mail order.)

P.O. Box 121-HHP-C
Homecrest Station
Brookly, NY 11229
(212) 743-5219

Crying Baby.

"The Doll Lady"

Loveable 12in (30.5cm) #115 Crying Baby, handcrafted (USA). Fine bisque porcelain, china painted head, turned down mouth and tears on cheek, hands and legs with soft body. Complete with body and clothing patterns. It will steal your heart away. $15.95 + $4.95 postage and ins. N.Y. residents add tax. Free catalog with purchase. For catalog and information (DISCOUNT) Doll Club, send $2.00.

P.O. Box 121-HHP-C
Homecrest Station
Brooklyn, NY 11229
(212) 743-5219

Her Royal Majesty - #H13421.

Holiday Handicrafts, Inc.

Li'l Missy beaded dolls, 5½in (14.0cm), can be made from kits in an evening. Just pin ribbon, sequins, beads, trims into foam doll body. No sewing required. Collectible. Retail price $4.49. Fifty-six kits available. Catalog available. (Wholesale and retail. Shop and mail order.)
**P. O. Box 470, West Hill Road
Winsted, CT 06098
(203) 379-3374**

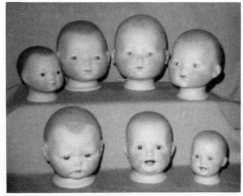

Flange neck babies.

Conni Lynch

Over 15 adorable bisque baby kits in flesh or black flesh. All have flange necks, set-in eyes, i.e. Kit includes porcelain head, hands (sometimes feet) and body pattern. Bye-Lo, Tynie Babe, Averille, etc. Signed and dated. Dress pattern $2.50 extra. Kits priced $25. - $50. Printed list $.50 + SASE (refundable first order). (Retail only. Shop and mail order.)
**205 East Main Street - P.O. Box 278
West Branch, IA 52358
(319) 643-2822**

Pincushion doll.

Rangely Arts & Crafts

Porcelain pincushion doll kits with fan, with mirror or hands behind head. Instructions. Bisque $15. each. China painted $55. each. 7¼in (18.5cm) high. Postage $2.50 per doll. Price list for other dolls $1.50. (Shop and mail order.)
**P. O. Box 966
Rangely, CO 81648**

Little Doll Studio

Phyllis Bashian

Reproduction kits, sizes miniatures and up. Replacement parts. Kid and muslin bodies. Custom wefted wigs (wigs made from your hair). Custom dressmaking. Over 100 kits priced at $20. and up. Printed list $1.00 (refundable on first order). (Retail only. Mail order only.)
**2113 Sunnybank Drive
La Canada, CA 91011
(213) 248-6602**

Carrie Cradle.

Fibre-Craft Materials Corp.

Carrie Cradle slumbers in her soft crochet cradle, which is also a purse! Easy-to-make with illustrated instructions from 100% acrylic yarn. Just one of five styles available. Retail price range $5.98 - $8.98; wholesale price range $3.29 - $4.93. Catalog available. (Wholesale only.)
**6310 West Touhy
Niles, IL 60648
(800) 323-4316 (4224)**

Haljo's Ceramics

Doll Kits, bisque or china painted from all of Bell's molds, many of Bryon's, others from Seeley, McNee, Small World, Sam's Ross, Robinhood and others by Hal & Jo Smith. Porcelain heads; porcelain, earthenware or composition bodies. Patterns available. 150 plus kits available retail $10. up. Discounts on volume $25. or more with sales number. (Shop and mail order.)

**1425 Linda Place
Tracy, CA 95376
(209) 835-1987**

DOLL MAKING SUPPLIES

All Prices Listed Are Subject To Change Without Notice.

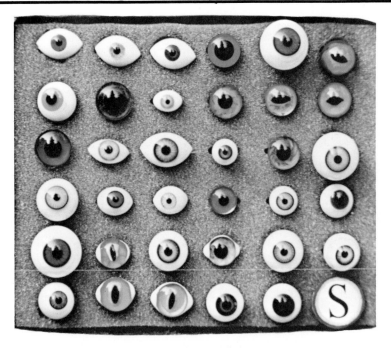

Schoepfer Eyes

We have in stock practically all sizes in round glass doll eyes in colors of brown and blue, also plastic eyes. Immediate delivery. Catalog and price list available. (Wholesale and retail.)

138 West 31st Street
New York, NY 10001
(212) 736-6934

Westwood Ceramic Supply Co.

Doll supply source for collectors and dealers. Fast service. We manufacture Sun Dynasty™ porcelain. Wigs, eyes, cord; all your doll needs. Dealers please write on letterhead. Catalog and printed list available. (Wholesale and retail.)

14400 Lomitas Avenue
Industry, CA 91746
(213) 330-0631

Doll Repair Parts, Inc.

Wigs, crowns, glass eyes, plastic eyes, doll shoes, socks, dress patterns, doll books, doll stands, reproduction bodies, hands and feet. Doll molds by American Beauty Ceramics, paints. Catalog $.50. (Wholesale and retail. Shop and mail order.)

9918 Lorain Avenue
Cleveland, OH 44102
(216) 961-3545

Les Bébé de Bea

Complete line of doll supplies. Glass eyes; compo slip, $15.95 gallon; human hair wigs from $12.; molds, compo bodies finished/unfinished; Bell porcelain; doll books; Lynn and Frankie's Patterns; greenware from over 100 molds; stands; brushes. Catalog $2.00. (Wholesale and retail. Shop and mail order.)

24302 West Warren
Dearborn Heights, MI 48127
(313) 563-0775

Victoria Anne, 18in (45.7cm) completed doll with clothing patterns - $29.95 + $2.50 shipping.

Cosi Cottage & Co.™

Send $2.50 for doll supplies and accessories catalog. Buttons, trims, fabrics, patterns, kits; over 80 sizes and styles of doll hats. Books on dolls, too, for the homemaker and doll sewer. (Retail only. Shop and mail order.)

326 North National Avenue
Fond du Lac, WI 54935
(414) 922-0027

The quality line of doll supplies from Doll Shop Enterprises.

Doll Shop Enterprises

Manufacturers/importers/exporters of doll supplies from our exclusive line of doll wigs to our "wood-n-comp"^C doll bodies. Everything that is needed for doll making is available from Doll Shop Enterprises. Catalog $2.00 (Int'l $3.50). (Wholesale and retail. Shop and mail order.)

**P.O. Box 1426
Smyrna, GA 30081
showrooms: 150-154 Washington Ave.
Marietta, GA 30060
(404) 428-3655**

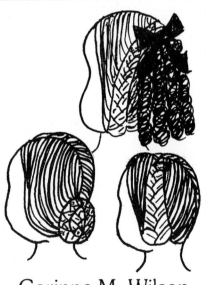

Corinne M. Wilson

Handmade mohair miniature wigs, 2in (5.1cm), 2½in (6.4cm), 3in (7.6cm), 4in (10.2cm) up to 6in (15.2cm). Blonde, medium brown, dark brown, black, gray, and white. Price $9.50 up + postage and insurance. (Retail only. Mail order only.)

**2608 Cheyenne
Wichita, KS 67216
(316) 682-2979**

La Ceramique Boutique

Quality originals created and sculpted by Berdell. Those paperweight eyes you have been looking for. Works of art --- not manufactured. Porcelain teeth for your antique dolls also. Retail price range $5.50 - $14. Fifteen percent discount on orders over $100. SASE for printed list. (Wholesale and retail. Shop and mail order.)

**C. R. B., Box 8485
Tucson, AZ 85738
(602) 791-7961**

The Doll's Nest

Doll making and repair supplies. Handmade leather bodies (jointed and gusseted styles). Patterns available. Acrylic eyes, German stretch wigs, straw hats, stands, mohair, shoes, socks, doll-size trims and buttons. Catalog $.75. (Wholesale and retail. Shop and mail order.)

**1020 Kenmore Boulevard, Dept. S
Akron, OH 44314
(216) 753-2464**

Doll Making Supplies

"BEC" DOLLS
BELLE EARL CHOHANIN
4048 W. Compton Blvd.
Lawndale, California 90260
(213) 679-3013

Doll Molds
Composition Body Compound
Catalog $3.50

A & D Ceramic & Doll Supply

- KILNS. 4 sizes specially built for your reproduction doll needs.

- Doll molds & composition bodies

- Porcelain casting equipment
- Doll patterns
- Shoe patterns & supplies to make them
- Eyes - stands - books & misc. doll supplies
- IMSCO synthetic & human hair wigs
- Shirley Augustine seminars

Send $2.00 for brochures to:

**A & D CERAMIC & DOLL SUPPLY
12600½ INTERURBAN AVE. SO.
SEATTLE, WASH. 98168
PHONE (206) 243-1445**

Doll's-N-Things

Greenware, books, patterns, molds, kilns. Complete line of doll supplies. Distributor for Seeley, Shirley Augustine patterns, Byron patterns, IMSCO products. Classes and seminars. SASE for printed list. (Wholesale and retail. Shop and mail order.)

**1416 Rees Street
Breaux Bridge, LA 70517
(318) 332-2622**

Crescent Bru reproduction.

Reja Dolls

Doll making supplies and professional instruction in porcelain doll making. Finished dolls and kits available. Finished doll brochure $.50. Shop hours: 10 a.m. -2 p.m. Tuesday through Saturday. Authorized Seeley distributor. (Retail only. Shop and mail order.)
**510 Ellington Road
South Windsor, CT 06074
(203) 289-8782**

FINE QUALITY **IMPORTED BUTTONS**
Designed for dolls dresses.

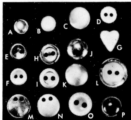

	No.	Size	Description	2 Dz.	6 Dz.	12 Dz.
A	9855	3/16"	Pearl with shank	2.00	5.25	8.25
B	4016A	1/4"	Pearl with shank	2.00	5.25	8.25
C	4016B	5/16"	Pearl with shank	2.00	5.25	8.25
D	5027	1/4"	Pearl w/2 holes	1.75	4.75	7.25
E	5684G	1/4"	Gold plated w/2 holes	2.75	7.25	13.50
F	5684S	1/4"	Silver plated w/2 holes	2.75	7.25	13.50
G	6335	5/16"	Pearl heart w/shank	DISCONTINUED		
H	9134G	5/16"	Gold plated w/2 holes	2.75	7.25	13.50
I	9134S	5/16"	Silver plated w/2 holes	2.75	7.25	13.50
J	7005G	5/16"	Hemisphere-shaped gold plated w/shank	2.75	7.25	13.50
K	7005S	5/16"	Hemisphere-shaped silver plated w/shank	2.75	7.25	13.50
L	9073	3/8"	Gold plated rim. Pearl inside w/2 holes	2.75	7.25	13.50
M	3098G	5/16"	Gold plated sequins with 2 holes	2.75	7.25	13.50
N	3098S	5/16"	Silver plated sequins with 2 holes	2.75	7.25	13.50
O	551	5/16"	Bakelite w/2 holes *Colors: see below	2.00	5.25	8.25
P	9340	5/16"	Bakelite hemisphere-shaped w/shank *Colors: see below	2.00	5.25	8.25

*No's. 551 & 9340 available colors: black, white, pink, blue, red, green, yellow. Minimum per color: per color.

Standard Doll Co.

**23-83 31st Street, Dept TCD82
Long Island City, NY 11105**

All the Trimmings

"All the Trimmings" is a converter and packager of fine laces, braids, elastics, embroideries, and buttons, plus 100% cotton specialty fabrics. Catalog $.50. (Mail order only.)
**P.O. Box 15528
Atlanta, GA 30333**

SAM™ MOLDS

©1982
Annoinette (A. Marque 18½″)
(#45A $115.00)

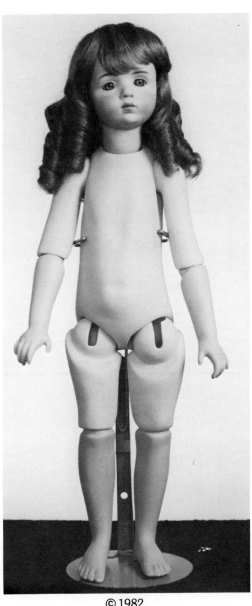

©1982
SA 168 *Annoinette* Pattern
(Includes shoe pattern)
$6.95

©1982
Annoinette Body
For porcelain casting
#45BCD $185.00
For casting composition
#44BCDE $185.00

Pictures are for molds and pattern *not* dolls.

Put Your Doll In The Finest, A Shirley Pattern

SHIRLEY™ DOLL PATTERNS

Doll Making Supplies

Fibre-Craft Materials Corp.

Create an Heirloom!

Create an heirloom! Individually painted bisque-look doll sets provide today's durability giving the impression of yesteryears' authentic treasures. Doll bodies and sets available in two sizes. Minimal assembly required. Retail price range $2.49 - $5.49; wholesale price range $1.37 - $3.02. Catalog available. (Wholesale only.)

**6310 West Touhy
Niles, IL 60648
(800) 323-4316 (4224)**

Sides Doll Supply

Reproduction molds, porcelain, wigs, instructions, elastic, hooks, criers, brushes, shoes, stockings, eye-sizers, china paint. Doll kits on order. Send for list of dolls available. Professional bisque.

**Box 376, Route 3
Clayton, NC 27520**

F. Jak Rogers - Wigmaker

Professionally licensed wigmaker making deluxe quality human hair doll wigs. Many styles available. Photograph/brochure with hair samples $1.00 (refundable first order). Little miniature wigs now available. Wigs $5.50 and up retail. (Wholesale and retail. Mail order and shows.)

**Star Route #1, Box 18
Niland, CA 92257**

Yesterday's Dolls Today

Will help you any way we can with your doll making or repairing needs. Classes in doll making and repairing. Everything needed to make a porcelain doll or repair a doll. (Wholesale and retail. Shop and mail order.)

**Cactus Alley
2610 Salem #6
Lubbock, TX 79410
(806) 797-9484**

Bring Your Artistry to Life!

Your models come alive with the fine precision tools from Kemper. For the dolls in your life . . . and for the life in your dolls . . . Kemper has the tools for every delicate detail of design. Model natural eyes with the Kemper eye sizer. Create vivid expressions with our cutting and detailing tools. Add the softest texture to your model's skin with Kemper fine sanders. Use our Lady Finger tools for the life-like hands and charming gestures.

For the liveliest dolls and the finest in crafts, remember Kemper, the quality manufacturers of precision tools for the ceramist and sculptor.

Dealer and distributor inquiries invited.

Write today for a FREE catalog.

KEMPER TOOLS®

Kemper Mfg., Inc., P.O. Box 696, Department DR, Chino, CA 91710.

Doll & Craft World, Inc.®

We offer French human hair and fine quality synthetic wigs, also blown glass and synthetic eyes. Composition and cloth bodies, stringing materials, Kemper tools, instruction books, stands and much more. Catalog $3.00. (Wholesale and retail. Mail order only.)

125 8th Street
Brooklyn, NY 11215
(212) 768-0887

Standard Doll Co.

New Catalog FREE

With order (of $15 or more). Hundreds of dolls (popular modern types to antique reproductions in bisque and china • parts • patterns • stands • shoes & accessories • books & kits • and much more.
For Catalog only Send $2.00.

23-83 31st Street, Dept TCD82
Long Island City, NY 11105

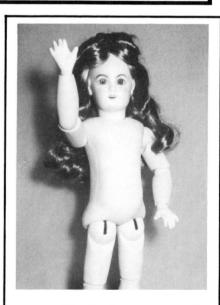

Lucy White

Mohair, top quality, for making doll wigs. Comes in straight and wavy; sold by the yard. Many beautiful shades to choose from. Send $1.00 plus large SASE for samples. (Retail only.)
135 Mark Street
Bristol, CT 06010

Doll Scope

25% discount on $50.00, up to 50% on $500.00 head molds: French fashions to characters - swivel to all-bisque. Body molds available. Our molds made for casting porcelain or compo. Molds: $10.00 and up. Catalog: $2.50
Route 3, Box 107-W
Mission, TX 78572
(512) 585-0257

GREAT DOLLCRAFTING VALUES!

GLASS-LIKE DOLL EYES

Unique quality acrylic material with the identical look, glisten, lusterous depth and feel of glass. Even the experts can't tell them apart.

No. 1940PE
Available: Blue or Brown

PUPIL SIZE		6 Prs.	1 Dz. Prs.	3 Dz. Prs.
3MM	(⅛″)	3.50	5.50	15.00
4½MM	(³⁄₁₆″)	3.75	6.00	16.00
6MM	(¼″)	4.00	7.00	18.00
8MM	(⁵⁄₁₆″)	4.75	8.50	23.50
10MM	(⅜″)	6.00	10.50	28.50
12MM	(⁷⁄₁₆″)	8.75	15.00	41.50

SPECIAL SAMPLER ASSORTMENT

2 pairs of eyes in each size—1 pr. brown, 1 pr. blue. TOTAL ONE DOZEN PAIRS.
No. 1950PE **10.50**

60-PC. ASSORTMENT PKG.

BONANZA! 60-pieces of accessories in one pack to fit all 11½″ high fashion dolls (Barbie, Maret, Twisti, Sindi, etc.). Includes: hi-boots, hats, pocketbooks, badminton sets, high-heel shoes (pumps), high-heel shoes (open toes), curlers, sunglasses, flower hatbands, hangers, necklace w/heart pendant, cameras, mirror and comb sets, binoculars.

No. EP8154
1 pack—1.95
6 packs—1.75 ea.
1 dz.—19.00
3 dz.—17.50 dz.

REPLACEMENT WIGS KIT

For all 11½″ high-fashion dolls (Barbie, Maret, Twisti, Sindi, etc.). Contains: 3 wigs on foundation (1 blonde, 1 brunette, 1 honey blonde), 3 hairpieces to match, 3 clips, one brush and comb set.

A BUY OF A LIFETIME!

No. EP8155A

1—1.95
6—1.75 ea.
1 dz.—19.00 dz.
3 dz.—17.50 dz.

8″ VINYL PLASTIC GIRL DOLL

Finest in imports, she has assorted, beautifully styled rooted hair, moving eyes, jointed head, arms and legs. Posable, she can sit or stand. Panties, shoes and socks included. A Great Value!

No. EP8709A

1—2.95
1 dz.—31.50
3 dz.—29.50 dz.
6 dz.—28.00 dz.

FINE QUALITY IMPORTED BUTTONS

Designed for dolls dresses.

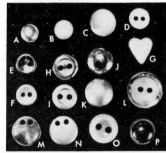

	No.	Size	Description	2 Dz.	6 Dz.	12 Dz.
A	9855	³⁄₁₆″	Pearl with shank	2.00	5.25	8.25
B	4016A	¼″	Pearl with shank	2.00	5.25	8.25
C	4016B	⁵⁄₁₆″	Pearl with shank	2.00	5.25	8.25
D	5027	¼″	Pearl w/2 holes	1.75	4.75	7.25
E	5684G	¼″	Gold plated w/2 holes	2.75	7.25	13.50
F	5684S	¼″	Silver plated w/2 holes	2.75	7.25	13.50
G	6335	⁵⁄₁₆″	Pearl heart w/shank	DISCONTINUED		
H	9134G	⁵⁄₁₆″	Gold plated w/2 holes	2.75	7.25	13.50
I	9134S	⁵⁄₁₆″	Silver plated w/2 holes	2.75	7.25	13.50
J	7005G	⁵⁄₁₆″	Hemisphere-shaped gold plated w/shank	2.75	7.25	13.50
K	7005S	⁵⁄₁₆″	Hemisphere-shaped silver plated w/shank	2.75	7.25	13.50
L	9073	⅜″	Gold plated rim. Pearl inside w/2 holes	2.75	7.25	13.50
M	3098G	⁵⁄₁₆″	Gold plated sequins with 2 holes	2.75	7.25	13.50
N	3098S	⁵⁄₁₆″	Silver plated sequins with 2 holes	2.75	7.25	13.50
O	551	⁵⁄₁₆″	Bakelite w/2 holes *Colors: see below	2.00	5.25	8.25
P	9340	⁵⁄₁₆″	Bakelite hemisphere-shaped w/shank *Colors: see below	2.00	5.25	8.25

*No's. 551 & 9340 available colors: black, white, pink, blue, red, green, yellow. Minimum 2 dozen per color.

FINE QUALITY WHITE DOLL (& all-purpose) BUTTONS

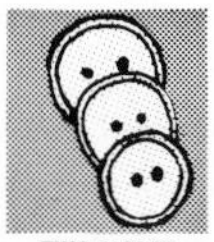

			3 dz.	6 dz.
No. 380/10	¼″		3 dz.–1.85	6 dz.–3.30
No. 380/12	⁵⁄₁₆″		3 dz.–1.85	6 dz.–3.30
No. 380/16	⅜″		3 dz.–2.00	6 dz.–3.65

TWO HOLES

No. 380/10 also available in: black, red, pink, blue, green, yellow. Price: 3 dz.— **2.50** 6 dz.—**4.50** (minimum 3 dz. per color).

Doll Stands

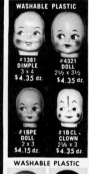

Adjustable. Sturdy steel construction

No.	FITS DOLLS	EACH	1 DOZ.
1½	3″ to 5½″	1.25	10.50
2	6″ to 11″	1.35	10.75
2L	8″ to 13″	1.45	11.00
2½	14″ to 18″	2.50	21.50
2½L	16″ to 22″	2.75	22.50
3	18″ to 24″	3.65	34.50
3L	25″ to 28″	3.85	37.50
4	26″ to 36″	7.25	73.50

✱ Dolls not included with stands

No. 1 — Doll Stands

Clear plastic with coil springs For 6, 8, 11 & 12″ slim dolls
For Flat-Soled Feet Only.

1-11 Pcs.	1 Dz. Lots	3 Dz. Lots	6 Dz. Lots	12 Dz. Lots
.40 ea.	3.00 dz.	2.75 dz.	2.50 dz.	2.25 dz.

DOLL SHOES & SOCKS ALL SIZES

Includes 24 prs. of assorted shoes (in white) & 17 prs. of socks in a full range of sizes to fit every type of doll.

SPECIAL OFFER No. 12
ONLY $16.50

Doll Faces

WASHABLE PLASTIC

#1381 DIMPLE 3 x 4 $4.35 dz.

#4321 DOLL 2½ x 3½ $4.35 dz.

#1BPE DOLL 2 x 3 $4.15 dz.

#1BCL CLOWN 2¼ x 3 $4.35 dz.

WASHABLE PLASTIC

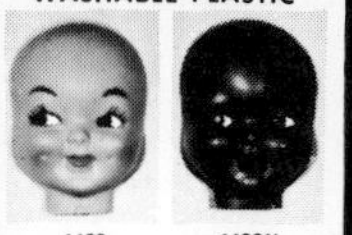

1402 DIMPLE 4½ x 3½ $5.00 dz.

1402N DIMPLE-Black 4½ x 3½ $5.00 dz.

New Catalog FREE WITH ORDER (of $15 or more)

Hundreds of dolls (popular—modern types to antique reproductions in bisque and china) • parts • patterns • stands • shoes & accessories • sewing & crafting supplies, books & kits • novelty & hard-to-get items, and much more.

For CATALOG Only—**send $2.00**
(RUSH 1st Class Mail —send $2.50)

ALL ORDERS—Add 10% for Postage & Handling. (Minimum Post. & Hndlg. **2.00** — Maximum **6.00**) N.Y. State residents add sales tax.

ORDER WITH CONFIDENCE . . . MONEY BACK GUARANTEE!

Standard Doll Co.

SINCE 1922 — THE DOLL-CRAFTER'S COMPLETE SUPPLY HOUSE

23-83 31st STREET, Dept. TDC82, L.I.C., N.Y. 11105

THE MOLD WORKS

10337A Jardine Avenue
Sunland, CA 91040

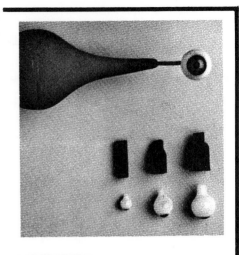

Pupil-Pluckers

The "Eye Ball Holder That Works", The PUPIL—PLUCKERS™. It's the only tool we know of on the market that securely holds round eyeballs during sizing and glueing . . . Even on closed crown heads . . . Fits most popular round eyeballs. Flexible and easy to use.

Screwgle-Mate

Introducing SCREWGLE - MATE™, another attachment that allows you to use SCREWGLES to quickly fasten heads to shoulder plate dolls. Because we cannot tell you which size SCREWGLE you need, . . . we have an introductory offer — "8 PAK" which contains one of each size for only $8. F.O.B.

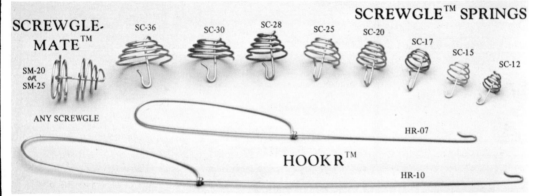

SCREWGLE™ SPRINGS

SCREWGLE-MATE™

SM-20 or SM-25

ANY SCREWGLE

SC-36 SC-30 SC-28 SC-25 SC-20 SC-17 SC-15 SC-12

HOOK R™

HR-07

HR-10

Send Large Double Stamped Self-addressed envelope for more information and nearest dealer.

QUALITY DOLL MOLDS AND COMPOSITION BODIES

Y109 JDK HILDA, HEAD CIRC. 14in (35.6cm)
Y109A JDK HILDA, HEAD CIRC. 12in (30.5cm)
Open crown socket head, open/closed mouth with two molded upper teeth. (MARKED: GERMANY JDK 245)
***Photograph courtesy of Chére Amie Dolls.*

NEW HEADS!!
Y123
Simon/Halbig 1079 (Takes our new GB-16 body) Pierced ears, four teeth.
Y124
JDK 260 (Takes our BB-16 body) Lovely baby or toddler, two teeth. (See these rare and beautiful dolls pictured in *Coleman's Doll Encyclopedia.*)

A beautiful reproduction brings the past into the present for the enjoyment of future generations. The doll you make today will be the heirloom of tomorrow.

For a free mold list, send SASE.

Illustrated catalog, send $2.50.

Catalog price will be deducted from your first order.

Yesteryear Products

**P.O. Box 13621
Dept. DC 982
Arlington, TX 76013**

"Suzy's Dolls"

Ethel Santarcangelo

Museum quality custom made reproduction dolls. No production wax, supplies including porcelain slip, molds, blanks, wigs, stands, bodies. Seeley books and plates. Catalog $1.00. (Wholesale and retail. Shop and mail order.)

**4 Monument Circle
Bennington, VT 05201
(802) 442-6095**

Doll Making Supplies

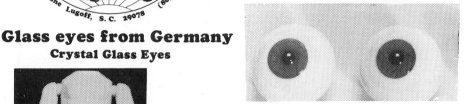
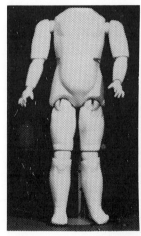
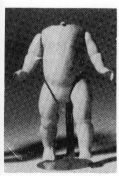
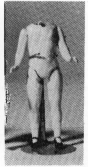

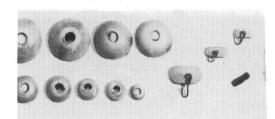

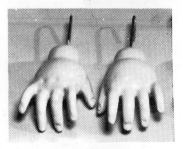

Bru Jne

Billie Pouty

K★R 117

S&H 949

Dolls by Judi™

Everything for the doll maker and doll collector. Doll making supplies as well as kits and completed dolls ready for any collection, and doll accessories. From bebees to Brus ranging in sizes from 3″ to 32″. Catalog and price list available - $2.00. Wholesale, retail and mail order.

Route 6, Box 327-C3
Fredericksburg, VA 22405
1-703-752-7361

Creative Silk

Pure China Silk . . .
For Elegant Doll Costumes

Chart of over forty colors includes many authentic hues. It is available with $8. refundable deposit. This fine silk fabric is only $8.95 per yard 36in (91.4cm) wide and discount is available on large club orders.

Dept. B-6, 820 Oakdale Road
Atlanta, GA 30307
(404) 378-7470

Josephine

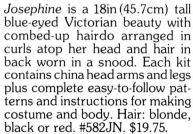

Your one shop for all doll maker's needs.

Bell Ceramics, Inc.

Bell's full color mold catalog features over 65 doll molds and includes information on White Orchid Porcelain and Bell's Premixed China Paint. Send $3.00 for catalog and doll technique sheets. *The Reproduction of Antique Dolls*, $7.95. *Practical Porcelain* instruction book, $3.95. (Wholesale and retail.)

P. O. Box 127
197 Lake Minneola Drive
Clermont, FL 32711
(904) 394-2175

Standard Doll Co.
China Doll Kits

Josephine is a 18in (45.7cm) tall blue-eyed Victorian beauty with combed-up hairdo arranged in curls atop her head and hair in back worn in a snood. Each kit contains china head arms and legs plus complete easy-to-follow patterns and instructions for making costume and body. Hair: blonde, black or red. #582JN. $19.75.

23-83 31st Street, Dept TCD82
Long Island City, NY 11105

Williams Doll Supply

Classes, seminars, patterns, supplies, wigs, eyes, composition bodies, workbooks, Seeley distributor, finished dolls. Printed list $1.00. (Wholesale and retail. Shop and mail order.)

1370 South Broadway
Denver, CO 80210
(303) 778-0599

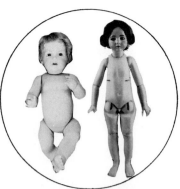

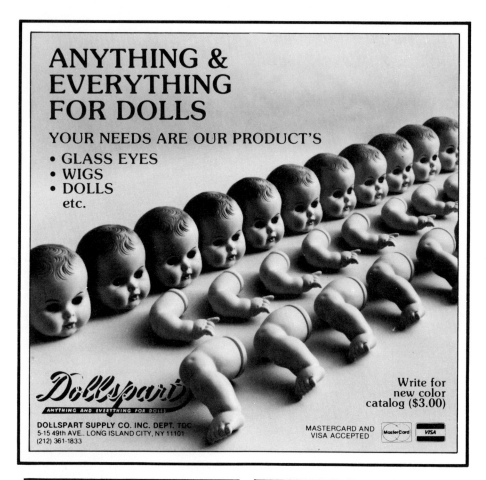

Windy Acres Doll Hospital

R.R. 1 (Carlos)
Lynn, IN 47355
(317) 874-2302

Catalog $1.00

(Catalog free with order.)

LS20
French Long
Curl with bang

LS10
Baby/Boy

LS30
Long Wave with
rooted front scalp

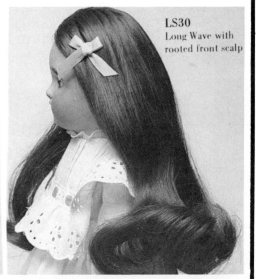

Ledgewood Studio

Period patterns for costuming dolls. Costuming supplies include silk fabric, silk and double-faced satin ribbons, French trims and lace, buttons, buckles, feathers, needles and thread for French hand sewing. Catalog $2.00 + $.50 postage. (Retail and wholesale. Mail order only.)

6000 Ledgewood Drive
Forest Park, GA 30050

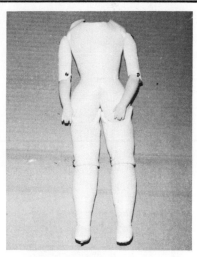

16in (40.6cm) universal jointed, all kid.

The Doll House

Beautifully handmade kid bodies, authentic copies of original, firmly sawdust stuffed. Body lengths: 6in (15.2cm) to 24½in (62.3cm), jointed and gusseted styles. Mary Steuber (ca. 1878) cloth with leather arms. Retail price range $49. - $112.50. Illustrated list $.50 + SASE. (Mail order only.)

1263 North Parker Drive
Janesville, WI 53545

DOLL RELATED ITEMS

All Prices Listed Are Subject To Change Without Notice.

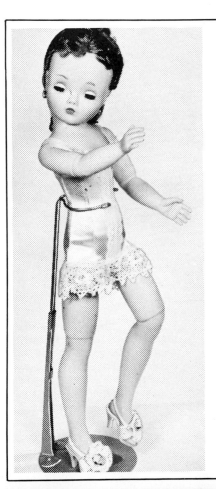

Doll & Craft World, Inc.®

125 8th Street
Brooklyn, NY 11215
(212) 768-0887

Especially for the doll maker and collector: fine quality wigs, glass eyes, stands, books, patterns, bodies, repair items, the widest assortment of shoes, Alexander catalog reprints and much more. Catalog $3.00. (Wholesale and retail. Mail order only.)

Custom designed bridal ensemble for 8in (20.3cm) Alexander doll.

Dolly H Fashions

Doll clothes. Custom designs and reproductions. Bring new life to a treasured doll of yesterday or today. Fine materials. Hand finished. Doll quilts hand pieced, appliqued and quilted. Dolls. Price range $15. and up. Printed list $2.00. (Wholesale and retail. Shop and mail order.)

Route #4 Lewis Street
Mt. Vernon, KY 40456
(606) 256-2415

Beautiful human hair Doll Wigs and Adjustable Stands at very <u>Affordable</u> Prices

Quality human hair wigs and stands at affordable prices.

Send stamped, self-addressed large envelope for further details. Quantity discounts available.

The Fashion Doll

P.O. Box 32663, San Jose, Ca. 95152 ·· (408) 259-8287 - evenings

Doll Related Items

"The quality line of doll supplies from Doll Shop Enterprises"

Doll Shop Enterprises

Manufacturers/importer/exporters of doll supplies from our exclusive line of doll wigs to our new "wood-n-comp" doll bodies. Everything that is needed for doll making, collecting is available from Doll Shop Enterprises. Catalog $2.00. (Int'l $3.50). (Wholesale and retail. Shop and mail order.)

**Post Office Box 1426
Smyrna, GA 30081
showrooms: 150-154 Washington Avenue
Marietta, GA 30060
(404) 428-3655**

Westwood Ceramic Supply Co.

Doll supply source for collectors and dealers. Fast, friendly service. We manufacture Sun Dynasty™ porcelain. Wigs, eyes, cord; all your doll needs. Dealers please write on letterhead. Catalog and printed list available. (Wholesale and retail.)

**14400 Lomitas Avenue
Industry, CA 91746
(213) 330-0631**

Eyes

Hand Painted Acrylic Eyes
COLORS: Blue, Brown, Green & Blue Gray
SIZES: 8mm $.60, 10mm $.70
12mm $.80, 14mm $.90
16mm $1.00, 18mm $1.10, 20mm $1.20

Send $1.00 & SASE for sample to:

**9630 Dundalk
Spring, TX 77379**
Minimum order 5 pair, 1 size, 1 color

Carol Foster

My Dolly ID tells of my life...
My name, my birthday and my height...It tells you even what's not in sight...So you can keep me tidy and bright...My value-priceless it may be...My Dolly ID describes every inch of me!
Ten ID's $1.25 plus LSASE (add postage for each sheet). Antique and collectible doll list $.50 and SASE. (Mail order only.)

**340 Pittsburgh Road
Butler, PA 16001**

The Clay Pigeon

A quick, simple method for making doll shoes in five sizes. Instructions, pattern and shoe last at a price that is less than one pair of leather shoes. $8.95 postpaid. (Retail only. Shop and mail order.)

**720 Cordova Drive
Orlando, FL 32804
(305) 423-2566**

Make leather shoes with an antique look.

168   Doll Related Items

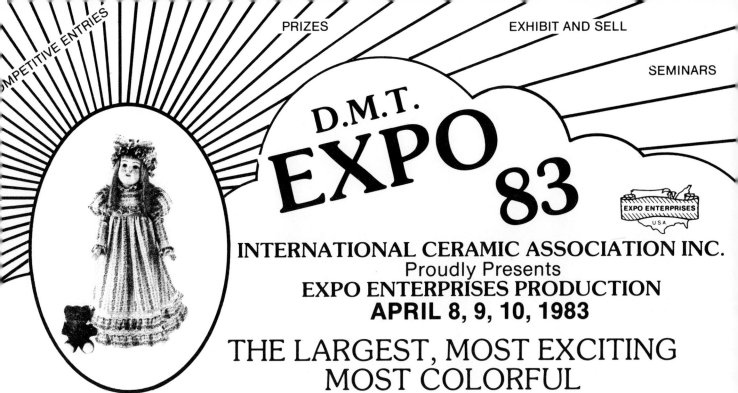

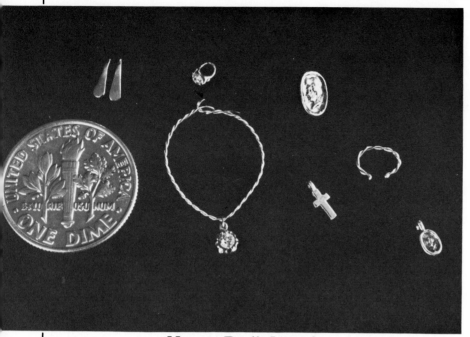

Karat Doll Jewelry

Authenticated 14K gold jewelry for miniature scale dolls. Larger scale available on special order. Some pieces include diamonds or other gemstones. All handcrafted, exclusive packaging. Retail price range $18. - $100. Wholesale price range $10. - $65. Printed list $1.00. (Wholesale and retail. Mail order only.)

Box 607
Hammondsport, NY 14840

Eyes

Old fashioned hand blown, hand painted ROUND glass doll eyes.

Colors: Brown, Blue, Blue Gray, Gray & Green

sizes & prices: 22mm $6.00 a pr.
20mm $5.50 a pr.
18mm $5.00 a pr.
16mm $4.75 a pr.
14mm $4.50 a pr.
12mm $4.25 a pr.
10mm $4.00 a pr.
8mm $3.75 a pr.
6mm $3.50 a pr.

Delivery time 1-2 weeks. Discounts available. Minimum order 3 pair. Send $11. for sample pair to:

EYES
9630 Dundalk
Spring, TX 77379

Large German nostalgic wicker doll carriage.

GTC German Toys & Crafts

No. 20 large German wicker doll carriage, iron spoked wheels and construction. Creme French lace, folding canopy, wooden handlebar, lace pillows and mattress. 39in (99.0cm) high, 35in (88.9cm) long, 14in (35.6cm) wide. Reproduction of 1880 Victorian. Catalog: $2.50. (Wholesale and retail.)

17415 Avilla Road
P.O. Box 50 L.V.
Lathrup Village, MI 48076
(313) 557-7764

Campbell's Dolls

Composition doll bodies, finest quality. German, French and toddler ball jointed. Toddler straight leg. Baby curved limbs. Sizes 7in (17.8cm) to 33in (83.8cm). Send $1.00 and LSASE for catalog. Glass doll eyes and stands. (Wholesale and retail. Shop and mail order.)

P. O. Box 3041
San Bernardino, CA 92413
(714) 882-6601

Aunt Jo's Doll Hospital

Handknit and fabric doll fashions by Aunt Jo. Doll shoes, hosiery, millinery, lingerie for antique to modern dolls. Custom costuming. Old fashioned toys, dolls, doll notecards, and Victorian miniatures. No catalog. (Retail only. SHOP ONLY.)

Hiway 69,
South of Smelter Stack
Mayer, AZ 86333

I-Draw Company (Division of Redor Co.)

How everyone can...
Design and create unlimited paper dolls and wardrobes, change heads and limb positions. (18 long lasting plastic templates with fine slots.) Kit #1: 2 Fashion-Guides★ (Town and Country Girl and clothes), stand-up paper doll paper (10 sheets), fine point pen, instruction booklet. $8. retail. Catalog page and price list free (line-drawing for reproduction) of entire line.

**2951 Randolph Avenue
Costa Mesa, CA 92626
(714) 557-2730**

Fashion-Guides★ Draw Paper Dolls.   ★ trademark

Hearth Side Shop

Furniture for your dolls. Oak rocker 16in (40.6cm) high, hand carved headrest $55. ppd. NYS residents add $3.99 tax. Send long SASE for our brochure. (Mail order only.)

**TDC Box 213
Brightwaters, NY 11718**

LeBob's Originals

Lapidary and Wood Crafts

Chairs made of hardwood veneer 14in (35.6cm) high and 10in (25.4cm) wide. They lock solid together without use of nails, screws or glue and can be taken apart for storage. Satisfaction guaranteed. Chair kit ready for sanding and finishing $16.75. Finished chair (lacquer) $36.75. Missouri residents add 3⅝% tax. Please allow 4-6 weeks for delivery.

**6517 Northwest Fairway Drive
Parkville, MO 64152**

*Original Certificates
for: Doll Adoption
       Doll-Birth
       Doll Creation
       Doll Records, more*

*Certificates with your Logo
~ or ~ let us design one.*

*Catalogue $1.25 LSASE
    Koskella
    215 Calle Diamante
    Tucson, Arizona 85704*

*Handlettered Calligraphy
    Parchment:
        white with black ink
        dk. cream with brown ink
on: White paper with black
    ink ~ suitable for
    printers copy for
                    clubs
                    classes
                    business*

GEORGENE AVERILL'S
"LAUGHING BABY"

S & CO.
"LORI"

GRACE
PUTNAM'S
"BYE-LO"

GRACE CORY
ROCKWELL'S
"GOLDIE"

JDK "HILDA"

$\mathcal{S}$EELEY'S
presents...
"The Old Baby Doll Collection..."

...a delightful new series of doll plates from "The Doll Collection"

Now the appealing elegance...the artistry... of some of the most loved baby dolls has been captured for your lasting enjoyment.

You'll display this charming plate collection with pride. Each beautifully executed piece portrays some of the finest porcelain baby dolls ever made—a legacy handed down to us by the famous old German dollmakers.

These very rare and valuable baby dolls are from Mildred Seeley's collection of antique dolls.

"JDK Hilda", the First Limited Edition plate, will be followed by the other four at intervals of approximately three months.

Each distinctive porcelain plate is 8½" in diameter, hand-bordered in 24K gold and features the story of the doll on the reverse side. Each Edition is limited to 9,500 individually numbered plates. Price $43.00 per plate.

Call or write Seeley's today for your informative, full color brochure at no obligation.

For your full color brochure on Seeley's "Old Baby Doll Collection," call toll-free 800-847-2547 between 8 AM and 5 PM, Eastern Standard Time. New York State residents call 607-432-3812.

 SEELEY'S
9 River Street
Oneonta,
New York 13820

Margaret Hydrick Bridgman

Doll stands, panties, Alexander shoes, other shoes, patterns, doll rubber stamps, laces, ribbons. Send SASE for reply.

**2824 Norbridge Ave.
Castro Valley, CA 94546
(415) 886-3980**

Uncut paper doll book.

Zelda H. Cushner

Old and new cut and uncut paper dolls, celebrities featured. Miniatures including furniture, accessories, occasionally doll houses. Featuring Brunswick doll needlepoints. Printed list $.25 + LSASE (3 ounces) (House, mail order and shows.)

**12 Drumlin Road
Marblehead, MA 01945
(617) 631-5819**

Doll Stands

Adjustable. Sturdy steel construction

No.	FITS DOLLS	EACH	1 DOZ.
1½	3" to 5½"	1.25	10.50
2	6" to 11"	1.35	10.75
2L	8" to 13"	1.45	11.00
2½	14" to 18"	2.50	21.50
2½L	16" to 22"	2.75	22.50
3	18" to 24"	3.65	34.50
3L	25" to 28"	3.85	37.50
4	26" to 36"	7.25	73.50

❋ Dolls not included with stands

No. 1 — Doll Stands
Clear plastic with coil springs
For 6, 8, 11 & 12" slim dolls
For Flat-Soled Feet Only.

1-11 Pcs.	1 Dz. Lots	3 Dz. Lots	6 Dz. Lots	12 Dz. Lots
.40 ea.	3.00 dz.	2.75 dz.	2.50 dz.	2.25 dz.

New Catalog. Free with order (of $15 or more). For Catalog only send $2.00.

Standard Doll Co.

**23-83 31st Street, Dept TCD 82
Long Island City, NY 11105**

Victorian

Ornaments

by Elspeth. Featuring full color ornaments for Antique Christmas, Valentines, Easter. Eleven different Victorian die-cut doll designs, countless variations by changing the period costume. Embossed and die-cut — just like the antique original Activated Paper Dolls. Beautiful Printing - Full-size patterns and instructions with pictures of finished hand-crafted doll. $6.00.

Hobby House Press, Inc.

**900 Frederick Street
Cumberland, MD 21502
(301) 759-3770**

In Harmony TOTE BAG

Tote Bags

14in (35.6cm) x 14in (35.6cm) Full color design on 100% polyester. No chipping or bleeding of design. Washable. Heavy duty construction, brown top trim and brown handles. $7.95.

Hobby House Press, Inc.

**900 Frederick Street
Cumberland, MD 21502
(301) 759-3770**

Fur further details see page 94.

TEDDY BEARS

Taken from A Collector's History of the Teddy Bear by Patricia N. Schoonmaker, page 115.

All Prices Listed Are Subject To Change Without Notice.

Steiff, long recognized as the premier stuffed toy in the world, has a range of teddy bears and other animals for young and old. A series of limited edition bears have been offered for the past two years, as is being offered again this year. The quality and life-like reproduction have always been associated with the "Button In Ear" brand of Steiff.

V.I.B. (Very Important Bear), Scarlett O'Beara.

North American Bear Co.

Scarlett O'Beara, one of 20 different styles of bears available. A hot pink bear, Scarlett is dressed in an antebellum gown and straw hat. Retail price $38. + $3.50 shipping charge. (Wholesale only.)
645 North Michigan Avenue
Chicago, IL 60611
(312) 943-1061

A lifetime of love.

Steiff is distributed in the United States by Reeves International, 1107 Broadway, New York NY 10010.

Cedric, the "English" teddy with molded-on shoes and spats. © 1980.

Carol-Lynn Rössel Waugh, (ODACA)

Original award-winning limited edition jointed character teddy bears of latex composition by ODACA artist. Some have molded-on garments. Cedric, Bearishnikov, Bearishnikova, Santa Bear, and Bearlock. Also professionally printed bear paper dolls to cover. Bears $50. - $100. Printed list $1.00. Photograph (specify bear) $1.00 each. (Retail only. Mail order only.)
5 Morrill Street
Winthrop, ME 04364
(207) 377-6769

Gigi's Teddy Bear Corner

Limited edition Steiff, Steiff bears, Kinser's Forever Toys, Bobtail Originals, Nisbet Baby Bully and Michard Originals. Send SASE for list.
Route 30 and Route 59
Plainfield, IL 60544
(815) 436-6488 or (312) 729-0187

A sample of Teddy Bear gift items.

Just Bears

Division of Ageless Treasures
Wide range of teddy bears from Hersey Bear to Steiff limited editions. Many teddy bear related items: cards, gift wrap, notes, gift and party items. SASE for list. (Wholesale and retail. Mail order only.)
403 Kingsbury Drive
Arlington Heights, IL 60004
(312) 870-8162

178

Teddy Bears

A COLLECTOR'S HISTORY of the TEDDY BEAR

by Patricia N. Schoonmaker

Through extensive research, the history of the Teddy Bear from its pre-Teddy days down to the present time has been traced. This richly illustrated volume features over 800 black/white and color illustrations showing thousands of bears including those manufactured by Ideal, Steiff and Horsman. Through the very detailed photographs of original catalogs and magazine articles collectors will be able to document and date the bears in their collections.

For the collector and/or lover of Teddy Bears this book will be THE resource guide plus a joy to read. 312 Pages, 8½ x 11". Cloth. $19.95.

Bible for Bear Collectors!

Available from distinctive dealers or directly from:
Hobby House Press, Inc.
900 Frederick Street
Cumberland, MD 21502
(301) 759-3770

Why Not, Inc.

Steiff Bears from 4½in (11.5cm) to 40in (101.6cm), including limited edition bears.

200 King Street
Alexandria, VA 22314
(703) 548-2080

JOEY BEAR AND YVETTE PRIVATE DETECTIVES

Copyright © 1982
by Monica Sullivan and
Steve Rubenstein

Steve Rubenstein, Publisher

Joey Bear and Yvette, Private Detectives is a photo story about a teddy bear and a doll who solve the mystery of a missing doll. The author is Monica Sullivan. $5.98. (Wholesale and retail. Shop and mail order.)
1445 Union Street #1
San Francisco, CA 94109

TOTE BAGS

FULL COLOR DESIGNS
14" by 14"
100% Polyester
Washable
no chipping or bleeding
of designs
Heavy duty construction, brown
top trim and brown handles.

BEAR PICNIC TOTE BAG $7.95

Available from Distinctive
Dealers or directly from:

Hobby House Press, Inc.

900 Frederick Street
Cumberland, Maryland 21502
(301) 759-3770

ANTIQUE BEAR TOTE BAG $7.95

Bears at Toy Fair 1982

Teddy bears, teddy bears and more teddy bears. That is what was found at the 1982 American Toy Fair. Teddy bear collectors will not be wanting for "new bears" for their collections this year.

Kisses, the Hershey bear by Ideal is 5½in (14.0cm) and made of soft, washable plush fiber. She comes with a Hershey T-shirt in yellow, red, blue or white and a candy kiss tag attached to her hand. As an added attraction, *Kisses* has a delicate chocolate scent. Also in the Hershey Bear line are two other citizens of Chocolate Town, USA. These two huggable bears are 10in (25.4cm) and 17in (43.2cm) sizes and are made of soft, washable plush fiber. They are dressed in T-shirts and have vinyl bear faces. They come with a special Hershey candy bar tag attached and also have the chocolate aroma.

Added to the already colorful line of collectible bears by the North American Bear Company, Inc., are *William Shakesbear, Sarah Bearnheart, Green Bearet, Bjorn Bearg, Bear-mitzvah* and *Theodore Bearington.* All of these 20in (50.8cm) bears are costumed in appropriate and colorful outfits and *Theodore (Teddy)* will be accompanied by his family, *Mama Bearington* and two children.

Fisher-Price has created plush toys from the storybook characters of the Berenstein Bears with both *Mama* and *Papa* bears having stitched-on clothing.

Trudy Toys is offering National Football League *Team Teddies* available in three sizes. Their little shirts indicate which team they represent such as the Steelers, Giants, Jets and so forth.

A complete line of licensed plush toys bearing the Jordache jeans name, and including bears, was introduced at Toy Fair in Toyland. Included in the group are the *Jordache Country Bears* with jeans and western vests and hats, the *Miss Jordache* series with bears wearing jeans and banners across their chests which say "Miss Jordache," and the *Jordache Preppies* series.

If you are a "M*A*S*H" fan, or even if you are not, you will want to watch for the *Gary Bear,* Gary Burghoff's (Radar's) bear. He comes hibernating in a tote bag, dressed in his tennis outfit. Included are humorous instructions on "The Care and Feeding of your *Gary Bear.*" Four additional outfits are available; a life guard outfit, winter outfit, army uniform and a pair of pajamas. This bear is represented by Cuddle Wit Inc., of New York.

Knickerbocker's contribution to the "1982 Bear World" is *Prayer Bear* and *Sweetheart Bear. Prayer Bear* wears a shirt embellished with its name, holds its front paws together in a prayer-like position and has its eyes closed. *Sweetheart Bear* is decorated with a heart saying "Sweet Velvet" and a ribbon is around its neck.

Budgie Bear from Princess Soft Toys is made of brown and cream colored long pile fabric and has a pretty satin ribbon tied in a bow around its neck. It is available in three sizes, 17in (43.2cm), 14in (35.6cm) and 10in (25.4cm). The smallest bear is available with a music box also.

Gargey Bear from Toys 'n Tapes is a 6in (15.2cm) pure wool bear whose back pack contains a cassette tape of four stories with songs sensitively written and beautifully told. The 30 minute tape is the same on both sides, eliminating rewinding and simplifying handling.

Atlanta Novelty has a variety of new bears between 9in (22.9cm) and 20in (50.8cm) in sitting positions. Among those most attractive were the *Ice Cream Bears* in various pastel shades.

From Animal Fair in Minneapolis, Minnesota, comes the quizical looking *Ted E. Bear. Ted E.* wears a vest, bow tie and stocking cap.

There will be several Steiff Limited Edition bears for 1982. One set of four 7in (17.8cm) bears has a table set with tea cups which have the Steiff insignia and name on each cup. A five-piece set of white mohair bears

Illustration 2. *Ted E. Bear* by Animal Fair.

that are fully-jointed and have "voices" and claws are in sizes of 4½in (11.5cm), 7½in (19.1cm), 10½in (26.7cm), 14½in (36.9cm) and 16½in (41.9cm). Two different bears, one of about 8in (20.3cm) and one of about 12in (30.5cm), will be made for the Margaret Woodbury Strong Museum in Rochester, New York, which is set to open in the fall of 1982. These teddys have hump backs and long arms that have felt pads and claws. A special three foot tall Steiff bear who carries the company tag in an ear, as all Steiff bears do, will retail for about $700.00.

The House of Nisbet has introduced a new bear by famous bear expert Peter Bull. This is *Young Bully,* who is a 12in (30.5cm) companion to Nisbet's popular *Bully Bear. Young Bully* wears the robes of "the Worshipful Company of Peanut Butter Eaters" and is also offered as a Limited Edition with a signed certificate by Peter Bull.

Sales representatives at the 1982 American Toy Fair reported that sales orders were larger than ever before. Many of the new teddy bears and dolls are manufactured with a child's playthings market in mind. Other dolls and bears are made with the collector in mind. The best of both types will be snapped up by collectors. There is such an extensive variation in the 1982 lines of merchandise from hundreds of different companies that there are plenty of desirable collectibles for collectors of every persuasion. We saw dolls that were exciting, unusual, clever, unexpected and surprising. There is a regular banquet of choices for doll and teddy bear collectors in 1982.

Illustration 1. 12in (30.5cm) *Young Bully* shown with *Bully Bear* from the House of Nisbet by Peter Bull. The bears are shown with the first three Bully Bear books which are by Peter Bull with illustrations by Enid Irving.

Lois Beck Originals

Twenty-five styles of bears from 6in (15.2cm) fully-jointed to 24in (61.0cm) fully jointed including a mechanical. Fake fur, mohair or seal fur bears available as well as bear repair. Price range $18.50 - $225. SASE for information. (Wholesale and retail. In home, shop and mail order.)

10300 Southeast Champagne Lane
Portland, OR 97266
(503) 777-2131

V.I.B. (Very Important Bear), Douglas Bearbanks.

North American Bear Co.

Douglas Bearbanks, one of 20 different styles of bears available. A classic tan bear, Douglas is suavely dressed in pin-striped pants, smoking jacket and ascot. Retail price $38. + $3.50 shipping charge. (Wholesale only.)

645 North Michigan Avenue
Chicago, IL 60611
(312) 943-1061

1in (2.5cm) to 1¼in (3.2cm) Bitsy Bears© Kimberlee Port 1976.

Kimberlee Port Originals

Miniature teddy bears, completely jointed. Limited editions. Creator of *UFDC Doll News* cover scene, winter issue 1976 (the teddy bear issue). Printed list $.50. Photographs available. (Retail only.)

P.O. Box 711
Retsil, WA 98378
(206) 871-1633

Collectible Bears by Dakin

R. DAKIN & COMPANY

P.O. BOX 7746, SAN FRANCISCO, CA 94120/(415) 952-1777

MERRYTHOUGHT

Merrythought Ltd. is one of England's oldest established toy manufacturers. For over 50 years their careful selection of materials, diligent design work and traditional craftsmanship have earned their toys the highest reputation for quality.

GT16

GT24

Panda — 15"
B182

GT14

LM16

TR18

TR12

TR14

TR16

GT10

Anniversary Bear*
AB16

GT12

GT08

LM14

Assembled here is a collection of Teddy Bears which should please the child and the collector alike. (The last two style no.'s indicate size in inches.)

The GT series is the well known Cheeky Bear. Made in a gold mohair and wool blend, Cheeky is fully jointed. Sizes GT14, GT16 and GT24 are fitted with music boxes. The TR series is pure gold mohair, fully jointed and of the highest possible quality. The LM series is champagne in color, fully jointed, in the highest quality plush. The LM16 comes with a bib and it's own "growl." The Anniversary Bear is Merrythought's recreation of their original Teddy, in commemoration of their 50th Anniversary. He is 16" and as AB16 is available in champagne plush, fully jointed and fitted with a growl. *There is also a special edition of 1000 pieces only, (AC16) signed and numbered, available in white pure mohair.

On Collecting Teddy Bears

by Patricia N. Schoonmaker

Illustration 1. *5in (38.1cm) antique bear of German origin thought by some to be an example of the 1907 (or earlier) Roosevelt bears. Pale gold mohair, hump on back, shoe-button eyes, red-brown embroidered nose and claws. Helen Sieverling Collection.*

Illustration 2. *15in (38.1cm) Winnie-the-Pooh of 1930 as advertised in* A Collector's History of the Teddy Bear, *page 178. Long gold plush, long of torso and short of leg, upturned nose, shoe-button eyes. Helen Sieverling Collection.*

How does one begin to collect teddy bears? That is the easiest part of all; go choose *one* bear that pleases you! However, to end up with a collection that gives joy and satisfaction takes a little thought and planning.

First, the writer would hope you would arm yourself with a copy of the book we have done on the subject as it contains much source material which will help with wise decisions in buying bears. The following letter just received gives a slight idea of the fun to be had in collecting teddies:

"I have been wanting to write to you for quite awhile now to say a big thank you for *A COLLECTOR'S HISTORY of the TEDDY BEAR.* What a treasure and pleasure! I love it.

"I have owned and read this book since last fall and I do not grow tired of it. You have so successfully combined information and entertainment. The only fault that I can find with the entire presentation is the book jacket--it should have carried a READER BEWARE label in bold red print! You see, since delving into your book I find my heart and home filled to the brimming with teddy bears. Whatever am I to do? I am certain that untold numbers of persons are suffering this same affliction (and addiction) since adding this book to their reading list.

"And to make matters worse--all bears seem to know about my malady. I find the little scamps tugging at my coat-tail and elbows whenever I go in the stores. They are finding their way to my front door via the mailman and friends. They are leaping up at me off the pages of catalogs and magazines. Several times they have even talked my husband into giving them a home with us. *And* I understand that a large Paddington is at this *very* moment making his way to my home from London.............."

Is your space limited? You may want to consider the delightful miniature versions. If you are already a doll collector, the bears are invaluable to pose with the dolls.

The search for very old bears of the early 1900s is perhaps the most challenging of all aspects of collecting. The earliest German Steiff specimens had a blank pewter button in the left ear for identification. Within a short time the firm added the logo "STEIFF" to the buttons. The front legs on early bears are somewhat longer than the rear legs. The backs have a realistic hump. They are usually fully-jointed in either short or long mohair wool from the angora goat, which is silky to the touch. All of the old bears have acquired considerable value and are not for those with limited funds. Yet no one need be excluded from this fascinating hobby, "Teddy Bear Hunting."

Never have manufacturers been more aware of collectors, and filling that need. One has to *ponder* which of the stars-of-the-season one can include and afford. Few people could buy or house them all, but some might try!

Association bears are very collectible, such as Peter Bull's *Bully Bear,* or Coach "Bear" Bryant's *The Winningest Bear.* The newest personality bear is the *Gary Bear* named for Gary ("Radar") Burghoff of the television "M.A.S.H." program. Toy Fair publicity states that *Gary Bear* comes hibernating in a tote bag, wearing his tennis outfit. The actor wrote, "Hi everyone, Here's my 'Gary Bear.' He's just my way of sending a *hug* to every kid in the world. Love, Gary." *Gary Bear* is represented by Cuddle Wit, Inc., New York.

Illustration 3. *12in (30.5cm) rare size Bellhop bear of 1923 as advertised in A Collector's History of the Teddy Bear, page 97. Gold mohair with red felt jacket and cap. Mechanical bear can say "Yes" or "No" by moving tail. Helen Sieverling Collection.*

Illustration 4. *16in (40.6cm) new fully-jointed bear from Dean's Childplay Toys, Ltd., England, an official toy maker to the British Crown. Honey brown mohair, dark brown pads. Courtesy of Ann Baxter.*

Illustration 5. *22in (55.9cm) bear, collector's item by Sue Kruse, California artist. Handmade, brown plush, jointed at shoulders and hips. Courtesy of Ann Baxter.*

Bears who are also featured in books are very desirable for hobby displays and sharing. One newest version is Theodore Edward Bear, better known as *Ted E. Bear* for short. Animal Fair is offering a new 10in (25.4cm) size as well as a *Patti Bear* edition.

Advertising bears, associated with a product or firm, are great fun and are amazing in variety. Some may wish to

Illustration 6. *16in (40.6cm) The Prince and Princess. Fully-jointed snowy white Hermann bears of West Germany. Prince wears gold ribbon and Princess a red ribbon plus impressive red company medallions. Currently available. Courtesy of Ann Baxter.*

Illustration 7. *10in (25.4cm) Hermann. Brown open-mouth with white collar, jointed with squeaker voice. 15in (38.1cm) Hermann. Brown, silver tipped fur, gold paper tags. Currently available. Courtesy of Ann Baxter.*

Illustration 8. *16in (40.6cm) mink-type brown and silver Hermanns made in West Germany. Squeaker voices, chain around necks and heavy red medallions. Currently available. Courtesy of Ann Baxter.*

specialize in these. Yet the average person will most likely find himself a general collector with some antiques, some moderns, handmades and miniatures.

Local clubs are invaluable help in learning of new bears or more about the older ones. In the Los Angeles area there is "Teddy Bear Boosters" with a semi-annual banquet, program and salesroom. In addition there is a monthly "Teddy Bear Collector's Club" for study purposes and fellowship. For those in other areas information about clubs near you can be obtained from the publication *The Teddy Tribune*. Bears are fun!

Recommended:
Teddy Bear Boosters, P. O. Box 814, Redlands, CA 92373. $2.00 a year to join. Club paper.
Teddy Bear Collector's Club, 6412 Cymbal Street, Anaheim, CA 92807. Open membership.
Good Bears of the World, P.O. Box 8236, Honolulu, HI 96815. Publication $4.00.
The Teddy Tribune, 254 W. Sidney Street, St. Paul, MN 55107. 5 fat, fat issues for $7.50.

PUBLICATIONS

All Prices Listed Are Subject To Change Without Notice.

The DOLL Artisan
1980

OCTOBER/NOVEMBER VOL 4 NO 1

Doll Artisan Guild

Bi-monthly magazine for members of the "Doll Artisan Guild," non-profit organization for the porcelain doll maker. Open to everyone. For membership information contact Doll Artisan Guild (607) 432-4977. Sample copy $2.50 ppd.

35 Main Street
Oneonta, NY 13820
(607) 432-4977

CARTE DE VISITE ALBUM DE LA POUPEE

Au Paradis des Enfants

Evelyn Jane Coleman

"Carte de Visite Album de la Poupee"

Fascimile of an 1870 French photograph album of dolls. Actual size 1¾ x 2-⅛" with a separate booklet describing the album and pictures in it. Both booklets are enclosed in a matching envelope. $3. 10 or more, 40% discount. (Mail order only.) **4315 Van Ness Street**
Washington, DC 20016

Carol Nordell

The Magic of Making a Miniature Nutcracker Ballet

Clear instructions for complete production in three-quarter scale. $7.70 including postage. SASE for brochure.

368 East Fifth Street
Mount Vernon, NY 10553

Madame Alexander Scarletts Calendar 1983

by Barbara Jo McKeon

Now Available A Collectors Item Limited
Calendar is full Color - 9 x 10"
Opened it Measures - 10 x 18"
The color photographs of Scarlett dolls from the past to the current are truly beautiful. Each calendar month has a different 5 x 7 Color photo of a Scarlett giving year type and value of each doll. First 500 will be numbered & Signed. Please order as soon as possible to insure your calendar $17.50ppd.

B.J.McKeon
P.O. Box 1481 - T.D.C.
Brockton, MA 02403
(617) 586-1279

Rosa N. Claridge

Studio portraits of antique dolls with informative descriptions of dolls and costumes. $7.95 & $.50 postage. (Wholesale and retail. Mail order only.)
P. O. Box 330
Newport, OR 97365

Albina Bailey

First Ladies Inaugural Gowns, Volumes I to V. Patterns, needlework and instructions, fits a 12in (30.5cm) doll. $7.98 & $.60 postage each. Massachusetts residents add $.40 sales tax. SASE for printed list of 10 publications. (Mail order only.)

Hayden Pond Road
Dudley, MA 01570

"Rare and Hard to Find Madame Alexander Collector's Dolls"

by Barbara Jo McKeon. A "must" for all doll lovers. New and exciting reference work. Her "Rare and Hard-to-Find Madame Alexander Collectors Dolls" contains over 80 dolls never seen before in reference books. Also, there are over 100 dolls never seen before in color! One outstanding feature is the set of Coronation pictures (15 in all), together with the composition Dolls of the Month, Fiction & Paintings. The rare Infant of Prague is also shown as well as the complete International and Americana Series. Surprises such as the Alexander Pig (in compo) and Poodle are in store for you. Too: Little Minister, 12in Lissy Graduation, Lissy Personalities, Portrettes, Portraits, Wendy and Alex-Kins, Cissettes, Scarletts, Little Women, Clover Kid, Tommy and Katie. There is also a rare 7in Sonja Henie, Scarlett, Nina Ballerina and Princess Elizabeth shown. 154 pages. Price guide included. $24.95 each. New Price Guide II $3.95 & $.75 postage and handling.

**Barbara Jo McKeon
P. O. Box 1481 - T.D.C.
Brockton, MA 02402
(617) 586-1279**

Emma Terry

Original Paper Dolls

Shirley Temple's Playhouse Paper Doll Card to Color $1.25. Shirley Paper Doll Calendar $1.25. Extras of either $.75 each. Illustrated listing/Shirley Paper Doll/stationery/newsletter $1.00. Commercial list $1.37. Checks payable to Emma Terry. (Mail order only.)

**P. O. Box 807
Vivian, LA 71082
(318) 375-4768**

Pat Frey

Limited edition paper dolls and costumes including Shirley Temple on card stock. All costumes from Shirley's movies. 8 page set 1980. $6.50 postage paid. SASE for complete list. (Mail order only.)

**9 Station Road
Cranbury, NJ 08512**

Shirley Temple paper doll.

Little Ranch Antiques, Inc.

1912 *Schoenhut Doll Catalog* bicolor reprint. Sharp black and red printing (no blurring). Over 50 dolls shown. $5.50 postpaid. West Virginia residents add 5% state tax. (Wholesale and retail. Shop and mail order.)

**1431 Washington Pike
Wellsburg, WV 26070**

DOLL READER

900 Frederick Street, Cumberland, Maryland 21502

The BEST doll magazine.

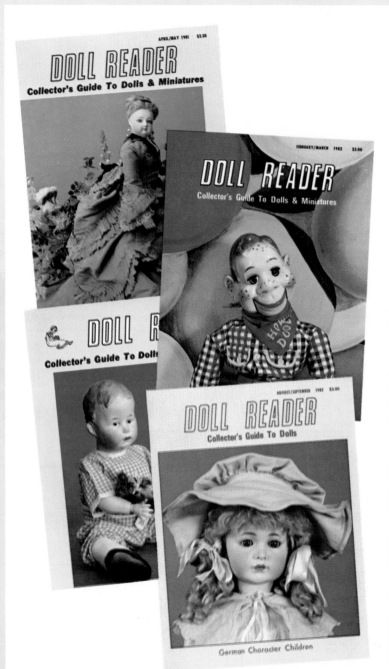

German Character Children

NOW 8 ISSUES

The BEST doll magazine. Nearly 200 pages -- eight times per year. Factual reference articles featuring photographs on doll collecting (antique and modern), artist dolls, doll making, paper dolls, dressing dolls and patterns. Doll advertisements galore. Beautiful color in magazine!

SAMPLE ISSUE

Try us and you will be enchanted.

$3.50

Subscription Price

$18.95

Save over $9.00 off
newsstand price
Foreign $29.95

Some recent issues... had over 600 detailed photographs!

Collector's Guide

to Dolls

Satisfaction Guaranteed!

If at any time you become disenchanted with our magazine, we will cheerfully refund unused portion of subscription!

Doll Times

44 page monthly newspaper, 70 word classified ad free each issue with subscription. Sample $1.50. Doll club page, shows, auctions, patterns, paper dolls. $16.50 first class per year; $8.50 half year. Free doll pin with subscription. Your choice - Bye-lo, Dream Baby, Terri Lee, Ginny, Schoenhut, S. Heine or Shirley Temple.

P. O. Box 276
Montgomery, IL 60538
(312) 355-0033

The Evergreen Press

Antique paper doll books by well known doll artists. Titles available: *French Paper Dolls, Paper Doll Wedding, Dolls of the 1930's, German Bisque Dolls, Little Women Paper Dolls.* Free catalog. (Wholesale and Retail.)

P. O. Box 4971
Walnut Creek, CA 94596
(415) 825-7850

Charles T. Branford Co.

Dolls in National and Folk Costume

by Jean Greenhowe. A fascinating collection of simple and inexpensive ideas for making 18 dolls of the world. Patterns, diagrams and detailed instructions. Exciting for older children as well as adults. List $11.75. Catalog $.25. (Wholesale only. Mail order only.)

P.O. Box 41
Newton Centre, MA 02159
(617) 964-2441

Laurel Dicicco

Doll Collector's Treasures

Vol. 3 featuring: Little Miss Shirley Temple. 162 pg. book. A pictorial history of child Shirley Temple and treasured collector's dolls. Includes Shirley Temple's own collection. Many pgs. in full color. Paperback $17.95. Hardbound $22.95. Post. $1. Send check or money order to:

14916 Cholame
Victorville, CA 92392

Grueny's, Inc.

How to booklet tells how to dress our tiny play-size dolls 1-2in (2.5-5.1cm). Kits are offered with porcelain doll to paint and all materials to complete. By Mary Ward. Booklet $8. (Wholesale and retail. Mail order and shop.)

P.O. Box 2477 - 917 West 2nd Street
Little Rock, AR 72203
(501) 376-0393

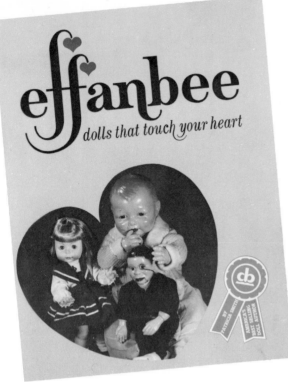

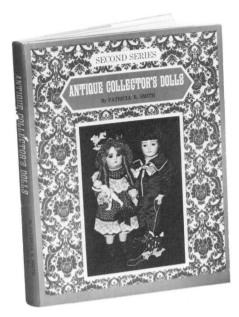

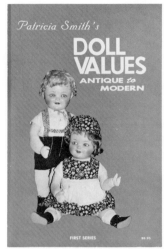

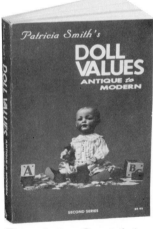

First Steiff Toy

100 Years of Steiff

by Shirley Conway & Jean Wilson.
Steiff company history, color pictures of old and new toys, black and white pictures, descriptions, price guide, teddy bear story. $9.95 + $1.50 postage and handling. Wholesale six or more.

Box 224
Berlin, OH 44610
(216) 893-2811

Kiddieland Souper Special

A publication to inform and share with other *Campbell Kid* collectors. Searching for old items and advising on items currently available. Not sponsored by the Campbell Soup Co. or affiliates. Bi-monthly newsletter $5. year (6 issues). $1. single issue. Since 1978.

11892 Bartlett Street
Garden Grove, CA 92645
(714) 892-5686

Ackert Enterprises

Antique Dolls Postcards

Doll post cards: 64 kinds and three advertising cards, $15.66 ppd. (Wholesale and retail. Mail order and shows.)

521 South 7th Street
DeKalb, IL 60115

Ackert Enterprises

"Through Post Cards of Our Antique Dolls"

Includes detailed descriptions and history of each doll and collectors reference for post cards. All color with 10 full page color enlargements. $19.95 + $2. postage and handling.

521 South 7th Street
De Kalb, IL 60115

Left: Mozambique.   Right: North Korea.

Nation-of-the-Month Club©

175 of the world's most authentic foreign costume patterns for 11½in (29.2cm) Barbie type dolls. Two patterns sent bi-monthly. $18. per year (USA); $27. per year (foreign). Back issues available including all United Nations. (Retail only. Mail order only.)

3755 Ruth Drive
Brunswick, OH 44212

The Doll Works

Paper Doll Notes

12 paper doll notes/envelopes, black on white, poly-pk. four antique dolls with authentic wardrobes. Schoenhut, boy and girl, S.F.B.J. girl, French, wood-body lady. $3. + $.85 postage. Dealer discounts. (Mail order.)

2203 North Hudson
Oklahoma City, OK 73103

Crown Publishers, Inc.

Collector's Encyclopedia of Dolls

by Dorothy S., Elizabeth A., and Evelyn J. Coleman. Covers all dolls, makers, materials, etc. to 1925. 2,000 illustrations and marks. $29.95. Free catalog. (Wholesale and retail.)

Developing Your Doll Collection: For Enjoyment And Investment

by Loretta Holtz. For the beginning doll collector. Covers the basic doll types and their sources. How to restore, preserve, display, store, catalog and exhibit a collection. Valuable tips and advice. $16.95. Free catalog. (Wholesale and retail.)

The Collector's Encyclopedia of Half Dolls

by Frieda Marion and Norma Werner. The first book that makes it easy to identify over 1,000 different half-dolls. These collectibles are illustrated, described and coded. Price guide included. $29.95. Free catalog. (Wholesale and retail.)

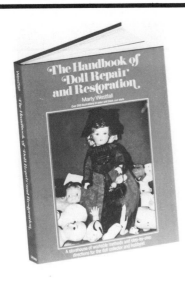

Handbook of Doll Repair and Restoration

by Marty Westfall. Step-by-step instructions provide simplified foolproof methods for quick repair and touch-up jobs. 200 color and black/white illustrations and photos. $15.95. Free catalog. (Wholesale and retail.)

The How to Book of International Dolls

A Comprehensive Guide to Making, Costuming & Collecting Dolls by Loretta Holtz. Dolls from all over the world, each with introductory text and step-by-step photos. Simple directions and patterns. 800 photos and illustrations. $19.95 cloth, $12.95 paper. Free catalog. (Wholesale and retail.)

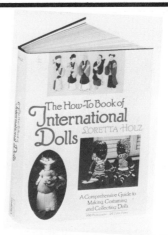

Making Original Dolls of Composition, Bisque and Porcelain

by Charlene Roth. An imaginative how-to presentation of original new dolls made according to antique doll making techniques. Over 200 color and black and white illustrations and photos. $12.95. Free catalog. (Wholesale and retail.)

1 Park Avenue
New York, NY 10016
(212) 532-9200

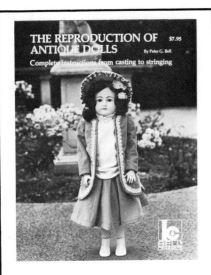

Bell Ceramics, Inc.

The Reproduction of Antique Dolls contains over 200 color pictures. The 48 page, 8½ x 11 book has detailed instructions on casting, firing, china painting, installing eyes and stringing. Send $7.95. *Practical Porcelain* instruction book $3.95. *Bell Mold Catalog* $3.00. (Wholesale and retail.)

**P.O. Box 127 - 197 Lake Minneola Drive
Clermont, FL 32711
(904) 394-2175**

Doll Castle News

Published bi-monthly, each issue of *Doll Castle News* contains 92 or more pages of interesting articles and columns covering dolls and miniatures, antique to modern. Now in its 22nd year of publication. One year subscription $9.; sample copy $1.50. (Wholesale and retail.)

**P.O. Box 247-CC
Washington, NJ 07882
(201) 689-7512**

The Dollmaker

The Dollmaker is the fastest growing publication of its kind. Each issue contains technical advice by professional doll artists for those who are creating dolls from rag to ceramic. Published six times a year. One year subscription $12.; sample copy $2. (Wholesale and retail.)

**P.O. Box 247-CC
Washington, NJ 07882
(201) 689-7512**

Doll Journal of Australia

Bi-monthly magazine for doll collectors. Interesting articles from around the world. Australia, New Zealand - $6.; U.S.A., Canada - $8.; England - £4.00. Bank notes accepted. Sample copy $2.50 airmail. (Mail order only.)

**Mrs. Beres Lindus
Box 97, P.O., Kensington Park
South Australia 5068
(08) 315073**

JOEY BEAR
AND
YVETTE
PRIVATE DETECTIVES

Quest-Eridon Books

Shirley Temple picture books and photos, reprints of old paper dolls, modern collector paper dolls, ladies' magazines, *Celebrity Doll Journal*, celebrity doll and toy research books, Kewpie paper doll reprint. Printed list $.25. (Wholesale and retail. Mail order only.)

**5 Court Place
Puyallup, WA 98371**

Steve Rubenstein, Publisher

Joey Bear and Yvette, Private Detectives is a photo story about a teddy bear and a doll who solve the mystery of a missing doll. The author is Monica Sullivan. $5.98. (Wholesale and retail. Shop and mail order.)

**1445 Union Street #1
San Francisco, CA 94109**

Better Books on Dolls and Doll Collecting!

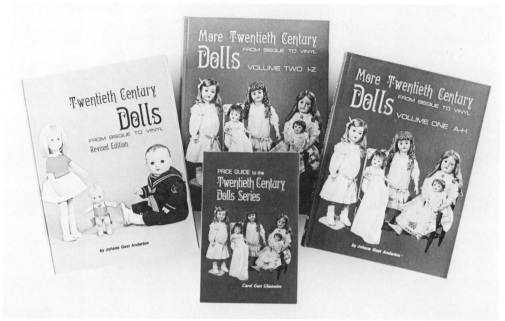

Twentieth Century Dolls, Anderton, $27.50
More Twentieth Century Dolls, Volume One,
    Anderton, $19.95
More Twentieth Century Dolls, Volume Two,
    Anderton, $19.95
Price Guide to the Twentieth Century Dolls Series,
    Glassmire, $9 95
Sewing for Twentieth Century Dolls, Anderton, $19.95
Much Ado About Dolls, Herron, $19.95
Herron's Price Guide to Dolls and Paper Dolls, $10.95
Dressing Dolls in Nineteenth Century Fashions, Bailey,
    $14.95
Dressing Dolls in Nineteenth Century Fashions, Vol.
    II, Bailey, $14.95
Wallace-Homestead Price Guide to Dolls, 1982-83
    Prices, Miller, $10.95

Watch for Barbara Ferguson's new book on *Collecting Paper Dolls* to be published in 1982.

These and other great books on collectibles available from your favorite doll dealer or the publisher. Dealer inquiries invited.

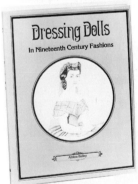

**1912 Grand Avenue
Des Moines, IA 50309**

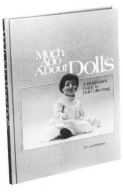

Write us for our FREE catalog!

Both Available now. . . and In Full Color

Madame Alexander Dolls in "Ladies of Fashion" and Madame Alexander Dolls "On Review"...a must for all doll lovers! These exciting book reference works are a must for all collectors of Madame Alexander Dolls. Both books are printed in full color. "Ladies of Fashion" has 163 pages...97 full pages, 251 photos...and carries a full collection of the Madame Alexander's 21" Portrait series started in 1965 through 1978 and a collection of Cissys created in the 1950s. Many of these are rare and are by far the most beautiful dolls of the Alexander line. Included are Godey Ladies, Beau Arts Dolls, Glamour Girl Walkers; also Maggie Mix-Up, Elise, Jacqueline, Piper Laurie, Polly, Sheri Lewis, Marlo Thomas Portrettes and many more.

"On Review" has 232 pages...623 photos and over 1025 dolls. Many never shown in a book before and many never in color. See the Alexander catalog come to life in color. Store specials such as F.A.O. Schwarz Katie and Tommie, 1962, one-hundredth year anniversary doll, Marshall Fields, Bullocks and others. Many surprises in hard plastic. See Cissy, Elise, Binnie and Jacqueline in trunks...Sonja Henie and Pamelas in suitcases. More than 100 Wendy-kins (Alexander-Kins) and over 100 Cissettes. Have a complete reference on Mimi, Elise, Cissy, Smarty, Janie, Portraits, Portrettes, Leslies, Polly, Maggie Mix-up and Brenda Starr all at your fingertips...all in color; Nina Ballerinas, Coronation Dolls, Princess Elizabeth, early cloth dolls, Maggie, and Smarty...all in one book. A section on Little Women dolls and a section on the collectable Lissy with full page picture of the Lissy Classics. All 12" dolls from Nancy Drew mold and the 14" Mary Ann Mold. Babies too.

"On Review" sells for $29.95...P.P. each. In lots of 6 or more plus UPS. "Ladies of Fashion" sells for $19.95...P.P., in lots of 6 or more $11.97 each plus UPS. Books autographed on request only.

Price guides may be purchased separately. Price guides sell for $3.95 each one copy, plus 65 cents postage. 6/or more copies send $2.25 each plus 65 cents first copy and for each additional copy add 30 cents. "Ladies of Fashion" has it's own price guide. "On Review" price covers more than 1200 dolls.

Send Orders to: Marjorie V. Uhl
811 Sioux Avenue
Mapleton, Iowa 51034   Phone 712-882-1517 or 712-882-2593

DEALERS MUST ORDER 6 or MORE BOOKS...
MIX OR MATCH.

1982 Peak Doll Directory

is NOT a "List of Dolls"
or just an "Address Book"
It is:

1. The 20th annual edition of the bests source of doll info available under one cover - Dolls to Buy, Places to visit, Publications, Supply Sources, Doll Friends & More!

2.   Purse size professionally printed guide to the doll world.

3.   An inexpensive place where you, too, can advertise your shop, dolls, wants and needs and much more!

1982 PPD now available $6.00 ppd.

Peak Doll Enterprises

P.O. Box 757
Colorado Springs, CO
80901
Shop address: **117 S. Main,**
Fountain, CO
80817
(303) 382-8750

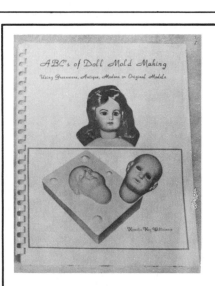

Doll Scope

With my two *A-B-C* books, you can build a hobby or business: *Doll Making Using Molds, Slip, China Paint & Kiln* (1973) and *Mold Making* (1979). No previous experience necessary: $18.50 and $16. + shipping and handling. Catalog $2.50.

Rt. 3, Box 107-W
Mission, TX 78572
(512) 585-0257

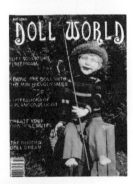
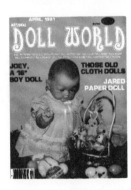

Yapoo's News Quarterly

Includes free patterns, "How-To" articles, historical information, readers' exchange and stories of contemporary dollers and miniaturists. Catalog includes originals, nationally known miniature supplies, doll supplies, books. $4. year; ($3.00 for catalog). (Wholesale and retail. Mail order only.)

Harrison Enterprises
1045 Allesandro Street
Morro Bay, CA 93442
(805) 772-7583

Doll Collector's Manual 1973

Limited editions of an official publication about dolls, doll collecting and related subjects. These manuals are beautifully illustrated and available to the general public. 1973 edition. $8.50pp.
The Doll Collectors of America, Inc.
Edgar Patry
11 Charlemont Road
Medford, MA 02155

Doll Collector's Manual 1967

Limited editions of an official publication about dolls, doll collecting and related subjects. These manuals are beautifully illustrated, and available to the general public. 1967 edition. $7.50pp.
The Doll Collectors of America, Inc.
Edgar Patry
11 Charlemont Road
Medford, MA 02155

Zelda H. Cushner

Largest selection of out-of-print doll books in the country. Many new doll and toy books; many old children's books. Printed list $.25 + LSASE (2 ounces). (Retail only. House, mail order and shows.)
12 Drumlin Road
Marblehead, MA 01945
(617) 631-5819

Modern Wax Doll Art

by Carol Carlton. 128 page paperback, color cover, 85 photos and diagrams; formulas, additives, interviews with other artists. Also, instructions in pouring, carving, modelling, dipping, wigging, body assembly, painting. $12. ppd. (Wholesale and retail. Mail order and shows.)
Carol Carlton
Box 159
Altaville, CA 95221
(209) 736-4702

"The Library"

From dolls and toys to glassware and furniture, reference books for all collectors. Privately published limited edition/import? Just released? We have it in stock. Prompt, personalized mail service since 1977. Catalog/printed list available, two stamps appreciated. (Retail only. Mail order only.)
P.O. Box 37
Des Moines, IA 50301
(515) 262-6714

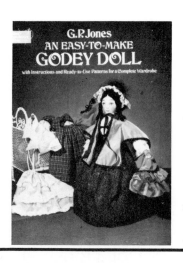

Publications

Books for Collectors by John Axe

Tammy and Dolls You Love to Dress

by John Axe. Story of Tammy and her "family" of teen fashion dolls. Over 215 black/white and color photographs. 81 Pages. Paper. $9.95.

Collecting Modern Dolls

edited by John Axe
How-to-Guidebook on Collecting Modern Dolls
Articles by favorite authorities on many different areas of collectible and modern dolls. Barbie, Alexander, Effanbee, Shirley Temple, Ginnys, Teddy Bears and other dolls by many noteable authors. Large detailed photographs. Limited supply left from Modern Doll Convention — hurry! 64 Pages, 8¼ x 10-⅞" Paper. $7.95.

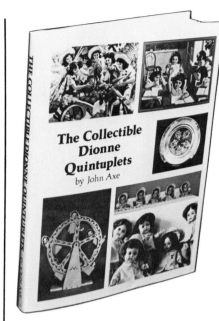

The Collectible Dionne Quintuplets

by John Axe. A comprehensive study of the Quints' lives as well as photographs and illustrations of Quint dolls and a large variety of other Quint collectibles. 154 Pages. Cloth. $9.95. 1980 Price Guide $1.50.

COLLECTIBLE SONJA HENIE
by John Axe. Reference on this celebrity includes dolls, paper dolls, movie memorabilia and a wealth of other Sonja Henie collectibles. 120 photographs. 48 Pages. Paper. $4.95.

COLLECTIBLE PATSY DOLLS AND PATSY-TYPES
by John Axe. Includes nearly every variation of Patsy dolls, most in original costume. Over 130 black/white and color photographs. 48 Pages. Paper. $4.95.

COLLECTIBLE BLACK DOLLS
by John Axe. Includes research data, makers and marks as well as perspective to black doll manufacture and advertising during 20th century. 116 detailed photographs. 48 Pages. Paper. $4.95.

COLLECTIBLE DOLLS IN NATIONAL COSTUME
by John Axe. Reflects a variety of commercially made regional costume dolls. 112 black and white photographs. 48 Pages. Paper. $4.95.

COLLECTIBLE BOY DOLLS
by John Axe. Nearly 100 photographs of boy dolls including turn-of-the-century bisques, composition, hard plastic and vinyl boy dolls. 32 Pages. Paper. $3.95.

Catalog free upon request.

Hobby House Press, Inc.

900 Frederick Street
Cumberland, MD 21502
(301) 759-3770

Books for Collectors by Hobby House Press, Inc.

ENCYCLOPEDIA OF CELEBRITY DOLLS

by John Axe

There are over one-quarter million adults who collect dolls. Collectors acquire dolls of many different mediums from bisque to vinyl and many styles from a woman to a baby, but the one thing that every collector has is a celebrity doll!

Also featured is a comprehensive look at celebrity dolls with over 1000 black/white photographs. 50 gorgeous full color photographs are on 16 pages. Arranged alphabetically this book provides easy access with very detailed listings and analysis of all dolls made in the image of a famous personality. The author, a Professor of History at Youngstown University, also gives a biographical insight into the life of the celebrity.

This book will be a "celebrity" to all those who have wished that detailed information be organized into one book and that the information be available for detailed study.

432 Pages. Index. Cloth. Write to Hobby House Press, Inc. for price and availability date.

Collector's Digest On German Character Dolls

by Robert & Karin MacDowell. This book provides a very detailed look at character dolls. Made by the German doll masters such as Bergner, Cuno & Otto Dressel, Heubach, Heubach/Köppelsdorf, Kämmer & Reinhardt, Kestner, Kruse, Armand Marseille, Schmidt, Simon & Halbig, Steiff, and Steiner, A closeup photograph of the face, markings, and body with many full length portraits. Nearly 240 black/white and color photographs. 160 Pages. 6 x 9". Paper. $9.95.

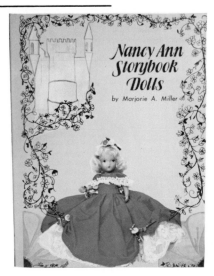

Nancy Ann Storybook Dolls

by Marjorie Miller.   A comprehensive study of Nancy Ann Storybook dolls; bisque, plastic and vinyl, also Nancy Ann style dolls. 480 black/white and color photographs. 240 Pages. Cloth. $17.95.

Hobby House Press, Inc.
900 Frederick Street
Cumberland, MD 21502
(301) 759-3770

Best of the Doll Reader

A thick book containing a compendium of special *Doll Reader* doll collecting article reprints from 1975 to 1980. These important research articles offer informative information and enjoyment for every doll collector. Included are 600 black/white photographs plus 12 pages of color photographs of collectible, modern, antique and artists' dolls. 250 Pages, 8¼ x 10-⅞ inches. Paper. $9.95.

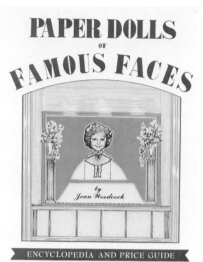

Books for Collectors by Hobby House Press, Inc.

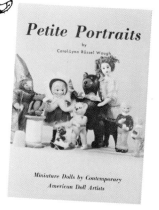

Petite Portraits
Miniature Dolls by Contemporary American Doll Artists
by CAROL-LYNN RÖSSEL WAUGH

The work of original doll artists is an up-and-coming collectible in the doll world today.

Petite Portraits is an informative and comprehensive guide to original miniature dolls and teddy bears in media from fibre to wax and ranging in a wide variety of styles and techniques. This valuable reference includes authoritative treatment of original dolls as well as costuming.

Over 450 black and white photographs and a color section illustrate the creative work of 52 talented doll artists.

224 Pages, 7 x 10", $12.95.

Mary Hoyer and Her Dolls
by Mary Hoyer

At last the complete story of the Mary Hoyer doll plus reprints of the famous knitting, crocheting and sewing projects for doll collectors and dressers has been published! The story is directly from the originator--Mary Hoyer.

- Over 200 color and black/white photographs.
- Original advertising and photographs show the dolls from 1937 through early 1970s. Identify and date your collection.
- Reprints of all Mary's Dollies Knit & Crochet books.
- Reprints of McCall/Hoyer dolls' clothes commercial patterns.

Clothes patterns will fit slim-bodied doll of the period -Alexander, R & B, Betsy McCall, Maggie, Alice, Harriet Hubbard Ayer and many others.

Over 100 knitting, crocheting, and sewing projects.
243 Pages, 8½ x 11". Cloth binding. $17.95.

On Making, Mending & Dressing Dolls

by Clara Fawcett. Valuable reference for the would-be doll maker and mender. Line drawings by this gifted doll, illustrator. 170 Pages. Paper. $6.95.

Kewpie Needlework Designs

KEWPIE DESIGN NO. I

"Days of the Week" patterns by Rose O'Neill. Sized for quilt blocks, tea towels, dollhouse size. Could applique on children's clothes. Reprinted from McCall's Pattern no. 342, ca. 1937. Original instructions and color guide included. $2.50.

KEWPIE DESIGN NO. III

Reprint of appliqued Kewpie coverlet pattern and downy pillow to match. Create as a gift to give a newborn baby but excellent for doll coverlet. $2.50.

KEWPIE DESIGN NO. II

Pattern for 14½" high stuffed Kewpie cloth doll designed by Rose O'Neill. Also included are patterns for romper, ruffled hat and panties. $2.50.

Hobby House Press, Inc.
900 Frederick Street
Cumberland, MD 21502
(301) 759-3770

Publications

209

Dolly Dingle

Dolly Dingle Transfer Designs

72 heat transfers -- 12 designs, 5 different sizes of the adorable "Campbell Kids" look. Finish with such needlework techniques as embroidery, quilting, sewing or fabric painting. 64 Pages. Paper. $3.95.

Sunbonnet Baby Transfer Designs Vol. I

Sunbonnet Babies Transfer Designs Vol. I

84 heat transfers -- 22 designs, 4 different sizes. Includes some scenes or settings. Finish by such needlework techniques as embroidery, quilting, sewing or fabric painting. 96 Pages. Paper. $4.95.

featuring "Days of the Week"

Sunbonnet Babies Transfer Designs Vol. II

84 heat transfers -- 27 designs, 5 different sizes. All different designs from Volume I. Features "Days of the Week Designs." 96 Pages. Paper. $4.95.

Kate Greenaway Transfer Designs

68 heat transfers -- 24 designs, 3 different sizes. Some scenes or settings. Finish by such needlework techniques as embroidery, quilting, sewing or fabric painting. 96 Pages. Paper. $4.95.

Hat Making For Dolls
1855-1916

Revised edition contains 18 doll hat patterns. Many patterns for child-type and lady-type dolls. All patterns authentic with helpful instructions and suggestions. Price: $2.75.

For free catalog write

Hobby House Press, Inc.

900 Frederick Street Cumberland, MD 21502 (301) 759-3770

Knitting & Crocheting for Antique Dolls

Darling clothes and accessories to knit and crochet for antique dolls. Reprint from old magazine articles and needlework books. Included are original patterns & illustrations. Tiny to large dolls included. Each is 8½ x 11". Paper. Approximately 80 items in each part.

KNITTING & CROCHETING FOR ANTIQUE DOLLS I - covers 1872-1898. 36 Pages, Paper. $3.95.

KNITTING & CROCHETING FOR ANTIQUE DOLLS II - covers 1898-1913 (Teddy Bear outfit included). 36 Pages, Paper. $3.95.

KNITTING & CROCHETING FOR ANTIQUE DOLLS III - covers 1914-1929. 36 Pages, Paper. $3.95.

DOLL REPAIR and RESTORATION

"Doctor Willie", from Our Darlings Story Book ca. 1890s.
All Prices Listed Are Subject To Change Without Notice.

"My repairs didn't hurt at all."

Dusty's Doll Hospital & Supply

Six doctors, each a specialist to give your dolls tender loving care. Custom costuming by two expert seamstresses. Buy, sell, and trade antique and collectible dolls. Supplies, accessories and appraisals. (Shop and mail.)

4425 Highway 78
Lilburn, GA 30247
(404) 972-5626

Plain & Fancy Doll Shop

General repairs, estimates given free, custom dressing. Antique materials used when possible. Antiques, collectibles bought and sold. Night appointments for your convenience. (Shop and mail order).

13505 Spriggs Road
Manassas, VA 22111
(703) 791-3364

Restoration of a Bye-Lo with a hole in top of head.

Vernal Restoration

Donna Vernal is a toy designer, a fine portrait artist and an impeccable restorer of fine antique dolls. Specializes in bisque character dolls and fine French dolls. Invisible and guaranteed. Will also buy damaged dolls. (Shop and mail.)

9325 Gary Avenue
Waconia, MN 55387
(612) 442-4984

Broken to beautiful.

Celinda's Doll Shoppe

Antique and collectible dolls restored, restrung, eye-setting. China and porcelain parts, heads. Bodies, new and restored. Wigs, new and restyled. Costuming and other accessories. Free estimates. Printed list $1.00 + LSASE.

4626 Northeast 4th Street
Minneapolis, MN 55421
(612) 572-1633

Doll's-N-Things

Custom dressing. Repair estimates by mail or at shop. Shoes, socks, eyes, wigs, etc. for your old doll.

1416 Rees Street
Breaux Bridge, LA 70517
(318) 332-2622

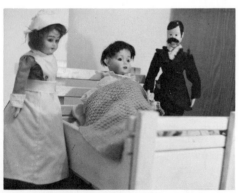

1898 doctor and nurse visiting patient.

Aunt Jo's Doll Hospital

Restore and authentically costume old and antique dolls. Repair stuffed animals, display mannequins, modern dolls, and statuettes. Receipts always given. Doll clothes and accessories for sale. No catalog. (Shop only.)

Hiway 69, South of Smelter Stack
Mayer, AZ 86333

212

Doll Repair & Restoration

Anne Luree Dolls

Professional bisque restoration, also china, composition and Schoenhut figures. Missing pieces modeled, parts matching. Museum quality work at reasonable prices. Free estimates.

**P.O. Box 7164
Sacramento, CA 95826
(916) 363-5733**

Learn doll repair. Free booklet describes fascinating and unique home study program. Learn to make, repair, restore and dress dolls, old and new. No salesman. (Mail only.)

NORM & MARGE MORRIS'
Lifetime Career Schools

**Dept. D-927
2251 BARRY AVE.
LOS ANGELES, CALIFORNIA 90064
(213) 478-0617**

Joan's Doll Hospital & Boutique

Effanbee's Mae West - John Wayne $62.95. Buy, sell, repair collectible and antique dolls. Make and sell doll clothes, specializing in *Barbie* and modern dolls. Free estimates given. (Shop and mail.)

**5900 86th Avenue North
Pinellas Park, FL 33565
(813) 546-3234**

M. Wynter Dolls

Expert, invisible restoration of collectible dolls by a doll artisan. All phases of restoration specifically designed to protect your dolls value and originality. Original dolls and restoration only. SASE for information. (Home studio.)

**3896-A Moran Way
Norcross, GA 30092
(404) 441-3276**

"Before" and "After," restored and dressed.

Poor Doll's Shop

Repair all types of dolls specializing in antique. 13 years experience. Do research and have doll kits. No job too small. Lifetime career. Graduate member of UFDA. Write for details and price, SASE please.

**Route 2, Box 58
Syracuse, IN 46567**

The Doll's Corner
Stage House Village

Complete hospital service. Expert restoration. Custom dressing, dolls accessories, supplies, wigs, shoes, stands, clothes, patterns, doll kits. Appraisal service. Repair estimates free. Hours 12:00 - 5:30 Tuesday to Saturday. We also carry Effanbee, Sasha, Gerber, Pauline, Z & Z dolls. SASE for information.

**Park Avenue & Front Street
Scotch Plains, NJ 07076
(201) 322-2025**

Dolls by Dottie

Porcelain reproductions, doll patterns, molds, kilns, supplies, classes, seminars. Seeley distributor. (Wholesale and retail. Shop and mail order.)

**2910 Centerville Road
Dallas, TX 75228
(214) 270-1851**

Doll Care
by Emily Manning

Check list form booklet telling in detail cleaning of all types doll surfaces, all types hair care, storage problems plus common errors and corrections. $3.50.

**Aunt Emily Doll Hospital
c/o Emily Manning
4809 Ravenswood Road
Riverdale, MD 20840
(301) 864-5561**

Anna Lou's World of Dolls

Handmade Leather Shoes

$ 8. up to 1½"
$10. 1½"--2¾"
$12. 2¾"-3⅞"
$14. 3⅞" up
Custom shoes your
fabric $15. any size
STYLES
German Sandal
Basic German
Hi. Button Boot
Toddler Tie
Basic French
Toddler Button Boot

Colors: White, Black, Brown

Add: lst. pr. $1. post.
$.20 ea. add. pr.
Trace foot for correct
size
Catalog: $.25 SASE.

**2907 Camino Calandria
Thousand Oaks, CA 91360
(805) 492-8025**

The Doll Savers

We do all types of doll repair and restoration as well as doll dressmaking, particularly bisques and Alexanders. Dolls costumed in modern or antique materials. Free estimates. All types, mechanical, composition, plastic, bisque.

**13220 Hanover Pike
Reisterstown, MD 21136**

ABC Doll
Shop & Repair

Quality repairs of bisque, china and composition; custom costuming; leather and cloth bodies; custom-made doll wigs and restyling; restringing; eye-setting; dolls and accessories for sale. Printed list: $1.00 and LSASE. Estimates given. (Shop and mail.)

**28 North Alma School Road, #C
Mesa, AZ 85201**

13½in (34.3cm) *Jackie Coogan*
by Horsman, 1921. *Photograph
by John Axe.*

SPECIAL DOLL ARTIST UPDATE

Why A Doll Artist Doll?

by
Carol-Lynn Rössell Waugh

Illustration 1. *About 7in (17.8cm) Garden Gal, dressed and undressed by Carol Carlton (ODACA). All hollow rigid wax; arms jointed with elastsic.*

Years ago--not so many years ago, really--before doll collecting reached its current level of popularity, it was relatively easy for a collector to obtain many of the dolls she wanted. Chiefly this was because hardly anyone else wanted them. Dolls that are now worth a ransom sold for shillings, we are told, when they could be unearthed.

However, this hobbyist's heaven was not without thorns. The earlier doll collector was on her own, without the network of knowledge which has grown out of the sharing of information on manufacturers and merchandise among dealers and dollers that we enjoy today. Sad to say, though, this very knowledge has added to the demand for dolls and to the rise in their prices.

So antique doll collecting has become somewhat of a specialized sport out of necessity. A collector often limits his hoard to one type of doll. The law of supply and demand has taken over the field; as the available number of antiques shrinks, prices soar.

Many collectors are, therefore, looking for alternatives to antique dolls. But they are still looking for the same qualities in dolls that they found in the antiques. These include beauty, scarcity of supply, limited editions, known makers and excellence of construction. This is why many doll collectors have begun to collect original doll artist dolls.

A doll artist doll has inherent rarity. It is a hand-crafted product, made by one artist or sometimes by a small team of artists for a limited amount of time. Sometimes these dolls are one-of-a-kind. Sometimes they are part of an "artist's edition" of anywhere from two to two thousand dolls. But, whatever the number of dolls in the edition, they all share common characteristics.

Chief in importance, perhaps, is the aesthetic stamp of the doll's creator. This is the big difference between original artist dolls and reproduction dolls. (Reproductions are proliferating now because of the increasing commercial availability of reproduction molds.) Since artist dolls are made by the artist or under his supervision, his original concept of the doll is protected. It is not watered down or distorted by the exigencies of mechanical reproduction and by the materials used by commercial doll producers. Every doll has a hand-done human touch that makes it one-of-a-kind even if it is one

of a series, because there is always variation in handwork.

There is a more important reason to buy an artist original doll if one is a collector--more important, I think, than its rarity. A doll artist doll is a work of art. It is sculpture in miniature on a very demanding scale of a very difficult yet universal subject--the human body. And what is even more amazing is that this sculpture is articulated. It moves! All the intricacies of movement have been worked out by the artist on an individual basis--not mass-produced. It is very special, very personal, very rare.

Okay, now. You say I have sold you on doll artist dolls. But how do you pick the best, the most beautiful? I can only give you guidelines that I would follow. Buying an artist doll is like buying any work of art. It is subjective, akin to the purchase of a painting. Everyone likes something different which makes it nice for both the collector and the artist, because there is such a wide range from which to choose.

Artist dolls are made in all media from fiber to wood and in all sizes. They depict everything from pilgrims to pixies and are serious or sappy or anything in between. Only the collector knows what he wants. One thing the buyer should insist upon, however, is that the doll he is buying is an ORIGINAL doll designed by the doll artist, not a reproduction of an antique or of someone else's work.

What I look for in an artist doll is something almost intangible. You could call it a sense of vision, a sense of aesthetic rightness in the doll. A doll that I would buy must "speak" to me in its own special way, and appeal, perhaps, to my sense of the absurd. (I am partial to animal dolls and fantasy folk, the smaller the better.) What I look for most of all is a well-made doll which shows that the doll maker knew what

he was doing with both his subject matter and his medium. The doll must show some sense of inner life, but not necessarily represent anyone of importance, or serve any high didactic purpose.

Knowledge of anatomy and proportion on the part of the doll maker-- or the lack of them--is always evident in his product. I look for dolls by people who know the rules, even if they choose later to ignore them for the purpose of exaggeration and caricature. Picasso knew the rules, too, as is evident in his early paintings. That is how he so successfully got away with rejecting them later on. He has a good foundation to build upon.

Doll artist dolls should be signed and dated. This adds to their value. If the doll is one of an edition, it is nice if it is numbered, but this is often not the

Illustration 2. *1in = 1ft scale (2.5 = 30.5cm) Gone with the Wind doll by Janna Joseph. Porcelain bisque.*

case. Sometimes the artist does not know how many dolls are in an edition he has made. Artist dolls have a way of dying on the way to completion, especially if they are made of porcelain. I used to have vast numbers of stillbirths when I worked in that medium.

A doll artist should stand behind his work. There are several organizations of professional doll artists which encourage integrity and professional dealings between their members and the general public. Among them are NIADA (National Institute of American Doll Artists), ODACA (Original Doll Artist Council of America) and BDA (British Doll Artists). Buying a doll from a member of these organizations carries with it an assurance of a certain level of competence and quality. But there are hundreds of unaffiliated doll artists making superior dolls who should not be ignored merely because they, for one reason or another, feel no need to be joiners. An "official name" on a doll is a meaningless status symbol if the doll does not reach out aesthetically to its owner.

That is the nice thing about doll artist dolls. They do reach out. They are such personal expressions, such mirrors of the artists' souls, that any one of them is bound to reach out to one person, but leave another cold. But when that doll and that person come into contact, it is love at first sight. When that happens to you--and don't think that it won't--you will never again have to ask "Why a doll artist doll?"

Illustration 4. *Sunny by Margory Hoya Novak (ODACA). Porcelain.*

Illustration 5. *Porcelain baby dolls by Lucille Garrard (ODACA).*

Illustration 3. *Plush bear by June Beckett (ODACA) and wooden dolls by Bob and June Beckett (ODACA).*

Illustration 6. *Granny by Lucille Garrard (ODACA). Porcelain and cloth.*

Illustration 7. *Dancer by Carol Nordell (NIADA). Composition.*

Illustration 8. *Flower Fairy by Tita Varner (ODACA).*

Illustration 9. *Porcelain doll by Sonja Bryer (ODACA).*

Illustration 10. *Porcelain dolls by Phyllis Wright (ODACA).*

Illustration 11. *Sailor by Margory Hoya Nova (ODACA). Porcelain bisque.*

Illustration 12. *Holmes and Watson by Sheila Kwartler (ODACA). Polyform on wire armatures.*

Illustration 13. *Elf by Susanna Oroyan (NIADA).*

Illustration 14. *Elf by Anne Luree Leonard (ODACA). All porcelain.*

Illustration 15. *All-porcelain artist's model doll by Annie Schickell (ODACA).*

221

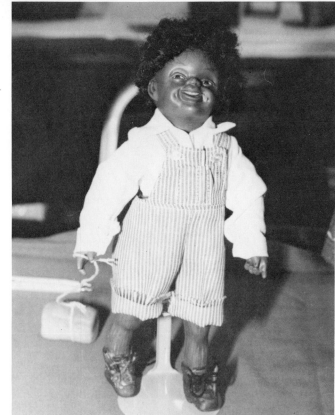

Illustration 16. *Porcelain doll by Tita Varner (ODACA).*

Illustration 17. *17in (43.2cm) St. Nicholas by Beverly Port (ODACA).*

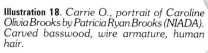

Illustration 18. *Carrie O., portrait of Caroline Olivia Brooks by Patricia Ryan Brooks (NIADA). Carved basswood, wire armature, human hair.*

Illustration 19. *6in (15.2cm) porcelain and cloth doll by Faith Wick (NIADA).*

Illustration 20. *1in = 1ft scale (2.5 = 30.5cm) lady doll by Deidra B. Spann. Porcelain bisque.*

Illustration 21. *Bearishnikov by Carol-Lynn Waugh (ODACA).*

British Doll Artists In 1982

by Ann Parker

Illustration 1. *Susi and Greta Fleischmann with a group of their Old Cottage dolls.*

make a doll of the glamourous comedienne Marti Caine, and it will be presented to her on her television show.

Greta and Susi Fleischmann have packed up their old doll workshop after more than 40 years - what a task! They have gone to live in Southampton to be near Greta's son who is a professor at the University, but they hope to continue their doll making on a very limited scale as soon as they have settled down.

They moved into their very quaint old cottage in Sussex after a hair raising escape from Czechoslovakia in 1938, when Susi was still a little girl; Mr Fleischmann died very soon and to make a living and keep her two children, Greta began to make dolls to sell. They were a tremendous success and sold all over the world, but in the last few years production has been reduced to just the number that Susi could manage to paint, so that with Greta's sculpture and design and Susi's painting, their dolls with the "Old Cottage Toys" label were able to be part of the original BDA display.

British Doll Artists main annual exhibition this year is from August 28th to September 30th at Burrows Toy Museum, Bath; there is not a great deal of space there but it is a lovely little museum and in a very convenient

As BDA puts on exhibitions and gets publicity, more and more of our isolated doll artists hear about us and join up; we have collected 44 members in two and a half years and regretfully turned many candidates down.

All the members to date have been making dolls for some time and have been relieved to find that they are not alone; as BDA becomes better known it is adding impetus to the explosion of interest in doll making and is tempting new artists to begin or to improve their existing dolls.

The making of reproduction antique dolls seems slower to catch on in Britain than in other countries, but at the same time the idea of the completely original doll has gained ready acceptance among the ordinary public and an increasing number of BDA members are teaching doll making to large classes, some at adult education centers and some privately; in 1982 most of our members are very busy people.

Most of the doll fairs in England are run by antique dealers and so far we still find that our original dolls are classed as "reproductions" and actually excluded from some fairs.

Paul Crees has begun to show his fabulous film stars at movie conventions and has had great success with them; he has just been commissioned to

Illustration 2. *Charlotte Zeepvat's dolls on display; on the left, Queen Victoria with baby Prince Arthur; center Emperor Franz Josef of Austria with Prince Rudolf; the adult figures are 11in (27.9cm); right, George who has a ceramic turning head, shoulder plate, arms and legs, soft body and real hair. Photograph by Andrew MacMillan.*

place. We are greatly assisted by Paul Crees and Thora Hughs who are lucky enough to live in beautiful Bath, the Georgian city, and we are looking forward to holding our annual general meeting there.

During June, July and August those of us who also belong to the Dollmakers Circle, which is an old established doll making club based in London, are taking part in the DMC display at a stately home, Hall Place, in Kent.

We have several BDA group displays planned at various events this year and find that we are beginning to be invited to display free at craft shows and charity events as an attraction to the public. Now that our membership has increased it is much easier to accept these offers as we often have a member living nearby who can take charge of the necessary organization involved.

BDA members recently voted to introduce special silk labels for BDA dolls and about half the members are already using them; their use will remain optional as they are much too big for tiny dolls.

We have also brought our directory up to date and the 1982 edition is available airmail, price two dollar bills, from: Ann Parker, 67 Victoria Drive, Bognor Regis, Sussex, England. PO21 2TD.

Illustration 3. *A display of dolls by Marjorie Harris. They are 14in (35.6cm) and individually modeled. On the left The Cribbage Players; on the right, Fagin and The Artful Dodger. Photograph by Andrew MacMillan.*

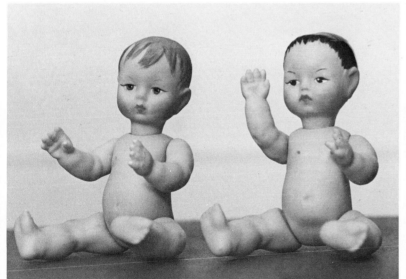

Illustration 4. *2in (5.1cm) porcelain babies by Jane Davies. They are highly detailed for their small size and as Jane has been in Bangcock for the last year, the baby on the right is Asian. She also makes a black baby in the same size.*

Illustration 5. *Julia Hills painting one of her famous clowns. Julia has moved to an artist's workshop at Stow-on-the-Wold and is making some very beautiful and unusual figures in her special ceramics.*

225

Illustration 6. *One of Sheila Wallace's beautiful wax figures, Marie Antoinette. It is individually modeled and 20in (50.8cm) tall.*

Right Illustration 7. *12in (30.5cm) costume figures by Vivienne Preece. They have polyester resin heads and limbs. Vivienne has now begun to make delightful tiny flower fairies at a very reasonable price.*

Illustration 9. *New member, Carol Eadon, with her graduation display at the end of her three years at art school studying ceramics. Her figures of the pop group, ABBA, can be seen hanging against the wall.*

Illustration 8. *Jay Harrison making one of her needlesculptured figures.*

Illustration 10. *Teresa Thompson demonstrating her charming historic costume dolls.*

Illustration 11. *An unusual Dutch doll seated on a painted Dutch chair by art teacher, Margaret Hickson. Margaret specialises in unusual and ethnic dolls.*

Above: Illustration 12. *Ellen Bedington and Kath Beech inspecting a porcelain fashion lady made by Kath.*

Right: Illustration 13. *8in (20.3cm) Clemmie, one of the bridesmaids at the Royal Wedding, made in porcelain by Ellen Bedington.*

Illustration 14. *One of Sheena MacLeod's Highland Characters. When standing, they are 8in (20.3cm). This one is a crofter making a creel.*

Illustration 15. *New member, Helene McLeod, has been selling a lot of her molded cloth play dolls.*

Illustration 16. *16in (40.6cm) The Old Broom Maker, individually modeled in self-hardening clay by Violet Oram of Scotland. This doll won first prize at the Royal Highland Show in Edinburgh.*

Illustration 17. *Two delightful 4in (10.2cm) Victorian children with molded cloth heads made by Thora Hughs of Bath.*

Illustration 19. *New member, Linnet Gotch, makes highly unusual cloth sculptures. All of them are in different styles and many are Art Deco.*

Illustration 18. *Ann Parker and Gillie Charlson at the Leeds show. Gillie is holding one of Sarah Jane Fisher's pretty dolls. On the left you can see a display of Brenda Pennington's costume dolls.*

Illustration 20. *Catherine Knight is one of the newest member of BDA. She has been making her lovely wax dolls for only a short time, but has made a variety of dolls and puppets ever since she was 14 years old.*

ODACA's New Members

by Carol-Lynn Rössel Waugh

Illustration 1. *Terol Lynn Reed, doll artist.*

In December 1981, ten artists gained membership in the Original Doll Artist Council of America. Though their work shows a healthy diversity in medium and technique, a common bond seems to link them. This is a sense of joy and wonder--an embracing of childhood and of fantasy.

The most popular medium again this year among new members is clay--either natural or synthetic. Wood came second and needlesculpture third. But listing media this way is akin to saying that pansies, daisies and roses are all flowers. The work of all these women must be seen to be appreciated.

Ruth Brown of San Diego, California, has been carving since 1967. She makes one-of-a-kind children of basswood that are approximately 16in (40.6cm) tall. They are jointed at hip, shoulder, elbow and neck. Some are portraits; some are just interesting faces that she likes. The dolls' photographs are so appealing and lifelike that they look like snapshots of idealized real children. This is appropriate. When she is not making dolls, Ruth Brown works as a black and white photographic printer.

Bella Authement's dolls are about the same size as Ruth Brown's but very different in concept. She has been making dolls since 1975 and specializes in lovely ladies from 14in (35.6cm) to 19in (48.3cm). Her early dolls were Cajun (Louisiana) ladies. In addition to these, Mrs. Authement makes dolls dressed in 19th century costumes, especially Godey and French fashions. The dolls are carved of tupelo wood with an X-acto knife. Some are all wood. Others have cloth bodies with wooden lower limbs and wooden heads. Their hair is either carved or made of bleached goat hair dyed with hair dye. The State of Louisiana bought four Authement Ladies for the mini-museum, a traveling van which displays the work of native artists and craftsmen.

Virginia "Ginna" Baldwin, of California, works in polyform and in porcelain, but most of all in needlesculpture. She has been doing needlesculpture for about six years and her dolls are largeish. They average between 15 and 25in (38.1cm and 63.5cm) in height. She works with nylon and uses a special treatment on the dolls' faces to make them last. She says that "each needlesculpture is one-of-a-kind in face, like people....To form the dolls in 3-D and design the clothes from the fantasies and reflections of the mind is IT for me."

From her Santa Clauses and pirates to her fairies, Ginna Baldwin's dolls take the viewer back to childhood dreams and give him a glimpse of those special times and places he secretly has always wanted to revisit.

Two other doll makers with similar motives are Cathy Ellis of Portland, Oregon, and Jean Heighton of San Mateo, California.

Cathy Ellis has been making dolls since 1980 and works in Super Sculpey, a synthetic low-fire clay. She draws upon her experience, working summers with a traveling carnival to create her colorful people and puppets in miniature size. Her largest doll is 5½in (14.0cm) to 6in (15.2cm) high. "What interests me most about doll making is getting people to laugh or at least smile at themselves. My hope is that an individual may recognize a silly or sentimental feeling possibly from childhood, and just for a second or two drop that 'serious adult' front we all have and relax," she says. Her menagerie of clowns, storybook people and typical doll house people--some so small they could easily qualify as secret pocket companions--easily do the job for her.

Jean Heighton calls her dolls "Fantasy Folk." They are, in my opinion, wonderful. Jean is always coming up with crazy lovable combinations of critter and costume that should not work but do. She works in various clays--mostly porcelain. And she makes storybook people you would not believe. *Sherlock Hound* is my favorite of her current bunch. He is a mixture of porcelain head, paws and feet, and real fur (from the waist to the ankles). He is 9¾in (24.9cm) tall and wears a deerstalker cap, Sherlock cape and sports a pipe in his mouth. The *Big Bad Wolf* is dressed in Granny's nightgown. He has a porcelain head, hands and feet and a furry body. *Billy the Kid* is, of course, a cowboy goat, complete with vest, chaps, guns and cowboy hat. Jean Heighton just gets better and better.

Terol Lynn Reed of Colorado has been making dolls of porcelain for three years. She embraces fantasy of a somewhat gentler vein. Her all porcelain fairy *Canda* has a delicate, late 19th century flavor. She could be right out of a juvenile book illustration. Terol's porcelain headed jesters live in that same storybook world. And her porcelain headed (and footed!) teddy bears are delightful. "If I could use one word to describe my dolls--the way that they look--the way that I feel about them--why they are--it would be FANTASY," she confides.

Illustration 2. 9¾in (24.9cm) Sherlock Hound by Jean Heighton. Porcelain head, paws and feet; real fur from waist to ankles.

Illustration 4. *Jean Heighton cleaning goose to go with 15in (38.1cm) Mother Goose.*

Wendy Brent of Eureka, California, combines rose petals and ceramic to create her dolls.

Barbara Jenkins, of San Anselmo, California, is a miniaturist who works in porcelain. She creates diminutive families in 1in = 1ft (2.5cm = 30.5cm) scale. This is just right for doll houses. They are beautifully dressed in turn-of-the-century fashions. She strives for "reality to the point of make-believe" in her dolls.

Jeanette Price works in Sculpey and in porcelain. She has been making dolls for six years. Some of her porcelain dolls are all-bisque; some have polyester fabric bodies. Her Sculpey dolls have Sculpey heads, arms and legs and felt and wire armature bodies. The latter are one-of-a-kind. She prefers them because she can get more detail into them without worrying about molds, undercuts and all the other limitations of molded porcelain work. Many of her

dolls are children. Some are portraits. Some are just for fun. They have won many awards.

Judi Somerville began working in porcelain three years ago and was certain she would make figurines. That was until she tried making a doll--just for the challenge. However, that portrait of her youngest daughter, Missy, changed her outlook on art. She is now a full-time doll artist. She excels at designing "little people"--children of all descriptions. Her early training as a painter comes through and still colors her preferences in doll making. She says: "I always look forward to painting the faces. This is when they come alive to me and I don't think I'm ever going to tire of that thrill."

Imagination and talent--these are the keynotes of our new members. We of ODACA are proud to welcome each of these artists into our ranks.

Illustration 3. 14in (35.6cm) Tevye. Limited edition with porcelain head and hands, composition boots and violin. Music box plays "If I Were a Rich Man."

Illustration 5. *Cathy Ellis at work.*

Illustration 7. 1in = 1ft scale (2.5-30.5cm) clown of Super Sculpey by Cathy Ellis.

Illustration 6. 1in = 1ft scale (2.5=30.5cm) doll house dolls by Cathy Ellis.

Illustration 8. 21in and 23in (53.3 and 58.4cm) Mr. and Mrs. S. Clause and 21in (53.3cm) Geosephe, the Organ Grinder, with their maker, Virginia "Ginna" Baldwin.

Illustration 9. 21in (53.3cm) Mrs. Peggotty, the Flower Peddler in needlesculpture by Virginia "Ginna" Baldwin.

Illustration 10. 8in (20.3cm) Fairy, needlesculpture doll with egg shell cradle by Virginia "Ginna" Baldwin.

Illustration 11. Bella Authement carving a boy doll.

Illustration 12. *14in (35.6cm) doll with blonde goat hair wig, wire armature body, wooden lower limbs and 1800 costume by Bella Authement.*

Illustration 14. *Doll artist, Ruth A. Brown.*

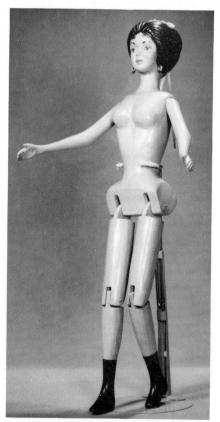

Illustration 13. *19in (48.3cm) all tupelo wood doll by Bella Authement.*

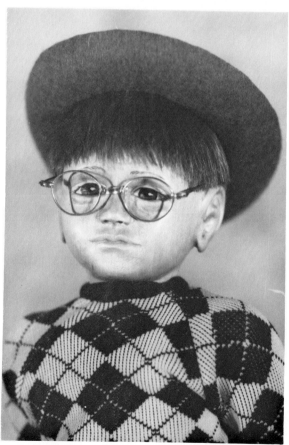

Illustration 15. *16in (40.6cm) John by Ruth A. Brown.*

234

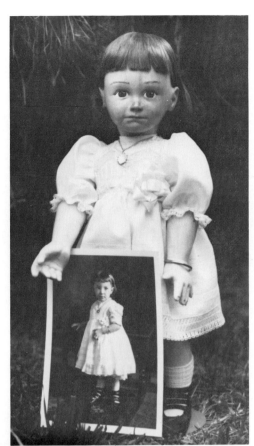

Illustration 16. *16in (40.6cm) Portrait of Dorothy by Ruth A. Brown.*

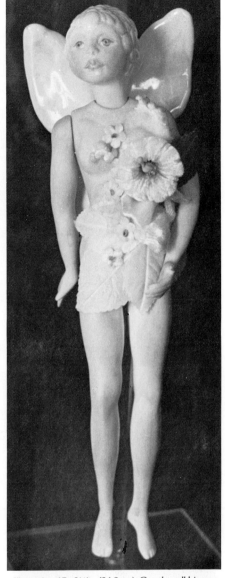

Illustration 17. *9½in (24.2cm) Canda, all-bisque fairy. Pearlized nouveau style hat and wings; jointed head and arms; clothing made from antique millinery.*

Illustration 18. *Jester on a dowel by Terol Lynn Reed. Hat of cotton velvet decorated with bells, ribbons and feathers. One-of-a-kind painting with art nouveau designs and flowers.*

Illustration 19. *Barbara Jenkins, doll artist.*

Illustration 20. 5½in (13.4cm) 1880 lady by Barbara Jenkins. Porcelain head, arms and legs; silk evening dress with lace and ribbon trim.

Illustration 21. 6in (15.2cm) 1890 man and 4in (10.2cm) 1890 boy by Barbara Jenkins. Porcelain heads, arms and legs; dressed in cotton.

Illustration 22. Judi Somerville working on a doll head.

Illustration 23. *12in (30.5cm) Bitsy by Judi Somerville. All bisque, bent leg, dressed in yellow batiste and white lace sun suit and bonnet; holding "pearl" bead necklace.*

Illustration 24. *16in (40.6cm) Shannon O'Malley by Judi Somerville. Bisque head and limbs; cloth body.*

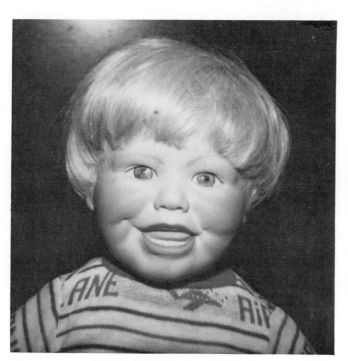

Illustration 25. *Kirk by Jeanette Price.*

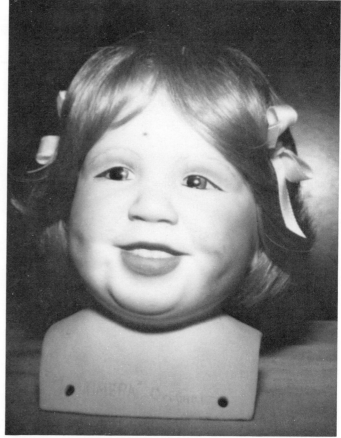

Illustration 26. *Kimera by Jeanette Price.*

Be sure to tell that
You found it in
THE DOLL CATALOG

INDEX

CROSS INDEX

GEOGRAPHICAL INDEX

Palm Desert
Georgianne's Dollhouse Dolls by
Georgianne
73-981 Highway 111
Palm Desert, CA 92260
Page 58
Palm Springs
Second Childhood
473 North Palm Canyon Drive
Palm Springs, CA 92262
Page 38
Pittsburg
Pittsburg Historical Museum
40 Civic Avenue
P.O. Box 1816
Pittsburg, CA 94565
Page 127
Poway
Pendlebury, Penny
13305 Alpine Drive
Poway, CA 92064
Page 20
Redwood City
McAdams, Ellen
by Terri people
3711 Page Street
Redwood City, CA 94063
Page 15
Riverside
Corning, Barb
7727 Bolton Avenue
Riverside, CA 92503
Page 25
Sacramento
Luree, Anne Dolls
P.O. Box 7164
Sacramento, CA 95826
Pages 23, 213
San Bernardino
Campbell's Dolls
P.O. Box 3041
San Bernardino, CA 92413
Page 170
San Diego
Fantl, Bess
18175 Parvo Court
San Diego, CA 92128
Page 20
San Francisco
Dakin, R. & Company
P.O. Box 7746
San Francisco, CA 94120
Page 181
Rubenstein, Steve Publisher
1445 Union Street #1
San Francisco, CA 94109
Pages 179, 198
Stanislaus Imports, Inc.
75 Arkansas Street
San Francisco, CA 94107
Page 101
Valentine's Ladies
P.O. Box 6340
San Francisco, CA 94101
Page 24
San Jose
Fashion Doll, The
P.O. Box 32663
San Jose, CA 95152
Page 167
San Rafael
Leuzzi, Marlene
#4 Fernwood Way
San Rafael, CA 94901
Page 51
Santa Barbara
Santa Barbara Museum of Art
1130 State Street
Santa Barbara, CA 93101
Page 127
Santa Clara
Gooch-Zamzow, Claudia
P.O. Box 4610
Santa Clara, CA 95054
Page 34
Santa Monica
Hawkins, Bulah Doll Museum
1437 6th Street
Santa Monica, CA 90401
Page 127
Simi Valley
Servant's
2124 Stow Street
Simi Valley, CA 93063
Page 64
Studio City
Doll Emporium
11354 Ventura Boulevard
Studio City, CA 91604
Page 55
Sunland
Mold Works, The
10337-A Jardine Avenue
Sunland, CA 91040
Page 156
Sunnyvale
Cupid's Bow Doll Museum
117 South Murphy Avenue
Sunnyvale, CA 94086
Pages, 127, 128
Sommars, Jewel
P.O. Box 62222
Sunnyvale, CA 94088
Pages 24, 204

Tehachapi
Gaillorraine Originals
407 Brentwood Drive
Tehachapi, CA 93561
Page 185
Temple City
Antique Doll Replicas by Yolanda
6021 North Encinita Avenue
Temple City, CA 91780
Page 11
Memory's Doll Hospital & Shop
P.O. Box 684
Temple City, CA 91780
Page 42
Thousand Oaks
Anna Lou's World of Dolls
2907 Camino Calandria
Thousand Oaks. CA 91360
Page 214
Tracy
Haljo's Ceramics
1425 Linda Place
Tracy, CA 95376
Page 145
Ventura
Doll Gallery, The
Florence Kotanjian
1276 East Main Street
Ventura, CA 93001
Page 37
Walnut Creek
Doll Faire Miniatures
1270-A Newell Avenue
Walnut Creek, CA 94596
Page 49
Dolls for You
1942 Pomar Way
Walnut Creek, CA 94598
Page 59
Yuba City
Milano's Creative Clay Cottage
625 Rowe Avenue
Yuba City, CA 95991
Pages 16, 102, 144

COLORADO

Colorado Springs
Original Porcelain Character Dolls
by Filis Coit
1846 Fuller Road
Colorado Springs, CO 80918
Page 30
Peak Doll Enterprises
P.O. Box 757
Colorado Springs, CO 80901
Shop address: 117 South Main
Fountain, CO 80817
Pages 101, 200
Quality Gifts & Imports
6850 North Academy Boulevard
Colorado Springs, CO 80918
Page 58
Denver
Lyn's Doll House
P.O. Box 8341 C
Denver, CO 80201
Page 112
Williams Doll Supply
1370 South Broadway
Denver, CO 80210
Page 158
Fort Collins
Plain Folk, The by Jan Painter
900 Cheyenne Drive
Fort Collins, CO 80525
Page 23
Tinker's Corner
129 South Whitcomb (Dept. DB)
Fort Collins, CO 80521
Page 114
Manitou Springs
Cameron's Doll & Carriage Museum
218 Becker's Lane
Manitou Springs, CO 80829
Pages 128, 129
Rangely
Rangely Arts & Crafts
P.O. Box 966
Rangely, CO 81648
Pages 35, 143, 145

CONNECTICUT

Bristol
White, Lucy
135 Mark Street
Bristol, CT 06010
Page 154
New Britain
New Britain Youth Museum
30 High Street
New Britain, CT 06053
Page 128
New London
Allyn, Lyman Museum
625 Williams Street
New London, CT 06320
Page 128
Niantic
Alice's Wonderland
P.O. Box 45
Niantic, CT 06357
Page 8

Riverton
McIntyre, Elizabeth Winsor
Antique Shop
Riverton, (Hitchcocksville), CT
06065
Page 44
South Windsor
Reja Dolls
510 Ellington Road
South Windsor, CT 06074
Pages 14, 150
Wethersfield
Olde Towne Doll Shoppe
217 Main Street
Wethersfield, CT 06109
Page 48
Winsted
Holiday Handicrafts, Inc.
P.O. Box 470, West Hill Road
Winsted, CT 06098
Page 145

District of Columbia

Washington
Coleman, Evelyn Jane
4315 Van Ness Street
Washington, DC 20016
Page 188
DAR Museum
1776 "D" Street, Northwest
Washington, DC 20008
Page 128
National Museum of History &
Technology
14th Street & Constitution Avenue,
Northwest
Washington, DC 20560
Page 128
Washington Dolls' House & Toy
Museum
5236 44th Street, Northwest
Chevy Chase, Washington, DC
20015
Pages 128, 129

FLORIDA

Clermont
Bell Ceramics, Inc.
P.O. Box 127
197 Lake Minneola Drive
Clermont, FL 32711
Pages 158, 159, 198
Deland
Deland Museum
449 East New York Avenue
Deland, FL 32720
Page 128
Homosassa
Homosassa Doll Museum
Route 2, Box 6
Homosassa, FL 32646
Page 129
Jacksonville
Jacksonville Museum of Arts and
Sciences
1025 Gulf Life Drive
Jacksonville, FL 32207
Page 129
Lakeland
Museum of Collectible Dolls & Doll
Shop
1117 South Florida Avenue
Lakeland, FL 33803
Pages 62, 129
Orlando
Clay Pigeon, The
720 Cordova Drive
Orlando, FL 32804
Pages 168, 174
Pinellas Park
Joan's Doll Hospital & Boutique
5900 86th Avenue North
Pinellas Park, FL 33565
Page 213
St. Petersburg
MAm Porcelain Dolls
2117 - 68th Terrace South
St. Petersburg, FL 33712
Page 11
Silver Springs
Florida's Silver Springs Antique Car
Collection
State Road 40
P.O. Box 370
Silver Springs, FL 32688
Page 129
Umatilla
Stevens, R. H.
Route 1, Box 476D
Umatilla, FL 32784
Page 37
Winter Haven
Museum of Old Dolls & Toys
1530 Sixth Street, Northwest
Winter Haven, FL 33880
Page 129

GEORGIA

Alpharetta
Trenholm's Treasures International
160 Sedalia Court
Alpharetta, GA 30201
Page 41

Atlanta
All the Trimmings
P.O. Box 15528
Atlanta, GA 30333
Page 150
Creative Silk
820 Oakdale Road, Northeast
Atlanta, GA 30307
Page 158
Toy Museum of Atlanta, The
2800 Peachtree Road, Northeast
Atlanta, GA 30305
Page 129
Forest Park
Ledgewood Studio
6000 Ledgewood Drive
Forest Park, GA 30050
Page 165
Lilburn
Dusty's Doll Hospital & Supply
4855 Highway 78
Lilburn, GA 30247
Pages 45, 212
Norcross
Wynter, M. Dolls
3896-A Moran Way
Norcross, GA 30092
Page 213
Savannah
Museum of Antique Dolls
505 East President
Savannah, GA 31401
Page 129
Smyrna
Doll Shop Enterprises
P.O. Box 1426
Smyrna, GA 30081
Showrooms: 150-154 Washington
Avenue
Marietta, GA 30060
Pages 148, 168

ILLINOIS

Arlington
Ageless Treasures
403 Kingsbury Drive
Arlington, IL 60004
Page 54
Arlington Heights
Just Bears
Division of Ageless Treasures
403 Kingsbury Drive
Arlington Heights, IL 60004
Page 178
Kingdom Doll Company, Inc.
1414 East Davis Street
Arlington Heights, IL 60005
Page 60
Klehm's Pink Peony Doll & Mini
Museum
2 East Algonquin Road
Arlington Heights, IL 60005
Page 130
Unicorn, The
Arlington Market
28 North Dryden
Arlington Heights, IL 60004
Pages 46, 171
Chicago
Chicago Historical Society
Clarke Street and North Avenue
Chicago, IL 60614
Page 130
North American Bear Co.
645 North Michigan Avenue
Chicago, IL 60611
Pages 178, 181
Danville
Vermilion County Museum
116 North Gilbert Street
Danville, IL 61832
Page 130
DeKalb
Ackert Enterprises
521 South 7th Street
DeKalb, IL 60115
Page 196
Frankfort
"Remember Me" in The Grainery
Connie Kaffel
Oak and Elwood Street
Frankfort, IL 60423
Page 54
Milan
Doll-Lain Originals
P.O. Box 910
308 West 4th Avenue
Milan, IL 61264
Page 88
Naperville
Enchanted Doll, The
1038 Heritage Hill Drive, Apt B
Naperville, IL 60540
Page 32
Niles
Fibre-Craft Materials Corp.
6310 West Touhy
Niles, IL 60648
Pages 145, 152
Niota
Ochsner, Grace Doll House
R. R. 1
Niota, IL 62358
Page 42

Normal
University Historical Museum
200 Block S. School
Illinois State University, Williams
Hall
Normal, IL 61761
Page 130
Northfield
Bard's Products, Inc.
1825 Willow Road
Northfield, IL 60093
Page 173
Park Ridge
DiAnn's Originals
P.O. Box 694, Dept. HH
Park Ridge, IL 60068-0694
Page 142
Plainfield
Gigi's Dolls
Route 30 and Route 59
Plainfield, IL 60544
Page 39
Gigi's Teddy Bear Corner
Route 30 and Route 59
Plainfield, IL 60544
Page 178
Rochelle
Ragbabies
Route 3
Rochelle, IL 61068
Page 115
Urbana
Taylor's Cutaways & Stuff
2802 East Washington Street
Urbana, IL 61801
Page 164
Waukegan
H and el & Associates
1010 Westmoreland Avenue
Waukegan, IL 60085
Pages 48, 173
Wheeling
Shirley's Dollhouse
20509 North Hiway 21, P.O. Box
99A
Wheeling, IL 60090
Page 37

INDIANA

Ellettsville
Kay's Doll House
P.O. Box 367, 222 East Vine
Ellettsville, IN 47429
Pages 10, 45
Indianapolis
Children's Museum of Indianapolis,
The
3000 North Meridian Street
Indianapolis, IN 46201
Pages 129, 130
Lynn
Windy Acres Doll Museum
R.R. 1 (Carlos)
Lynn, IN 47355
Pages 130, 165
Middletown
Burton's, Sarah, Doll Depot
560 Locust Street
Middletown, IN 47356
Page 15
Doll Depot
560 Locust Street
Middletown, IN 47356
Page 52
Mooresville
Stewart, Brenda L.
The Peddler's Workshop
1562 Rooker Road
Mooresville, IN 46158
Page 28
Richmond
Doll Shop, The
903 South A Street
Richmond, IN 47374
Page 49
Wayne County Historical Museum
1150 North A
Richmond, IN 47374
Page 130
South Bend
Hobby Center Toys
Scottsdale Mall
Ireland & Miami Avenues
South Bend, IN 46614
Page 47
Syracuse
Poor Doll Shop
Route 2, Box 58
Syracuse, IN 46567
Page 213

IOWA

Burlington
Betty's Dolls
1244 Agency Street
Burlington, IA 52601
Page 34
Council Bluffs
Yesterdears Doll Shop
2410 West Broadway
Council Bluffs, IA 51501
Page 48

Princeton
Doll Carousel
P.O. Box 1377
Princeton, NJ 08540
Page 50

Scotch Plains
Decamp Classics
P.O. Box 372
Scotch Plains, NJ 07076
Page 100
Doll's Corner, The
Stage House Village
Park Avenue and Front Street
Scotch Plains, NJ 07076
Pages 61, 214

Somerville
Skydell's
71 West Main Street
Somerville, NJ 08876
Page 68

Somerset
Royal Doulton
700 Cottontail Lane
Somerset, NJ 08873
Pages 86, 87

Washington
Doll Castle News
P.O. Box 247-CC
Washington, NJ 07882
Pages 198
Dollmaker, The
P.O. Box 247-CC
Washington, NJ 07882
Page 198

NEW MEXICO

Albuquerque
Betty's Doll Haven
1020 California Southeast
Albuquerque, NM 87108
Page 56
Terian
Box 318
Albuquerque, NM 87106
Page 113

Las Cruces
Playhouse Museum of Old Dolls &
Toys
1201 North 2nd Street
Las Cruces, NM 88001
Page 132

Santa Fe
Museum of International Folk Art
P.O. Box 2087
Santa Fe, NM 87501
Page 132

Tucumcari
Tucumcari Historical Museum
416 South Adams Street
Tucumcari, NM 88401
Page 132

NEW YORK

Avon
Joy's Lamplight Shoppe, Inc.
5480 East Avon Road
Avon, NY 14414
Page 61

Baldwin
Tiderider, Inc.
Eastern and Steele Boulevards
P.O. Box 9
Baldwin, NY 11510
Pages 82-85, 182

Binghamton
Dolls by Dolores
112 Dunham Hill Road, RD4
Binghamton, NY 13905
Page 17
Ives, Geraldine
18 Asbury Court
Binghamton, NY 13905
Page 32

Brightwaters
Hearth Side Shop
TDC Box 213
Brightwaters, NY 11718
Page 172

Brockport
Main Street Emporium
41 Main Street
Brockport, NY 14420
Pages 28, 58

Brooklyn
Doll & Craft World, Inc.
125 8th Street
Brooklyn, NY 11215
Pages 154, 167
Doll Lady, The
P.O. Box 121-HHP-C
Homecrest Station
Brooklyn, NY 11229
Page 144
Loretta's Adopt-A-Doll Shop Ltd.
Box 259, Gravesend Station
Brooklyn, NY 11223
Page 60

Buffalo
Yesterday's Children
P.O. Box 233
Buffalo, NY 14226
Page 39

Chittenango
Jean's 20th Century Dolls and
Decorated Eggs
Chittenango R#2, NY 13037
Page 54

Clarence Center
Delightful Dolls
P.O. Box 152
Clarence Center, NY 14032
Page 173

Clyde
MacLennan, Linda
183 Glasgow Street
Clyde, NY 14433
Page 56

East Meadow
Orso, Ida
423 Bellmore Road
East Meadow, NY 11554
Page 53

Elizabethtown
Adirondack Center Museum
Court Street
Elizabethtown, NY 12932
Page 132

Elmira
Arnot Art Museum Shop
235 Lake Street
Elmira, NY 14901
Page 64

Fort Salonga
Farran, Eleanor J.
33 Fieldview Drive
Fort Salonga, L. I., NY 11768
Page 42

Garrison
Something Special
Route 9
Garrison, NY 10524
Page 38

Great Neck
Kwartler, Sheila
10 Chadwick Road
Great Neck, NY 11023
Pages 20, 142

Hamburg
Carolena's Precious Dolls
5684 Sterling Road
Hamburg, NY 14075
Page 142

Hamilton
Claridge Dolls
RD #2, Route 12B, Box 190
Hamilton, NY 13346
Pages 9, 10

Hammondsport
Karat Doll Jewelry
Box 607
Hammondsport, NY 14840
Page 170

Holbrook
Mikuen's
1394 Coates Avenue
Holbrook, NY 11741
Page 14

Jamestown
Benner-Disbro Studio
373-B West Oak Hill Road-RD 2
Jamestown, NY 14701
Page 22

Kew Gardens
Herman, Roslyn Linda
124-16 84th Road
Kew Gardens, NY 11415
Page 37

Kingston
Fantastical Doll House
Route 28
Kingston, NY 12401
Page 51

Long Island City
Dollspart Supply Co. Inc.
Dept. TDC
5-15 49th Avenue
Long Island City, NY 11101
Pages 89, 164
Signature Collection
Dept. TDC
5-15 49th Avenue
Long Island City, NY 11101
Page 57
Standard Doll Co.
23-83 31st Street, Dept. TCD82
Long Island City, NY 11105
Pages 150, 154, 158, 176

Melville
Mella's Doll Shelf
Box 751
Melville, Long Island, NY 11747
Page 52

Merrick
Ronelle Sales
1841 Stanley Drive
Merrick, NY 11566
Page 42

Mount Vernon
Nordell, Carol
368 East Fifth Street
Mount Vernon, NY 10553
Page 188

New Lebanon
Cohen, Marvin Auctions
Routes 20 and 22, Box 425
New Lebanon, NY 12125
Page 139

New York
Atlanta Novelty
200 5th Avenue
Suite 1372
New York, NY 10010
Page 71

Crown Publishers
1 Park Avenue
New York, NY 10016
Page 197

Dover Publications
180 Varick Street
New York, NY 10014
Page 203

Effanbee Doll Corporation
200 Fifth Avenue
New York, NY 10010
Page 90

Penny Whistle Toys Inc.
1283 Madison Avenue
New York, NY 10028
448 Columbus Avenue
New York, NY 10028
Page 61

Reeves International
1107 Broadway
New York, NY 10010
Pages 98, 99, 178

Schoepfer Eyes
138 West 31st Street
New York, NY 10001
Page 147

Sotheby Parke Bernet Inc.
1334 York Avenue
New York, NY 10021
Page 138

North Chili
Victorian Doll Museum & Chili Doll
Hospital
4332 Buffalo Road (Route 33)
North Chili, NY 14514
Pages 131, 133
Victorian Doll Museum
4332 Buffalo Road (Route 33)
North Chili, NY 14515
Page 133

Norwich
Guinn, Donna G.
RD #4 · Box 154-B2
Guinn Ridge Road
Norwich, NY 13815
Page 22

Norwood
Maribeth Doll Clinic
3 Bicknell Street
Norwood, NY 13668
Page 48

Oakfield
Joyce's Dolls
6435 Knowlesville Road
Oakfield, NY 14125
Page 52

Oceanside
Berv, Maxine
Box 341
Oceanside, NY 11572
Page 40

Old Chatham
Shaker Museum, The
149 Shaker Museum Road
Old Chatham, NY 12136
Page 133

Oneonta
Doll Artisan Guild, The
35 Main Street
Oneonta, NY 13820
Pages 32, 33
Seeley's Ceramic
9 River Row
Oneonta, NY 13820
Pages 162, 163, 175

Pearl River
Gordon, Rita
19 Valley Court
Pearl River, NY 10965
Pages 8, 10

Palham
Dolls by Pauline
14 Pelham Parkway
Pelham, NY 10803
Page 96

Poughkeepsie
Burger, Doralee
37-E Colburn Drive
Poughkeepsie, NY 12603
Page 56

Rochester
Strong, Margaret Woodbury Mu-
seum
One Manhattan Square
Rochester, NY 14607
Page 132
Trauger, Peggy, Dolls Patterns
Costumes
20 Wendover Road
Rochester, NY 14610
Page 112

Staten Island
Dolls by Renée
16 Orchard Lane
Staten Island, NY 10312
Page 33
Staten Island Historical Society
Richmondtown
Staten Island, NY 10314
Page 132

St. James
House of Wright
P.O. Box 456
St. James, NY 11780
Page 27

Williamson
Doll House, The
6195 Willow Drive
Williamson, NY 14589
Page 66

NORTH CAROLINA

Camden
Doll Carriage, The
Highway 158
Camden, NC 27921
Page 65

Charlotte
Dolls by Jerri
P.O. Box 9234
Charlotte, NC 28299
Pages 72, 75

Clayton
Sides Doll Supply
Box 376, Route 3
Clayton, NC 27520
Page 152

Statesville
Arts and Science Museum
Museum Road
Statesville, NC 28677
Page 133

OHIO

Akron
Doll's Nest, The
1020 Kenmore Boulevard, Dept.
D
Akron, OH 44314
Pages 44, 114, 148
Hobby Center Toys
Chapel Hill Mall
Brittain Road
Akron, OH 44310
Page 47
Hobby Center Toys
Summit Mall
3265 West Market Street
Akron, OH 44313
Page 47

Berlin
100 Years of Steiff
Box 224
Berlin, OH 44610
Page 196

Brunswick
Nation-of-the-Month Club
3755 Ruth Drive
Brunswick, OH 44212
Page 196
Wonderful World of Dolls©
3755 Ruth Drive, Dept. DC82
Brunswick, OH 44212
Page 114

Canton
Hobby Center Toys
Belden Village Mall
Everhard and Whipple Roads
Canton, OH 44718
Page 47

Chesterland
Staufen Studio
8564 Mulberry Road
Chesterland, OH 44026
Page 92

Cincinnati
Hobby Center Toys
Beechmont Mall
7500 Beechmont Avenue
Cincinnati, OH 45230
Page 47
Kenner Products
1014 Vine Street
Cincinnati, OH 45202
Pages 76, 77

Cleveland
Doll Repair Parts, Inc.
9918 Lorain Avenue
Cleveland, OH 44102
Pages 39, 147
Hobby Center Toys
Randall Park Mall
Route #8
Cleveland, OH 44128
Page 47
Western Reserve Historical Society,
The
10825 East Boulevard, University
Circle
Cleveland, OH 44106
Page 133

Dayton
Hobby Center Toys
Dayton Mall
2700 Miamisburg-Centerville Road
Dayton, OH 45459
Page 47

Elyria-Lorian
Hobby Center Toys
Midway Mall
Midway Mall Boulevard
Elyria-Lorian, OH 44035
Page 47

Enon
Byerman, Elizabeth
P.O. Box 216
Enon, OH 45323
Page 51

Findlay
Hobby Center Toys
Findlay Village Mall
1800 Tiffin Road
Findlay, OH 45840
Page 47

Fremont
Hobby Center Toys
Potter Village
1136 Oak Harbor Road
Fremont, OH 43420
Page 47

Greenville
Garst Museum
205 North Broadway
Greenville, OH 45331
Page 133

Holland
Hobby Center Toys
7856 Hill Avenue
Holland, OH 43528
Page 47

Lima
Doll Corner
940 Richie
Lima, OH 45805
Pages 17, 144
Hobby Center Toys
Lima Mall
2400 Elida Road
Lima, OH 45805
Page 47

Milan
Milan Historical Museum
10 Edison Drive
Milan, OH 44846
Page 133

New Philadelphia
Hobby Center Toys
Monroe Mall
Monroe Avenue
New Philadelphia, OH 44663
Page 47

New Springfield
DeVault's, Barbara Dolls
Box 138
New Springfield, OH 44443
Page 48

North Canton
Dollie Dear
P.O. Box 2383
North Canton, OH 44720
Pages 40, 42

Tiffin
Hobby Center Toys
Tiffin Mall
870 West Market Street
Tiffin, OH 44883
Page 47

Toledo
Arden 1 Originals
1969 Potomac Drive
Toledo, OH 43607
Page 23
Blair Museum of Lithophanes and
Carved Waxes
2032 Robinwood Avenue
Toledo, OH 43620
Page 133
Hobby Center Toys
Franklin Park Mall
Monroe and Talmadge Road
Toledo, OH 43623
Page 47
Hobby Center Toys
North Towne Square Mall
343 North Towne Square Drive
Toledo, OH 43612
Page 47
Hobby Center Toys
Southland
1435 South Byrne Road
Toledo, OH 43614
Page 47
Hobby Center Toys
Southwyck Mall
2040 South Reynolds Road
Toledo, OH 43614
Page 47
Hobby Center Toys
West Gate
3301 West Central Avenue
Toledo, OH 43606
Page 47
Hobby Center Toys
Woodville Mall
3725 Williston Road
Toledo, OH 43619
Page 47

Waynesville
Stetson House, The
Box 235, 234 South Main Street
Waynesville, OH 45068
Page 64

Willoughby
Byron Molds
4530 Hamann Parkway
Willoughby, OH 44094
Page 161

Worthington
Old Rectory, The
Worthington Historical Society
50 West New England Avenue
Worthington, OH 43085
Page 133

Youngstown
Wanda's Dolls
274 Benita
Youngstown, OH 44504
Page 38

OKLAHOMA

Oklahoma City
Doll Works, The
2203 North Hudson
Oklahoma City, OK 73103
Page 196
Reeder, Betty
Bru-Bet's Dolls
2737 Southwest 63rd Street
Oklahoma City, OK 73159
Page 17

OREGON

Beaverton
Cookie's Dolls
15315 Southwest Village Lane
Beaverton, OR 97007
Page 38
Corvallis
Yesterday's Charmers by Charleen
Thanos
1525 Northwest Woodland Drive
Corvallis, OR 97330
Page 34
Cottage Grove
Dunham Porcelain Art
36429 Row River Road
Cottage Grove, OR 97424
Page 50
Eugene
Fabricat Design - Susanna Oroyan
1880 Parliament Street
Eugene, OR 97405
Page 33
Precious Babes by Beth
980 Robin Hood Avenue
Eugene, OR 97401
Page 26
Florence
Dolly Wares Doll Museum
3620 Hiway 101 North
Florence, OR 97439
Pages 132, 133
Grants Pass
Connie's Dolls & Co.
421 Southeast 6th Street
Grants Pass, OR 97526
Pages 63, 174
Newport
Claridge, Rosa N.
P.O. Box 330
Newport, OR 97365
Page 188
Portland
Beck, Lois Originals
10300 Southeast Champagne Lane
Portland, OR 97266
Pages 9, 181
Irma's Gallery Molds©
Pacific Business Park
4910 Northeast 122nd Avenue
Portland, OR 97230
Page 160
Kezi Works, The
P.O. Box 17062
Portland, OR 97217
Pages 18, 19
Miller, Jane
10347 Southwest East Ridge
Portland, OR 97225
Page 40
Pipsqueekers
Cathy J. Ellis
6335 North Moore
Portland, OR 97217
Page 22

PENNSYLVANIA

Beech Creek
Little, Virginia
Locust Lane Dolls
R. D. 1, Box 207
Beech Creek, PA 16822
Page 22
Bensalem
Mandeville's Antiques and Collect-
ibles
380 Dartmouth Court
Bensalem, PA 19020
Page 39
Butler
Foster, Carol
340 Pittsburgh Road
Butler, PA 16001
Page 168
Douglassville
Merritt, Mary Doll Museum
RD 2
Douglassville, PA 19518
Page 133
Doylestown
Rothschild
42 East State Street
Doylestown, PA 18901
Page 29

Edinboro
Nerissa ™
P.O. Box 200
Edinboro, PA 16412
Page 16
Flourtown
Mostly Dolls and Toys
1518 Bethlehem Pike
Flourtown, PA 19031
Page 59
Glenshaw
Pittsburgh Doll Company, The
Buchholz, Shirley
2814 Herron Lane
Glenshaw, PA 15116
Page 39
Grove City
Wallace, Sheila
407 Garden Avenue
Grove City, PA 16127
Page 8
Mechanicsburg
Colonial House of Dolls
300 South York Street
Mechanicsburg, PA 17055
Pages 69, 174, 215
Middletown
Welker, Lauren
77 Hanover Street, Dept. DC
Middletown, PA 17057
Page 174
Moscow
Tovcimak, Lucille Sabad
401 North Main Street
Moscow, PA 18444
Page 15
New Hope
Shoppe Full of Dolls
39 North Main Street
New Hope, PA 18938
Page 65
Philadelphia
Perelman Antique Toy Museum
270 South 2nd Street
Philadelphia, PA 19106
Page 133
Pittsburgh
Pittsburgh Doll Company, The
Kintner, Joyce
4 Old Timber Trail
Pittsburgh, PA 15238
Page 39
Sharon
Boycan's Craft & Art Supplies
Dept. HHP-2, P.O. Box 897
Sharon, PA 16146
Page 164
West Chester
Chester City Historical Society
225 North High Street
West Chester, PA 19380
Page 133
York
Moore's Lois House of Dolls
19 Crestview Drive
York, PA 17402
Pages 32, 33

RHODE ISLAND

Cranston
Conn, Jo Dolls
2548 Cranston Street
Cranston, RI 02920
Page 10
Providence
Gorham Texton
Dept. DR
Providence, RI 02907
Page 78

SOUTH CAROLINA

Charleston
Dolls by Penny
414 Cessna Avenue
Charleston, SC 29407
Page 50
Lugoff
European Doll Supply
35 Wildwood Lane
Lugoff, SC 29078
Page 157

SOUTH DAKOTA

Murdo
Camp McKen-Z Doll Museum
Murdo, SD 57559
Page 133

TENNESSEE

Antioch
Dainty Darling Dolls
by Jeri Ann Ray
645 Roxanne Drive
Antioch, TN 37013
Page 14
Chattanooga
Ancraft Company
305 Nye Drive
Chattanooga, TN 37411
Page 91

TEXAS

Arlington
Yesteryear Products
P.O. Box 13621
Arlington, TX 76013
Page 156
Austin
Heirloom Dolls by the DeAngelos
5003 Tahoe Trail
Austin, TX 78745
Page 50
Corsicana
Playhouse Designs, Inc.
920 North Main Street
Corsicana, TX 75110
Page 110
Dallas
Barnard Originals
3065 Sumter Drive
Dallas, TX 75220
Page 44
Dolls by Dottie
2910 Centerville Road
Dallas, TX 75228
Pages 164, 214
Fort Worth
Audria's Crafts, Inc.
913 East Seminary
Fort Worth, TX 76115
Page 143
Fort Davis
Neill Museum
7th and Court
Fort Davis, TX 79734
Page 134
Garland
Harris, Marilyn
1833 Cripple Creek
Garland, TX 75041
Page 54
Houston
House Beautiful of Texas, Inc.
13017G Clarewood
Houston, TX 77072
Page 114
Museum of American Architecture
and Decorative Arts
7502 Fondren Road
Houston, TX 77074
Page 134
Tyner, Boots Originals
5027 Whispering Falls
Houston, TX 77084
Page 31
Kerrville
Story Book Museum
620 Lois Street
Kerrville, TX 78028
Page 133
Lampasas
Doll Emporium, The
Route 2, Box 187, South Hiway
183
Lampasas, TX 76550
Page 30
Treasures by Trulove
101 East Avenue C
Lampasas, TX 76550
Page 28
Lubbock
Yesterday's Dolls Today
Cactus Alley
2610 Salem #6
Lubbock, TX 79410
Page 152
Mission
Doll Scope
Route 3, Box 107-W
Mission, TX 78572
Pages 154, 200
Rosenberg
Fain Auction Way
1420 Mimosa
Rosenberg, TX 77471
Page 138
Mail-Order Doll House DC
1613 Walger
Rosenberg, TX 77471
Page 204
Silsbee
Lynne's Doll House
P.O. Box 1637
Silsbee, TX 77656
Page 38
Spring
Eyes
9630 Dundalk
Spring, TX 77379
Pages 168, 170

UTAH

Provo
McCurdy Historical Doll Museum
246 North 100 East
Provo, UT 84601
Pages 133, 134

VERMONT

Bennington
Bennington Museum
West Main Street
Bennington, VT 05201
Page 134

Suzy's Dolls
Ethel Santarcangelo
4 Monument Circle
Bennington, VT 05201
Page 156
Calais
Kent Tavern Museum
Kents' Corner
Calais, VT 05648
Page 134
Herrick
Springfield Art & Historical Society
Elm Hill
Herrick, VT 05156
Page 134
Montpelier
Vermont Historical Society
109 State Street
Montpelier, VT 05602
Page 134
Waterbury Center
Barrie, Mirren
Route 1, Box 328
Waterbury Center, VT 05677
Page 33

VIRGINIA

Alexandria
Angie's Doll Boutique
1114 King Street, Old Town
Alexandria, VA 22314
Pages 44, 114
Why Not, Inc.
200 King Street
Alexandria, VA 22314
Pages 59, 179
Chesapeake
Melton's Antiques
4201 Indian River Road
P.O. Box 13311
Chesapeake, VA 23325
Page 53
Fredericksburg
Dolls by Judi
Route 6, Box 327-C3
Fredericksburg, VA 22405
Page 158
Harrisonburg
Hawkins, Susan Dolls
Route 4, Box 256-B
Harrisonburg, VA 22801
Page 32
Manassas
Barbara Anne's Babies
13820 Spriggs Road
Manassas, VA 22111
Page 11
Plain & Fancy Doll Shoppe
13505 Spriggs Road
Manassas, VA 22111
Pages 40, 212
Richmond
Laughon, Jr., Dr. Fred
8106 Three Chopt Road
Richmond, VA 23229
Page 10
Marandy Dolls, Etc.
Bridgers, Eleanor G.
Studio - 2811 Jeffers Drive
Richmond, VA 23235
Page 15
U.S. Historical Society
1st and Main Streets
Richmond, VA 23219
Pages 80, 81
Valentine Museum, The
1015 East Caly Street
Richmond, VA 23219
Page 134
Salem
C & W Enterprises
Mary Ann Cook
2700 Titleist Drive
Salem, VA 24153
Page 56
Schuyler
Sweeney, Patricia Frances
Strawberry Fields Doll Studio
Route #1, Box 207
Schuyler, VA 22969
Page 60
Suffolk
Aston, Janet G.
1236 Buckhorn Drive
Suffolk, VA 23437
Page 67
Dolls of Yesteryear by Robert
Archer
420 North Broad Street
Suffolk, VA 23434
Page 26
Vienna
Bonnie-Lee Portrait Doll Makers
2005 George Washington Road
Vienna, VA 22180
Page 14
Wytheville
Marcelle's Doll Shoppe & Hospital
170 West Main Street
Wytheville, VA 24382
Page 49

WASHINGTON

Bellevue
Kahler Kraft
9605 Northeast 26th
Bellevue, WA 98004
Page 113
Coupeville
Waverly Lynn
P.O. Box 762
Coupeville, WA 98239
Page 119
Kelso
Cowlitz County Historical Museum
405 Allen Street
Kelso, WA 98626
Page 134
Port Orchard
Judi's Dolls
P.O. Box 607
Port Orchard, WA 98366
Page 112
Port Townsend
Granny & Me
René E. Wells
136 "F" Street
Port Townsend, WA 98368
Page 30
Puyallup
Quest-Eridon Books
5 Court Place
Puyallup, WA 98371
Page 198
Retsil
Port, Beverly Originals
P.O. Box 711
Retsil, WA 98378
Pages 22, 185
Port, Kimberlee Originals
P.O. Box 711
Retsil, WA 98378
Page 181
Seattle
A & D Ceramic & Doll Supply
12600½ Interurban Avenue South
Seattle, WA 98168
Page 150
Collectible Doll Company
6233 2nd Avenue Northwest
Seattle, WA 98107
Page 14
Empire Antiques & Dolls
6740 Empire Way South
Seattle, WA 98118
Page 45
Spokane
Tif N' Todds
731 West Knox
Spokane, WA 99205
Page 13
Sunnyside
Stefanie's Treasures
P.O. Box 904
Sunnyside, WA 98944
Page 45
Tacoma
Weems, Elva
10510 East Polk Street
Tacoma, WA 98445
Page 26

WEST VIRGINIA

Charleston
Henderson, Edna Dolls
200 Swarthmore Avenue
Charleston, WV 25302
Page 12
Wellsburg
Little Ranch Antiques, Inc.
1431 Washington Pike
Wellsburg, WV 26070
Page 189

WISCONSIN

Fond du lac
Cosi Cottage & Co.
326 North National Avenue
Fond du lac, WI 54935
Pages 91, 147
Janesville
Doll House, The
1263 North Parker Drive
Janesville, WI 53545
Page 165
Portage
Bobi's Doll Creations
306 Riverview Court
Portage, WI 53901
Page 21
Sheboygan
Oldenburg, Mary Ann
5515 South 12th Street
Sheboygan, WI 53081
Page 23

AUSTRIA

Salzburg
Spielzeugmuseum
Bürgerspitalgasse 1
Salzburg, Austria
Page 134

CANADA

Guelph
Guelph Civic Museum
6 Dublin Street, South
Guelph, Ontario N1H 4L5, Canada
Page 134

Hamilton
Dorvey's Antiques
29 Inverness Avenue West
Hamilton, Ontario, L9C1A1
Canada
Page 55

Kingston
Dolls International
412 Southwood Drive
Kingston, Ontario, Canada K7M
5P6
Page 48

DENMARK

Billund
Legoland Museum
Billund, Denmark
Page 134

EAST GERMANY

Dresden
Museum of Folklore
Dresden, DDR, East Germany
Page 134

ENGLAND

Bath
Burrows Museum
Roman Bath Building
Bath, Avon, England
Page 134
Museum of Costume
Assembly Rooms, Bennett Street
Bath, Avon BA1 2QE, England
Page 134

Bognor Regis
Parker, Ann
67 Victoria Drive
Bognor Regis, Sussex, PO212TD
England
Page 8

Bristol
Blaise Castle House Museum
Henbury
Bristol, England
Page 134

Bromsgrove
Playthings Past Museum
Beaconwood, Beacon Lane
Bromsgrove, England
Page 134

Dorset
Red House Museum & Art Gallery
Quay Road, Christ Church
Dorset, England
Page 134

Essex
Saffron Walden Museum
Museum Street, Saffron Walden
Essex, England
Page 134

Gloucestershire
Sudeley Castle
Gloucestershire, England
Page 134

Gwyneed
Museum of Childhood
Water Street, Menai Bridge
Gwynedd, England
Page 134
Penrhyn Castle
Bangor, Gwynedd
Wales, England
Page 135

Hove
Museum of Art, Hove
19 New Church Road
Hove, East Sussex BN3 4AB,
England
Page 134

Isle of Wight
Arreton Manor
Arreton
Isle of Wight, England
Page 135
Lilliput Museum of Antique Dolls,
The
High Street, Brading
Isle of Wight, England
Page 135

Kings Lynn
Museum of Social History
27 King Street
Kings Lynn PE30 1HA, England
Page 135

Kingsbridge
Cookworthy Museum
The Old Grammar School
108 Fore Street
Kingsbridge, S. Devon TQ7 1AW,
England
Page 135

Lancanshire
Gillie Dolls
69 Babylon Lane, Anderton, Nr.
Chorley
Lancanshire, England
Page 27
Judges' Lodgings
Church Street, Lancaster
Lancanshire, England
Page 135

Leeds
Abbey House Folk Museum
Abbey Road
Leeds LS5 3EH, England
Page 135

Lincoln
Usher Gallery
Lindum Road
Lincoln LN2 1NN, England
Page 135

Llandudno
Llandudno Doll Museum and Model
Railway
Masonic Street
Llandudno Gwynedd LL30 2DU,
England
Page 135

London
Bethnal Green Museum of Child-
hood
Cambridge Heath Road
London E2 9PA, England
Page 135
Gunnersbury Park Museum
Gunnersbury Park
London W3, England
Page 135
Museum of London, The
London Wall
London, EC2Y 5HN England
Page 135
Pollock's Toy Museum
1 Scala Street
London W.1., England
Page 135

Luton
Luton Museum and Art Gallery
Wardown Park
Luton LU2 7HA, England
Page 135

Manchester
Monks Hall Museum
42 Wellington Road, Eccles.
Manchester, M 30 ONP, England
Page 135

Middlesex
Glover, Margaret
42 Hartham Road, Isleworth
Middlesex, England
Page 27

Norwich
Stranger's Hall
Charing Cross
Norwich, NR2 4AL England
Page 135

Nottingham
Museum of Costume & Textiles
51 Castle Gate
Nottingham, England
Page 135

Oakham
Thompson, Teresa
35 Lonsdale Way
Oakham, Leicestershire
LE15 6LP England
Page 27

Oxford
Grove House
Iffley Turn
Oxford, England
Page 135

Preston
Harris Museum & Art Gallery
Market Square
Preston, Lancashire, England
Page 135

Salisbury
Salisbury and South Wiltshire
Museum
65 The Close
Salisbury, Wiltshire, SP1 2EN,
England
Page 135

Tunbridge Wells
Tunbridge Wells Municipal Museum
Civic Centre, Mount Pleasant
Tunbridge Wells, Kent TN1 1RS,
England
Page 135

Warwick
Warwick Doll Museum
Okens House, Castle Street
Warwick, CV34 England
Page 135

Weston-super-Mare
Woodspring Museum
Burlington Street
Weston-super-Mare, Avon BS23
1PR, England
Page 134

Winscombe
House of Nisbet
Dunster Park
Winscombe, Avon BS25 1AG,
England
Page 100

Tower Treasures
Dunster Park
Winscombe, Avon BS25 1AG,
England
Page 24

Worcestershire
Hereford and Worcester County
Museum
Hartlebury Castle, Hartlebury, Nr.
Kidderminster
Worcestershire DY11 7XZ,
England
Page 135

Worthing
Worthing Museum & Art Gallery
Chapel Road
Worthing, West Sussex, BN11
1HQ, England
Page 135

York
York Castle Museum
Tower Street
York, England
Page 135

FRANCE

Courbevoie
Musee Roybet - Fould
178 Boulevard St. Denis
92400 Courbevoie, France
Page 136

Paris
Musee Carnavalet
23, Rue de Sévigne
Paris 75003, France
Page 136
Musee de l'Homme
Place du Trocadero
Paris 75016, France
Page 136
Musee des Arts Decoratifs
107 rue de Rivoli
Paris 75001, France
Page 136
Musee National des Techniques
C.N.A.M. 292, rue Saint-Martin
Paris 75003, France
Page 136

Poissy
Musee du Jouet
1 Enclos de l'Abbaye
Poissy 78300, France
Page 136

IRELAND

Dublin
Museum of Childhood
20 Palmerston Park 6
Dublin, Ireland
Page 136
National Museum of Ireland
Kildare Street
Dublin 2, Ireland
Page 136

MONACO

Monte Carlo
Princess Grace's Doll Museum
Musee National de Monaco
Monte Carlo, Monaco
Page 136

NETHERLANDS

The Hague
Nederlands Kostuummuseum
Lange Vijverberg 14-15
2513 AC The Hague, Netherlands
Page 136

NOVA SCOTIA

Yarmouth
Yarmouth County Museum
22 Collins Street
(Postal address: Box 39)
Yarmouth B54 4B1, Nova Scotia
Page 134

SCOTLAND

Edinburgh
Museum of Childhood
38 High Street
Edinburgh, Scotland
Page 136

SOUTH AUSTRALIA

Kensington Park
Doll Journal of Australia
Mrs. Beres Lindus
Box 97, P.O., Kensington Park
3-5068 South Australia
Page 198

SPAIN

Barcelona
Museo Romantico Provincial
12 Calle Montcada
Barcelona, Spain
Page 136

SWEDEN

Stockholm
LeKaks Museum - The Toy Museum
Mariatorget 1
Stockholm, Sweden
Page 136

SWITZERLAND

Basel
Kirschgarten
Elizabethstrasse 27
Basel, Switzerland
Page 136

Riehem
Spielzeug und Dormuseum Reihem
Baselstrasse 34
CH4125 Riehem, Switzerland
Page 136

Zurich
Doll Museum - Barengasse Zurich
Sasha Morgenthaeler
Barengasse 20-22
8001 Zurich, Switzerland
Page 136
Zurcher Spielzeng Museum
Fortunagasse 15/Rennweg
8001 Zurich, Switzerland
Page 136

WEST GERMANY

Kevelaer
Niederrehinisches Museum fur
Volkskunde und Kulturgeschichte
Haupt Str. 18
D 4178 Kevelaer, West Germany
Page 136

Kreis Viersen
Klein, H. G. Collection
D 4155 Grefarth
Kreis Viersen, West Germany
Page 136

Neustadt
Neustadt Tract Museum
Neustadt near Coburg,
West Germany
Page 136

Nurnberg
Bayer, Dr. Lydia Museum
Theodorstrasse 7/11
85 Nurnberg, West Germany
Page 136

Other Companies or Individuals

Other Companies or Individuals

Other Companies or Individuals